Good Cooking from India

enjoy 200 kitchen-tested recipes from a centuries-old cuisine that matches today's interest in healthful eating

By Shahnaz Mehta
with Joan Korenblit

Editor: Charles Gerras

Book Design: Kim Morrow
Illustration: Jean Seibert
                Mary K. West

Rodale Press  Emmaus, Pennsylvania

Printed in the United States of America on recycled paper, containing a high percentage of de-inked fiber.

Editorial Assistance: Camille Bucci

Recipe Testing: JoAnn Benedick and Linda C. Gilbert
             Susan M. Hercek
             Yvonne Malloy

Props for the cover photograph: Helen B. Henry Antiques, Macungie, PA 18062

Library of Congress Cataloging in Publication Data

Mehta, Shahnaz.
  Good cooking from India.

  Includes index.
  1. Cookery, Indic.   I. Korenblit, Joan.   II. Gerras,
Charles.   III. Title.
TX724.5.I4M43   641.5954   81–8647
ISBN 0–87857–357–7 hardcover   AACR2

2 4 6 8 10 9 7 5 3 1   hardcover

For M. B.
and
for his grandchildren and great-grandchildren . . .

contents

acknowledgments

First, my mother, Birjees Jehan Kidwai, for being an inexhaustible source of ideas, a reference library, an excited encourager, and a painstaking partner in testing innumerable recipes.

My husband, Vijay Mehta, for enduring the dubious distinction of being my main taster. Many a recipe that did not pass his seasoned judgment was doomed to remain on the pages of my ancient, unbelievably tattered recipe notebook, dating from my childhood with Babuji.

My friends who so generously shared their recipes.

My children, Devika Laila and Nayan Tara, for putting up with a distracted mother who ate and dreamt recipes for two years.

Cathy Rose, Gerry, and especially Baba and Prita for their patient proofreading and suggestions.

Photographs, Ahmed Hossain and Mohsin Abdullah

Chini, my alter ego.

Shahnaz Mehta

My husband, Mike Korenblit, whose enthusiasm is an inspiration.

Joan Korenblit

The Rodale Test Kitchen staff for their conscientious effort to make everything right, and for their sensitivity to the special qualities of Indian cuisine.

Camille Bucci for her unstinting help and perseverance in working toward consistency.

Charles Gerras, our editor, for his faith, and for "ruling" with a light hand.

And most of all, to Babuji and Asho for their inspiration.

S.M. and J.K.

share our joys

The India of bejeweled Rajas riding in state atop ceremonial elephants and of tigers roaming free no longer exists. Today India, like many other countries in the world, is primarily concerned with the struggle to achieve economic self-reliance and dignity. This struggle can be seen in different ways through the eyes of India's varied people—those who live in the thousands of slowly changing villages as well as the city dwellers who experience the urgency of modern urban life.

One of our ancient and best-known stories illustrates how perceptions of reality (life) can differ. It is actually part of the *jain* creed that all judgments are conditional. Absolute truth only comes to the periodic redeemers, or *jinas.* Four blind men encountered an elephant and each touched a different part of the beast. Every one of them arrived at a totally different "picture" of what he had "seen." The same is true of India which is many things to many people. Yet, in all our diversity, we have some strong common bonds and a shared heritage that make us all "Indians," and proud of it.

One of these bonds is the attitude all Indians have toward food. Our sages stated simply: *Annam Brahma,* "Food is God." This philosophy gives rise to a deep regard for hospitality, a word known in its truest sense by all Indians. We consider it a privilege and a sacred duty to give shelter to any guest, to give alms, and to offer food to household deities.

This sense of sharing oneself through food blossoms into joyful form during our many colorful festivals and ceremonies. People sing and dance, adorn their homes and themselves, and exchange a dazzling variety of savories and sweetmeats with friends and relatives. An oft-sung Indian lullaby illustrates vividly our love for sweetmeats:

> *Chanda Mama Duur Kay*
> *Baray pakaain buur kay*
> *Aap khaain thali may*
> *Hum ko day dain pyali may*

> Uncle Moon, dwelling far away,
> Is preparing sweets of fine jaggery.
> He, himself, eats in a *thali* (plate)
> And gives to us in a *pyali* (cup).

But even on an ordinary day, mealtime is an "occasion." This is largely because of the atmosphere created by the woman of the house who lovingly serves each member of the family, uniting all of them in an act of sharing.

Servants Become a Part of the Family

In our household my mother was assisted in this task by Babuji, our cook, who did not perceive his duties as ending in the kitchen. Babuji belonged to a feudal tradition in which servants working for a family became a real part of it. The lives of dozens of servants, with their dependents, were inextricably linked with the lives of their employers. In a real and practical sense, and in the absence of government welfare systems, the servants depended on those they served for their well-being.

Babuji was nurtured in this atmosphere. His father and grandfather had worked for my father's family, a typical Muslim Zamindar (land-owning) family of Lucknow, in north India; so Babuji was now an "old hand." When he came to Assam (in east India) with my father, he came not as a servant, but as a member of the family. He was very conscious of his rights and quickly carved out an important position in the household for himself. Asho, Hansraj, and Hussain, who later came to work for us and gradually became part of our lives, always recognized Babuji's place in our home. For example, if it came to a question of their doing something that I wanted that was contrary to Babuji's wishes, it was Babuji's will that would prevail!

Babuji was a precious link for all of us between the feudal days he had known with my father and the modern life we now lived in Shillong. Somehow we knew that if Babuji was in his kitchen, all was right with the world! Separated from the main house by a covered passageway, his kitchen was a little building which we associated with the most tantalizing aromas emanating from the dozens of spices with which he surrounded himself.

Spices—the Fabled Riches of India

Spices, synonymous with India since antiquity, are mainly responsible for the superbly varied flavors of our cuisine. India is a land rich in jewels, ivory, perfumes, silks, the finest muslins, and no less precious, the fabulous spices of the Orient. Even before the time of Alexander the Great, who came to India in 327 B.C., India had found a market for her treasures in most of the then known world.

In ancient times, these treasures found their way by camel and mule over the historic Khyber Pass and the legendary Silk Route. Centuries later, the pursuit of its magnificent riches brought British, French, Dutch, and Portuguese traders to the shores of India. Fenugreek, turmeric, clove, cardamom, saffron, and peppercorn are just a few examples of the endless aromatic wealth that India has traditionally enjoyed and now shares with the rest of the world.

Spices have three important functions: as a preservative, as a medicinal, and as a seasoning. Ancient Sanskrit writings of India describe many of the best known spices, emphasizing their value as food preservatives—an important consideration in warm climates. These writings also attach importance to the purported medicinal properties of spices, as did the Hakims, traditional Muslim doctors.

The tremendous range of spices at our disposal allows full creative freedom to the cook. With all this fragrant wealth to choose from, it is no wonder that "instant" mixtures such as "curry powder" are almost never used in India. Instead, each cook creates a unique blend of spices which imparts an individual flavor to each dish.

Regional Variations Lend Depth and Interest to the Cuisine

Together with the scope for individual creativity, there are great regional variations in Indian cooking, lending to the interest and depth of the cuisine, for Indians and foreigners alike. Locally grown ingredients play a large part in shaping the flavor of different types of regional foods. It is no accident that people from northern India count wheat as one of their basic sources of grain, since it grows most easily in that area. South Indians rely on rice because it can be cultivated locally.

In luxuriant Assam forests, a large sweet-sour fruit known as *o tenga* grows abundantly. Not unexpectedly, there is a traditional Assamese specialty dish that features this fruit. Along India's coastal regions, coconut palms are a familiar sight, so naturally coconut is well reflected in the cooking of this area.

My family has been particularly fortunate in absorbing some of this regional diversity in cuisine. Although we come from north India, we spent many years in the east and later in west India, and our background exposed us to influences from all parts of the country.

Because our large extended family also embraced "uncles" and "aunts" (close friends from different parts of India who were considered members of the family) our inventory of favorite family dishes kept expanding. We have accumulated recipes through many generations, some of which we kept as closely guarded secrets.

Cooking Indian Dishes in America

When we came to the United States, I enjoyed serving some of these dishes to our American friends, but initially I was faced with a challenge. This country does not have the same range of vegetables and fruits that we were used to, though I was delighted to discover fruit like avocado, which we do not have in India. Thus, I began to experiment with the vegetables that I could find and soon discovered many new, exciting ways to prepare them. I already had a treasure trove of traditional Indian recipes, together with the basic culinary skills. I built on this wealth to create variations using vegetables available here (instead of the typical ones used in India) and found the results very satisfying. For example, in India we have about a hundred varieties of mango. Here I have found mainly one kind, and it tastes completely different from the mangoes we are used to. However, upon using the mango in chutneys, in fruit salad, in *Aam Kulfi* (A Mango Ice Cream) and in our well-loved cool drink, *Mango Fool* (see Index for these mango recipes), I found ways to make the best possible use of the fruit available here.

In response to the Rodale Press guidelines for health, I excluded salt, sugar, and processed flours from the recipes for this book. In the beginning I thought this would be a tremendous obstacle. I was finally convinced that we could indeed live without salt when I cooked a salt-free meal for my family one day. We quietly enjoyed it—and no one reached for the salt shaker!

In this book I feel I have succeeded in presenting our typical Indian dishes in a manner that preserves their authenticity, yet allows for individual variation. The recipes reflect the wide variety of our cuisine, while eliminating much of the painstaking work we take for granted in India. The chapter, "Feeling at Ease with Indian Cookery," provides readers with the opportunity to experience the range and diversity, the hustle and bustle, and the love and care that go into preparing a meal in an Indian kitchen.

To get an idea of the kind of meals we serve every day and the special meals we prepare for a party, consult the selection of complete menus that are provided. Whether you choose to prepare the menus I suggest or make up your own, the section will be a helpful guide in presenting a typical Indian meal. Then, if you use today's modern gadgets for preparing the dishes, you will find it is very simple to produce Eastern magic in Western kitchens!

feeling at ease with indian cookery

In Indian cooking as in Indian classical music, the art of improvisation is encouraged. Imaginative innovation and experimentation, within certain limits, can bring delectable results! It is difficult to set down rules for Indian cooking because no two experts agree about the preparation of a particular dish. However, we can offer a few general observations.

Presentation of a Meal

A typical Indian meal consists of about five or six dishes. As a rule, these are not presented as separate courses, but are served all at once, arranged on tables or on mats on the floor. Often both rice and *roti* (bread) are served. However, there are regional differences in the style of serving. For example, a meal generally ends with the serving of one or two sweet dishes, except in some parts of India where the sweet is presented at the beginning of a meal or, as in Maharastra, where it is often served along with other dishes.

Probably because so many Indian dishes have lots of gravy, we invented a whole new set of eating utensils. The *thali* is a plate made of silver, stone, brass, stainless steel, or aluminum with a rim around it. On the *thali* are placed little *katoris,* or bowls, each filled with a different meat, lentil, vegetable, or yogurt-based preparation. We break off pieces of our *rotis* and use them to scoop up the contents with our fingers in small mouthfuls. We also generally have a small mound of rice on the *thali,* over which we pour contents from one or two of the *katoris.* In this way we can enjoy a neatly organized meal in spite of having so many dishes to choose from!

Curried Dishes

There are many ways of preparing meats, fowl, fish, and vegetables. *Korma, pasanday, saalan, kabab, kofta, keema, tandoori, raan,* and *vindaloo* are some of the names by which we identify different types of curried meats. Some of these, like *saalan, korma, vindaloo,* and various *keema* preparations, have gravy and would probably be called a curry by Westerners.

Bharta, bhaji, sabzi, katlay, and *tarkari* are some of the names by which different vegetable preparations are known. (See the Glossary.)

It is not true that Indian food has to be "hot." A curry need only be as "spicy" as you want it to be. Among the main ingredients that impart a certain "hotness" to a dish are red chilies, chili powder, green chilies, peppercorns or black pepper, ginger, and *garam masalla* (a blend of freshly ground spices). In chilies, the seeds are the hottest part. The quantity of any of these called for in different recipes may be substantially reduced, if you wish, without altering the character of most of our recipes.

Some of the ingredients we use to thicken or flavor a gravy for a typical curry are ground or chopped onions, fresh ginger root, garlic cloves, tamarind juice, coconuts, tomatoes, white poppy seeds, cashew nuts, and jaggery. Yogurt, chick-pea flour, ground coriander, and cumin are also used frequently for this purpose.

Onions, garlic, and the like often need to be fried for about fifteen minutes, so if while frying you find the *masalla* sticking to the pan, sprinkle a little water from time to time as you fry so that these spices do not burn. Generally, when oil appears at the sides of the pan, the *masalla* is properly fried and you can then add to it the meat or vegetable. In most cases, tamarind juice should be cooked for at least twenty minutes. Coconut milk should be brought to a boil very gradually and thick coconut milk should be added during the last stages of cooking. Most preparations that include yogurt should be heated gradually, then cooked on low heat.

The Varied Use of Spices

Certain spices that have a sharp or even bitter flavor, like turmeric, fenugreek, asafetida, or pepper and chilies, will never be used when making a sweet dish. Yet, spices like cardamom, cinnamon, and saffron, which are used in sweet dishes, are also used in savory preparations. For instance, tradition requires that the glorious fragrance of saffron heralds to guests that one of two typically north Indian delicacies, *pullau* (a savory) or *sivain* (a sweet) is ready to be served.

In India, with few exceptions, we use whole spices, freshly ground each day. However, in this book we have used the readily available powdered forms in a number of recipes for our readers' convenience. Keep in mind that the powdered spices, cumin and coriander for instance, are less flavorful than freshly ground cumin and coriander seeds. If you decide to use the whole spices and grind them yourself, remember to use slightly less than the prepared amount mentioned in recipes. The freshly ground spices will be more potent than those previously ground. Whole peppercorns, cardamoms, cloves, and other spices are often added to pilafs and other preparations as a sort of extra garnish. However, these whole spices are not meant to be eaten.

There are a few spices, like oregano seeds and onion seeds that have such a distinctive flavor that when they are used in a dish, you need add only one or two other spices (such as turmeric). On the other hand, coriander powder and turmeric powder, for example, can be used along with numerous other spices, as their flavors will blend easily.

Among the spices that, after being lightly fried or roasted, can be added at the last minute to season a dish are mustard seeds, asafetida, oregano seeds, cumin, chilies, cardamom, garlic, cloves, and homemade *garam masalla*. Others, like coriander powder, turmeric powder, onions, and store-bought *garam masalla*, need a longer cooking period.

Weights and Measures

In India we generally do not weigh or measure the ingredients. Most Indians have developed an ability to guess the correct proportions. This can be quite an obstacle when attempting to explain a recipe to a Western friend. I know what it feels like because often when I would ask Babuji or Asho for a recipe, they would tell me the ingredients but not the exact proportions or other details, assuming that I knew all this. If I persisted they would look pityingly at me and say, *"Aare bhai, andaze say dalo"*—"Oh, just add by judgment." *Andaz* means idea, but used colloquially it means "inspired guesswork!"

However, I don't intend to leave you guessing; I have used a simple method for the measurements throughout this book. For instance, in India, ginger and garlic are ground on a stone slab called the *sil,* often with other spices. In this book I specify either grated or minced ginger and garlic separately, so that I can measure the exact amounts.

Cooking Oils Used

A variety of oils and fats are used in India, including mustard oil, sesame oil, almond oil, peanut oil, coconut oil, and various vegetable oils. Some special dishes are cooked in *ghee,* a type of clarified butter. *Ghee,* which is relatively expensive, is not used as freely as it was in earlier times when we always served food cooked in the purest homemade *ghee.*

Availability

Ingredients named asafetida, *chana daal,* tamarind, fenugreek, and jaggery sound exotic and some people might wonder if they are available in this country. Many of the items necessary for my recipes are available at local grocery stores, and natural foods stores. Ethnic food stores are good places to look for unfamiliar items. However, all ingredients needed for my recipes can be found at Indian stores. For those who live in cities where there is no Indian store, I provide a list of retail and wholesale mail-order outlets (see list following the Glossary). Spices, lentils, and other dry ingredients can be mailed safely, but it is wise not to order fresh ingredients by mail.

Substitutions

Whenever possible, I offer alternatives for some typically Indian spices. However, if you want the authentic character of the Indian recipes I present, do not substitute various ingredients on your own.

You will notice I use fresh green coriander leaves in a large number of recipes. They impart a subtle and delicate flavor to a dish, enhancing the taste. These fragile leaves are available, in season, at most Indian and Spanish stores. You can also grow your own from coriander seeds available at local supermarkets or from seeds sold as Chinese parsley. When not available, use the substitutes in the recipes, or your favorite fresh herbs.

In a number of dishes, I use fresh green chilies, most commonly the serranos. Should these be unavailable, jalapenos or anaheims can be substituted. The jalapenos are quite "hot" and roughly half or less of a jalapeno pepper may be equal to one serrano.

With anaheims you will need to use double or more of the quantity of the smaller, "hotter" serranos. There will be, however, a subtle change in the flavor of the dish if you use chilies other than serranos.

I use fresh tomatoes in my recipes. If you want to substitute canned tomatoes, drain thoroughly, then use in the proportion indicated. If you use canned kidney beans or chick-peas, drain well and add them to the preparation after first frying all the spices called for in that recipe. Then simmer all for a shorter period than you would if uncooked beans or chick-peas were being used.

inside an indian kitchen
the tools and the techniques of indian cooking

When you walk into a typical Indian kitchen, the first thing you will notice is that it is very clean. Traditionally, Indians have regarded cooking with a certain reverence. In many homes you are not permitted to enter the kitchen without removing your shoes at the doorstep.

Inside, the stove is often a simple clay or earthen construction, built into a corner of the kitchen. In certain households this is "cleaned" almost every day by spreading a thin layer of fresh, wet clay over the entire surface. This homemade stove is fired by wood, coal, or charcoal, as is the *angeethi,* which is a small cylindrical stove made of metal. The *angeethi,* like the kerosene stove, is very convenient as it can be placed anywhere or even carried for a picnic. Gas and electric ranges are now becoming increasingly popular. In north India and some affluent homes in other parts of the country, there might be a *tandoor,* a special type of clay oven, used to cook a variety of dishes that thus acquire the name *tandoori.*

On the stove you will notice a *karhai,* a *tava* and several *degchis.* Hanging by nails on the walls you will probably see a *karchi,* a *tambakhash,* a *ghotni,* and tongs and pincers of different sizes. Perhaps you will see a *soria,* a *himam dasta,* some *mitti kay bartan,* a *chalni,* a *kaddu kash,* an assortment of *thalis, katoris,* and one or two hand-held coconut graters. In a corner of the kitchen, in every Indian home, there is the *sil batta* used for grinding spices, for each day's meal.

Many of our Indian tools and the cooking processes we use are unique. I believe that a description of them will give you a "feel" for the atmosphere in our kitchens. I think this background will give you the confidence you need to tackle even a large dinner party with flair and confidence!

Tools and Utensils Used for Cooking and Baking

Karhai

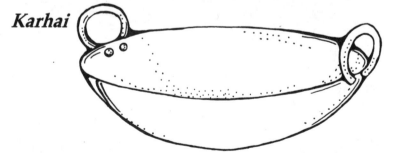

This is a deep, bowl-shaped pan with rounded bottom, made of iron, silvered brass, or heavy aluminum. The *karhai* is used for both shallow- and deep-frying. The advantage is that a relatively small amount of oil is needed, and stir frying is facilitated by the rounded shape. The size range is enormous—from four inches to three feet in diameter. The larger *karhais* are important during marriages and other big feasts, when large quantities of food have to be prepared. They are also used by restaurants and and roadside sellers of a variety of snacks.

Any deep frying pan will serve the same purpose. However, larger amounts of oil will have to be used to achieve the same results. Probably the best substitute for the *karhai* is the Chinese wok, which is very similar in shape, but has a shallower bowl.

Tava

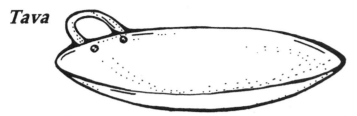

The *tava* is an iron disc, slightly concave, measuring about ¼ inch thick and 9 or 10 inches in diameter. It is placed directly on the stove burner. The main purpose of the *tava* is to cook a variety of breads. For making *Chapati* (Whole Wheat, Flat Round Bread) the convex side is used. To cook *Parathas* (Shallow-Fried Bread), *Dosas,* (Thin Ground Rice and Lentil Bread) and a simple version of *Naan,* (Leavened, Baked, Whole Wheat Bread) the concave side of the *tava* is used. Spices, nuts, and flours can be roasted or shallow-fried on the *tava.* See Index for the recipes of these breads.

In most cases, you can use a heavy, cast-iron or well-seasoned griddle, instead of a *tava.*

Degchi, Sometimes Called *Patila*

Essentially, the *degchi* is just an ordinary pot or pan without handles, used for the bulk of our cooking. The distinguishing feature of the Indian *degchi,* however, is the heavy metal of which it is most often made, and its extended rim into which its special lid fits securely, minimizing loss of flavor and nutrients in cooking. The lid is slightly concave, almost saucer-shaped. This has the specific purpose of enabling live coals or water to be placed on top of the lid during the last stages of cooking.

Chimtay

Tongs are used for lifting the lids from *degchis* and for picking up pieces of glowing charcoal. Large curved pincers are used to grip entire *degchis* (which have no handles) and to lift them off the burner.

Karchi

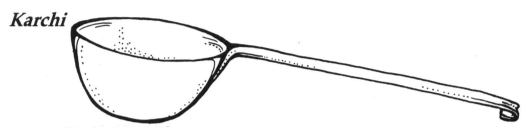

The *karchi* is a heavy iron spoon, shaped like an ice cream scoop or an old-fashioned ladle. It is used for frying small amounts of different spices, that are then added to various dishes. It is also used for ladling out foods that contain a large amount of liquid or gravy.

Ghotni

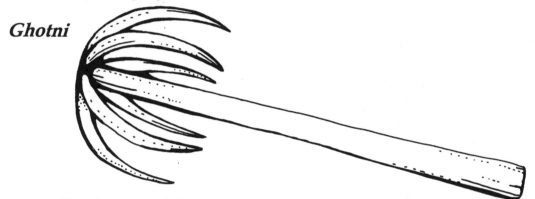

The *ghotni* is used for making butter as well as for stirring and mashing lentils, or certain vegetables. It thus combines the jobs that a regular masher and a stirrer will do. It is a very versatile tool, found in practically every Indian household. It consists of a straight wooden handle, with a "head" at one end. This head has different shapes or designs. Some are like a plain "X" attached to the handle; others are more elaborate, sometimes carved like a cluster of large rosebuds; still others take on any shape that takes the carpenter's fancy.

Chalni

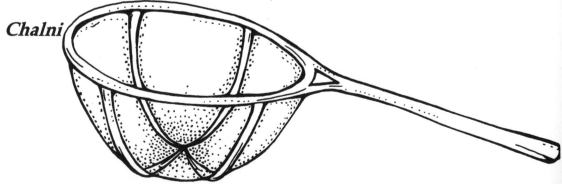

Sieves or strainers of various sizes, are used in much the same way as in the United States. My own favorite is the tea strainer. In Assam, the land of sprawling tea estates, a visitor would be greeted with cups of steaming tea and *paan* (beetle nut and leaf with various condiments), an ever-present accompaniment to the serious business of small talk which would ensue!

Tambakhash

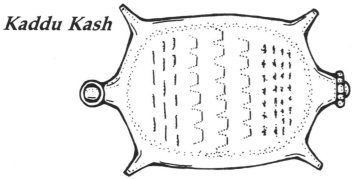

This is a flat iron or metal disc, with or without perforations, attached to a long handle. It is used for extracting foods from hot oil, or stirring foods that need air while cooking.

Kaddu Kash

The *kaddu kash* is a grater, used for grating vegetables, similar to the graters we use in the United States. This tool derives its name from the vegetable, *kaddu* (pumpkin), which is grated to make a popular *halva* (a sweet) and *Khat Mithi Kaddu* (Sweet and Sour Pumpkin or Acorn Squash). Recipes for these are listed in the Index.

Soria

The *soria* is a special tool used for pressing different kinds of premixed batters through holes into hot oil. In general, it works like a cookie press or a cake-decorating tube, but is much larger and has interchangeable plates at the lower end. The *soria* is cylindrically shaped. The plates, which are circular rounds, have perforations of various designs and thicknesses, which allow batters to be pressed through for deep frying. On top is a lid with a screwlike handle attached, which, when turned, presses the batter through the perforations at the lower end.

Tandoor

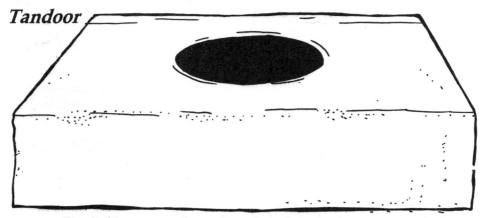

The Indian cuisine has adopted cooking tools and methods from many surrounding countries, making them uniquely its own. One such addition is the *tandoor,* a clay oven.

Since the *tandoor* is not easy to install, most modern cooks use a gas or electric oven in place of the *tandoor.* The culinary results when using the ordinary oven are good, but cannot be compared to those achieved when using the *tandoor.*

Mitti Kay Bartan

These earthen pots are found in almost all Indian village homes. They are simple, unglazed, round pots with saucer-shaped lids that fit very tightly. The earthen pots are inexpensive and readily available in India. They are used widely as cooking vessels.

A pottery enthusiast can easily make a couple of these pots. No glazing is required, so they are ready for use after the initial firing.

Tools Used for Grinding

Sil Batta

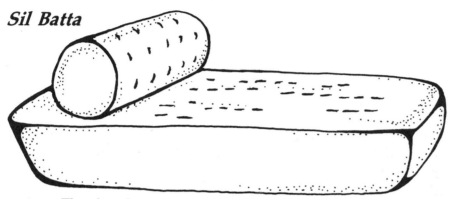

The *sil* is a large, heavy stone slab which can be oval, rectangular, or shaped like a Gothic arch, i.e., rectangular with an arch shaped over one width. Tiny grooves are chipped into the surface of the *sil* to facilitate grinding. The grooves are rechiseled from time to time, as they become blunted with constant use.

Along with the *sil,* the *batta,* which is a small rounded stone, is needed. This little stone also has grooves cut into its surface. Spices or fresh herbs are placed on the *sil* and ground with the help of the *batta.*

Himam Dasta

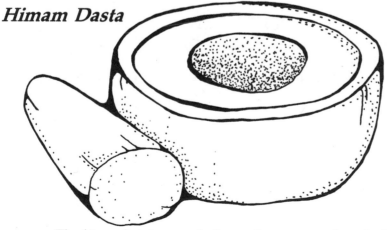

The *himam dasta* is very similar to the mortar and pestle. It is used mostly for grinding whole dry spices.

The electric grinder or blender can replace the *sil* or *himam dasta* in most instances, and is becoming increasingly popular in India.

Turapni

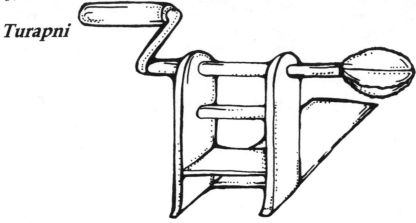

There are many kinds of coconut graters. They are made of iron, attached to a platform which is held securely underfoot, with the user sitting in a squatting position. The halved coconut is held over the grating part, which is an iron rod with a conveniently shaped rounded head with sharp jagged edges. Some graters are operated by a little crank turned by one hand, while the other hand holds the coconut at the cutting edge.

Chakki

Huge stone discs form the *chakki,* which is mainly used for grinding large quantities of grain.

Techniques of Indian Cooking

In Indian cooking, the selection and preparation of spices and other ingredients prior to the actual cooking needs special attention. Many of these procedures constitute some of the most delightfully picturesque, traditional and typically Indian sights and sounds. The aromas that emanate from the kitchen during the preparation of food are part of the magic of a family meal, which I now share with you.

Every Indian child has awakened to the sound of a coconut being grated and of fresh coriander or mint leaves being ground on the *sil batta.*

Preparation Procedures

This familiar pleasure, this comfortable ritual Indian cooks enjoy, is sure to find favor with anyone who loves working with food. The simple physical task that calls forth such captivating scents and marvelous flavors quickly becomes a labor of love.

Peesna (Grinding)

A unique feature of Indian cooking is that the spices used are freshly ground each day. Herbs and spices, such as ginger, garlic, coriander leaves, and cumin seeds, are placed on a flat heavy stone slab, the *sil.* A little tamarind juice, vinegar, or water is sprinkled on the spice which is then ground with the help of the *batta.* A movement that simultaneously presses down and moves back and forth is used, holding the *batta* firmly to do the grinding. The spice is repeatedly gathered into one spot on the *sil* and then the process of pressing down and grinding with the *batta* is repeated. The spice is thus reduced to a soft puree. Grinding the whole spices in this way, with liquid, to make a wet *masalla,* mellows their raw flavors.

If a dry spice, lentil, grain, or nut is needed, it is reduced to a powder, or coarsely ground as required, without the addition of any liquid, in the *himam dasta.* This includes spices such as cloves, cardamoms, peppercorns, and whole dried red chilies. Freshly ground (whole) spices taste and smell incomparably better than commercially sold preground spices.

The electric mixer with an extra attachment for grinding or a spice grinder can be used in place of both the *sil batta* and *himam dasta.* If a puree is required, a little liquid needs to be added in the mixing jar, along with the spice being prepared. A spice mixture that is not dry, but still does not have sufficient liquid content, does not process well in the grinder or blender. Whenever possible, add some liquid from the main body of the dish being prepared to facilitate the grinding of the spices. Also, when only a small amount of the spice is needed, it is quicker and easier to use the *sil batta* or *himam dasta,* as the electric mixer cannot efficiently grind very small amounts of spices.

Saaf Karna (Winnowing, Cleaning)

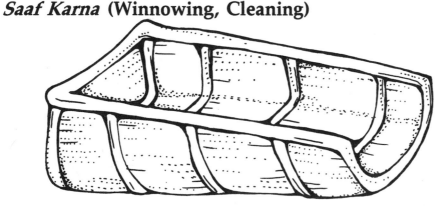

Indians use a large number of grains and cereals daily, mostly in their natural forms. It is often necessary to separate the outer husk from the grain and also the lighter "debris"—stones and sticks, for example—from grains. This is done by winnowing. It is a common sight to see a woman standing outside her kitchen using the *soup,* a flat, large, squarish, woven cane tray to throw the grains in the air skillfully and repeatedly. As she does this, she pulls the *soup* a fraction backwards. This enables some of the foreign matter to accumulate gradually toward the front, while the rest of it is blown away. (You may recall that from biblical times there have been references to chaff, husks of grain, blowing in the wind.) The heavier grain falls to the back of the *soup* and it is then easy to see the few remaining sticks or stones that have accumulated in front, to discard them.

This last step, of picking out the remaining sticks and stones, is essential even in the United States. Many lentils and beans are mixed with small stones which have to be removed before cooking. This is especially true of some small black lentils where it is not easy to see the stones without careful scrutiny.

It is always wise to pick over the lentils carefully before they are needed for cooking. The lentils can then be stored away and only need to be washed thoroughly, and sometimes soaked before they are cooked.

Bhigona (Soaking)

When a cuisine relies heavily on pulses (lentils and beans), the process of soaking is very important. The beans that are very hard should be soaked anywhere from a few hours to overnight. In general, the whole beans such as chick-peas and kidney beans or the small whole black beans are soaked overnight. Other grains and lentils, including rice and split lentils, benefit from as little as an hour or less of soaking. The soaking makes the actual cooking easier, saving both time and fuel.

Khamir Tyyar Karna (Fermentation)

In north India, the popular breads such as *Naan,* Leavened, Baked Whole Wheat Bread, *Tandoori Roti,* Whole Wheat, Leavened, Quick-Baked Bread, and *Bhatura,* A Leavened, Deep-Fried Bread (see Index) are made from flour to which a natural yeast is added. The yeast is fermented overnight and then added to the bulk of the flour, together with yogurt. It is kneaded and made into a dough which is then allowed to rest for a few hours and the process of fermentation continues. It is then kneaded again, formed into flat round shapes and either deep fried or baked in the *tandoor* to make the different types of breads.

The *chapati* is a whole wheat bread that is popular throughout north India. Many health-conscious people eat this bread on the day after it is cooked. It is believed that the yeast, that is naturally inherent in the whole wheat, gets a chance to become further activated overnight. This simple bread, which is often the sole breakfast with a glass of tea, for many Indians, is thus utilized to its best advantage.

In south India, where rice is the main staple, it is used as the base for dozens of different dishes. *Idli* and *dosa* are among the most popular south Indian preparations, where rice combined with lentils is made into a bread. The rice and lentils are soaked separately for a few hours. They are then ground to a paste with the addition of some water, combined, and allowed to rest or ferment for 12 to 24 hours, lightly covered. In a colder climate it is necessary to allow the rice and lentil mixture to ferment for 48 hours or sometimes longer. During this period, the process of fermentation takes place with the enzymes being activated. The mixture takes on a frothy appearance, and turns just a bit sour, as required. The mixture is then cooked (*idlis* are steamed and *dosas* are shallow fried) until a light nutritious "bread" is formed. For making *dosas* which are similar to crepe suzettes, the rice is ground finer than is needed for making *idlis*.

Masalla Lagana (Marinating)

In India, artificial tenderizers are unknown. Yet, often, meat needs to be softened before it is cooked. Raw papaya was always one of Babuji's important ingredients. He would mix the meat well with ground, raw papaya and leave it to marinate for a few hours or overnight, making good use of one of nature's best tenderizers. The meat tenderizers sold commercially in the United States rely heavily on papaya.

Indians also marinate many of their meat or fowl dishes in yogurt. The well-known tandoori chicken is marinated with lemon juice or yogurt or both. In some tribal areas, meat is marinated for up to four or five days in a thick tamarind sauce with a generous dash of jaggery.

Indian pickles are famous the world over. Pickling is a form of marinating, which preserves food and intensifies flavors. However, most pickles need salt, an ingredient we try to avoid due to its poor effect on health, so pickles are not included in this book. Still, they are very popular in India.

Masalla Chunna (Selecting Spices)

A typical sight in many households is a wide array of spices arranged on a *thali*, ready for the day's cooking. The spices are carefully chosen and placed side by side in the required quantities for the dishes to be prepared. This process of selection and arrangement is a time-saving device that is quite important in Indian cooking where so many dishes are prepared for a meal and so many different spices are used. This little detail can be fruitfully copied for Western cooking as well.

Actual Cooking Processes

Talna (Frying)

In most Indian homes teatime snacks are a way of life. A large number of these snacks are prepared by the process of deep frying, using the *karhai*.

The oil or *ghee* is heated in the *karhai* and when it is almost at smoking point, various batters are dropped in and the snacks are ready in a few minutes. *Puri,* a whole wheat bread, is also cooked in one or two minutes, using this method. Along with snacks and breads, some desserts are also made by deep frying different combinations of grains, lentils, and thickened milk.

Perhaps a major part of Indian cooking begins with the process of shallow frying. A relatively small portion of oil is heated in a *karhai* or pan, and then different spices are added at various stages. The main ingredient is then added to the pan and also fried. Some dishes, including a large number of vegetable dishes, are cooked entirely by shallow frying, sometimes with a small amount of liquid being added. Certain breads such as *parathas* and *dosas* are shallow fried by adding a minimum amount of oil to the *tava* or griddle.

Bhun-na (Roasting)

Roasting as a cooking process is regarded differently in India than it is in the West. When an Indian speaks of roasting, or *bhun-na* as we call it, it generally means quickly "browning" lentils, flours, spices, or nuts, without the addition of oil. The process of quickly frying meat (with oil) is also called *bhun-na.*

The *tava* or griddle is placed directly on the fire, and heated. The ingredient to be roasted is then placed on the *tava* and tossed a few times, until it is lightly browned. Often the roasted ingredient is used as a garnish. Otherwise it is added to the main dish, either whole or ground, to enhance the flavor.

This method lends itself excellently to the idea of the quick yet nutritious meal that is so popular nowadays. Wheat, soya, and chick-pea flour that are so healthful can be "roasted" in a matter of a few seconds and added to the main course. Also, the roasted flours and nuts can be used as a garnish to enrich and enliven a simple salad, or dessert.

Tandoor May Lagana (Baking, Grilling)

Traditionally, in India as in the Middle East, the process known as baking is done mainly in the *tandoor,* an earthen oven.

Bhap Dayna (Steaming)

Steaming as a cooking process is widely used in south India and by tribal groups. South Indians use a special steamer known as as the *idli* steamer for cooking their nutritious bread, *idli.*

Tribal groups and Indian settlers from Nepal, China, and Tibet steam one of their most popular dishes, *momos.* This is a kind of pastry-wrapped meatball, similar to the wonton that is known in the United States.

Dum Dayna (Natural Pressure Cooking)

Dum literally means breath. Rice *pullaus* (pilafs) and certain meats and vegetables benefit greatly in added flavor by being given *dum*. The process is similar to steaming, but liquid does not have to be added.

After a dish has been partially cooked by other methods, like shallow frying, and during the last half hour or so of cooking, the lid is sealed very tightly, the fire is turned to its lowest point, and the dish is allowed to cook in its own juices. The idea is to catch the "breath" or essence of the food.

I remember Babuji making a dough from a mixture of flour and water, and forming long strips of it to seal the lid tightly. Then live coals or very hot water was placed on the lid and the dish was left to stay warm, on the lowest heat. He did this every time he made *pullaus* (pilafs). This whole process is known as giving *dum*, and is uniquely Indian. By using a combination of shallow frying or another method, and the *dum* process, the major part of the food value is retained.

Ubalna (Boiling)

If there is one process that is almost never solely used in the preparation of a dish, it is boiling. Plain boiled rice is an exception. Otherwise, after potatoes and occasionally other vegetables are parboiled, they are always cooked by another process as well, before they are served. A number of other ingredients are then added to them, thus changing their flavor and appearance.

Baghar, Tarka, or *Chonk* (A Kind of Fried Garnish)

Another process which is unique to the Indian subcontinent is the process known as *chonk* or *baghar*. Some oil is heated in the *karchi* or a pan, and a chosen spice, or spices, are quickly fried on high heat and immediately added to the already cooked lentils or other dishes. *Chonk* is similar to adding a garnish, but it is not always added at the very last minute as a garnish is, and of course, does not have uncooked ingredients in it.

The sizzling sound associated with *chonk* is one of the most pleasant sounds typical of an Indian kitchen. It heralds to the family that the meal is well in progress, whetting all appetites for the approaching feast!

herbs and spices

Most of the herbs and spices used in Indian cuisine are familiar to western-ers. Still, you will find pleasure in the beguiling flavor combinations Indian cooks have devised for using them. Be bold in testing flavorings that are new to you. They will bring a fresh dimension to food preparation in your kitchen.

Anise *(Suva)*

Anise seeds are golden brown in color and are delicately tear-shaped. They have a subtle sweet flavor which is very pleasant.

This delicate plant has a fragrance I remember as a child. My mother would boil a few anise seeds together with some mint leaves in water and give the strained liquid to my brother, Baba and me when our stomachs were upset. The properties attributed to anise are varied. It is believed to promote digestion, stimulate the appe-tite, alleviate cramps and nausea and to help increase the milk supply of nursing mothers and wet nurses.

Asafetida *(Heeng)*

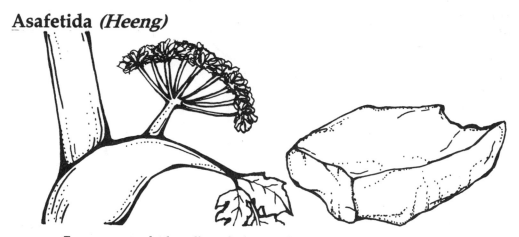

For every roadside seller of *alu puri* this spice is indispensable. It adds an unmatchable, exotic, tangy flavor to the potato.

Asafetida is an oleo-gum resin extracted from an herb that grows plentifully in Asia and the Middle East. This spice is available in two forms, as a powder and in slightly sticky lumps. However, the recipes in this book use only the powdered form of asafetida.

Asafetida relieves gas, acts as a nerve tonic, has carminative qualities, and, when applied to a painful cavity in a tooth, can relieve the ache.

Bay Leaf *(Tez Patta)*

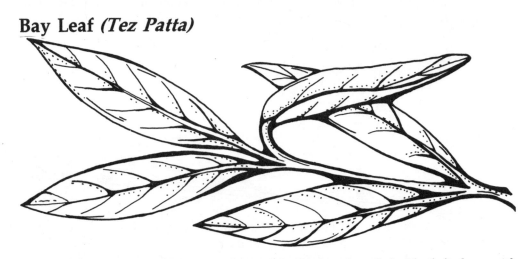

Bay leaves were always prominently displayed on Babuji's *thali* along with other spices necessary for making a *pullau.* Besides *pullaus,* the bay leaf is used in dried form in numerous meat and fish dishes.

Cardamom *(Elaichi)*

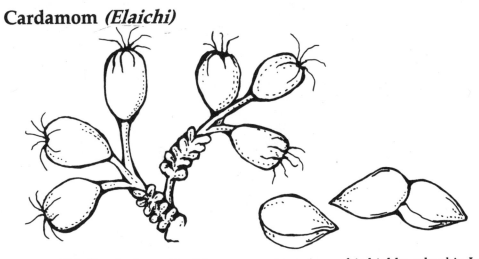

This "seed of paradise" is an expensive spice and is highly valued in India.

Indians use cardamoms for *pullaus,* meat, poultry, and fish dishes and in preparing sweetmeats or desserts. *Srikand,* A Light Dessert with Yogurt, Saffron, and Almonds (see Index), derives its subtle flavor mainly from this delicate spice. Often, the whole pod, including the skin, is used so as to extract all the flavors from this delightfully aromatic spice.

There are two main kinds of cardamom, large and small. Big cardamoms *(badi elaichi)* are dark brown and have 20 to 30 dark, highly flavored seeds. Small cardamoms *(choti elaichi)* are pale green, buff, or khaki-colored. Generally they have 10 to 15 subtly sweet-flavored, dark seeds.

A tea made from some crushed cardamom seeds (from small cardamoms) and water, with a few drops of honey, is a soothing, effective cure for queasiness or nausea. Cardamom is also believed to stimulate the appetite and is used as a mouth freshener.

Chilies and Pepper *(Mirch)*

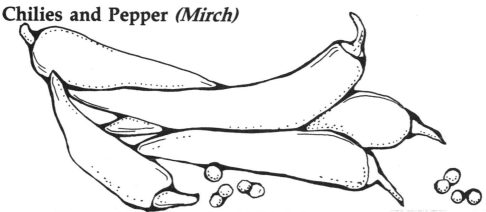

There are dozens of varieties of chili in India, comprising varying degrees of "hotness." As chilies are so widely used in India, people there are able to judge the hotness of a chili by its appearance. Chilies can be used fresh or dried.

Fresh green chilies *(hari mirch)* are used to provide hotness, to give flavor, or to garnish a dish. Generally, a green chili with seeds is hotter than one whose seeds have been removed. Once the seeds have been removed, the chili adds a beautiful, elusive flavor to a dish, without making it "chili hot." Whole green chilies (with or without seeds) are a traditional garnish for some lentils and potato dishes, and are used as an accompaniment to some kinds of *kababs.*

Dried red chilies *(lal mirch),* either whole, crushed, or ground, are used to add hotness to a dish, or they can be lightly fried and used as a garnish.

The mild-flavored, dried red chilies *(kashmiri mirch)* are used to add a lovely reddish color to a dish without imparting the usual hotness associated with chilies.

Black pepper *(kali mirch),* the dried berry of the pepper tree, grows plentifully on the Malabar (west) Coast of India. It has long been one of the oldest trade items from the East, being regarded as a basic condiment and a cure-all remedy among indigenous medicines. It is used to cure toothaches and other aches and pains. It is often used by midwives as a rejuvenating tonic for mothers who have just had a baby. A few grains of black pepper, mixed with honey, acts as an appetizer and promotes digestion.

To obtain white pepper *(safed mirch),* the peppercorns are allowed to ripen on the vine, and the black outer hull is removed. This leaves a white center that is milder than black pepper.

Both pepper and chilies are believed to be a cure for digestive ailments. This is especially true of green chilies, which are rich in chlorophyll. Chilies also are highly antiseptic and act as a preservative, which is an important consideration where the weather is very warm. Indians use chilies and pepper quite liberally. Any adverse effect from the regular use of these hot spices is neutralized by the Indians' equally heavy reliance on yogurt, which is well-known for its stabilizing qualities.

Take or leave chilies, but be sure you avoid *bichu chili!* This tiny but potent chili richly deserves its name—Scorpion chili!

Cinnamon *(Dal Chini)*

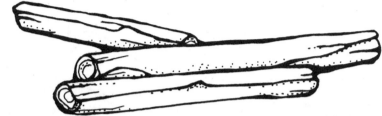

Often when Baba and I would walk into the kitchen, Babuji would offer us a cinnamon stick, which is known to sweeten breath. We use this popular spice in both sweetmeats and savory dishes.

The bark of the cinnamon tree is used as a tonic for the whole system; it may be used to relieve heartburn and nausea and is commonly administered as a sedative during childbirth.

Clove *(Lavang or Laung)*

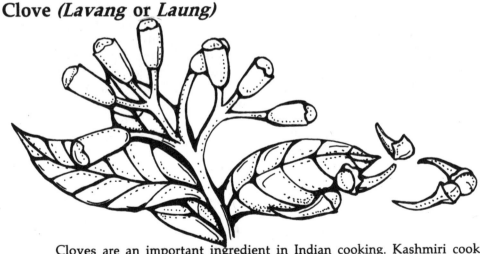

Cloves are an important ingredient in Indian cooking. Kashmiri cooking makes use of coarsely pounded cloves in a variety of dishes to great advantage. Whole cloves are used, producing excellent results, in a sweetmeat also known as *lavang.*

Whenever I had a sore throat or slight cough, my mother would give me a whole clove to suck. This would bring relief from the cough, as well as sweeten the breath. Clove tea, or a whole clove, chewed slowly, also relieves various stomach disorders. Used externally, clove oil is helpful in relieving pneumatic pains, headache, and lumbago.

Coriander *(Dhania)*

Among the first things my mother did when she arrived in the United States was to plant coriander seeds in a convenient corner of my garden. Since it is used so extensively in our cooking, it is practical to have home-grown coriander handy.

This versatile plant, a member of the parsley family, is used in three forms —whole leaves, seeds, and freshly ground—and functions as a spice and as an herb. The leaves *(dhania patta* or *hara dhania)* resemble flat-leaf parsley, but are more fragile-looking. Used extensively as a garnish, they impart a delicate, fresh fragrance, plus a dash of pleasing color. The off-white to yellowish-brown seeds are used as a spice. They are used freshly ground and impart a subtle flavor that does not mask the basic flavors of the dish to which they are added.

Coriander relieves stomachache. It is a wonderfully cooling, soothing herb that also acts as an appetizer and a carminative. It is sometimes applied externally to soothe the pain of rheumatism. Indians prepare it as an eyewash, to ease pain, swelling, and burning. Coriander vinegar was used to preserve meats in ancient times.

Cumin *(Zeera)*

One of the most delightful aromas associated with Indian kitchens is that of cumin seeds being roasted. Cumin that is freshly roasted and ground smells and tastes incomparably better than preground cumin.

Cumin has such a rich pleasant flavor that it can easily be used as the sole spice in many quick stir-fried vegetable dishes. It is also wonderful as a garnish, lightly roasted, sprinkled over savory yogurt preparations.

Slightly thinner than cumin, black cumin *(kala zeera)* gets its name from its color. It is a very important ingredient in the preparation of *garam masalla* (see Index) which is one of the most commonly used combinations of spices in India.

Cumin is beneficial to the heart and also acts as an appetizer and digestive. It is particularly useful for women, as it has properties that are believed to strengthen the uterus.

Curry Leaf *(Kardi Patta)*

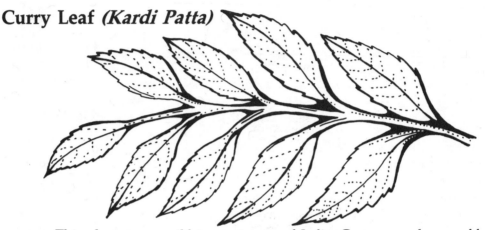

This plant grows wild in most parts of India. Green curry leaves add an exquisite, fresh flavor to a wide variety of dishes. It is always a great pleasure to begin cooking, walk out to the garden to pluck a few curry leaves, and add them to the particular dish being made. Fresh overlapping curry leaves are sometimes used as a wrap for meat or fish dishes.

Dried curry leaves are available in the United States. They are not to be confused with commercial curry powder, which is rarely used in Indian homes.

Dill *(Soya Saag)*

In India, nursing mothers find dill helpful in promoting the flow of milk, particularly when combined with anise seeds, coriander, fennel and caraway. Used for settling an upset stomach, as well as for gas pains, these feathery, succulent leaves are very quieting to the nerves when used as a drink.

Fennel *(Saunf)*

Fennel seeds are very widely used in India. Most restaurants keep a platter full, either on individual tables or at the counter, much as mints are used in the United States. After a meal, we pick up a handful, and chew on the sweet-tasting seeds to help digest the meal and freshen the breath. The flavor improves if the seeds are served lightly roasted.

Kashmiri cooking uses fennel to great advantage, in curries or breads. The tender shoots of this delicate plant are excellent used as a garnish for meat, fish, or rice dishes. The seeds are used in pickling certain foods, especially mango.

Both the seeds and the root of the fennel are useful in clearing stomach and intestinal problems. Fennel has basically the same beneficial effects as anise. Tea made from fennel seed is good for insect bites and food poisoning.

Fenugreek *(Methi)*

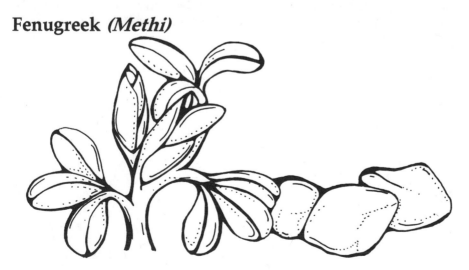

Fresh fenugreek leaves are considered a great delicacy. When the leaves are in season in India, people dry out quantities of them for use in winter when they are not available fresh. *Alu Methi*, a dish of potatoes with fenugreek leaves, is a very popular dish in the United Provinces and Punjab. In America, many Indians plant fenugreek seeds to ensure a supply of this delicious green. It is very helpful in toning down strong cooking odors, such as the smell of fish.

My grandmother made sure that she included lots of fenugreek in our food when any of us were recovering from an illness, for it is believed to have marvelous strengthening qualities. Fenugreek, a small rectangular-shaped mustard-colored seed, is taken for bronchitis or fevers and used as a gargle for sore throats. Powdered (ground) fenugreek seeds are used externally for some types of skin irritations.

Garlic *(Lassun)*

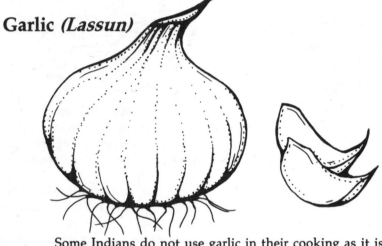

Some Indians do not use garlic in their cooking as it is thought to inflame the baser passions! For the rest, however, garlic is an indispensable kitchen herb, used both for its flavor and (usually raw) for its medicinal values. It relieves various problems associated with the digestive system. Garlic is a great invigorator, and its beneficial effect on blood circulation and the heart brings relief to common body ailments and has a soothing effect on nerves.

It has wonderful antiseptic qualities. When I had an earache as a child, my mother would heat mustard or sesame oil with whole cloves of garlic and place a few drops in my ear. This brought quick relief with no fear of infection.

Garlic is excellent pickled or made into a chutney, adding a powerful dose of both flavor and medicine to the meal.

Ginger *(Adrak)*

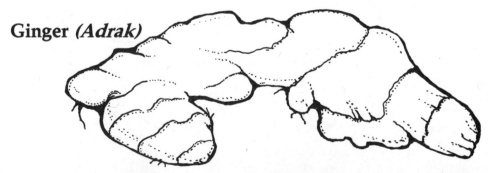

A pungent, spicy addition to food, fresh ginger is easily available in India, and is widely used. Ginger root, dried and powdered, is known as *sonth*. It is an important ingredient for a popular tamarind-based sauce which is also known as *Sonth* (see Index).

Finely chopped ginger mixed with honey brings almost immediate relief to a sore throat, cough, or cold, as it inhibits the production of mucus in the body. Boiled and drunk as a tea, it promotes cleansing of the system. Our *Masalla Tea* recipe (see Index) calls for generous amounts of ginger!

Kewra Water *(Ruh, Kewra)*

A flavoring obtained from the flower of a plant called *kewra* is known in India as *ruh, kewra,* which means "essence of *kewra.*" It comes in the form of a white liquid. It is valued for its cooling properties.

Lemon *(Nibu)*

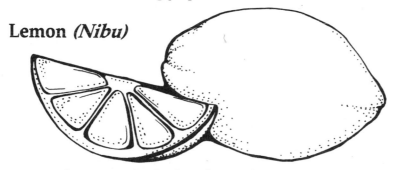

A very popular drink, *Nibu Pani* (lemon water) which is simply old-fashioned lemonade, is served in every Indian home in the hot summer months. After a heavy meal, a squeeze of lemon diluted in a little cold water works wonders to stabilize the stomach and cleanse the system. Applied externally, it is useful on sunburns. Lemon juice combined with thick (natural) cream, or glycerine and rose water, makes a wonderful facial pack, and it is the only beauty treatment my mother has ever used! A refreshing citrus, lemon is used as a remedy for many ailments, mainly colds and coughs. To relieve sore throat pain, dilute lemon juice with water.

Mace *(Javitri)*

Mace, the hard outer shell of nutmeg, is used sparingly because of its powerful flavor and its equally strong hallucinogenic effect when overused. A light orange-tan when dried, ground mace (or thin strands of mace) provides a golden color and an exotic flavor to numerous desserts and meat dishes.

Mint *(Pudina)*

Mint exists in a wide variety in India, as in the United States, and most types are good for relieving indigestion, gastric upsets, and nausea. It is soothing, helpful in easing pain, and acts as an antacid. Of course, it's also a wonderful breath freshener.

Aside from adding a splash of color as a garnish, mint forms the base for a popular chutney, *Pudina Chutney* (see Index).

Mustard *(Rye* or *Sarson)*

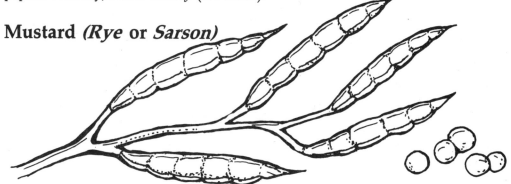

Mustard seeds are one of our most commonly used spices. In Eastern India (Assam, Bengal) mustard is known as *rye.* In Punjab, Bihar, Rajasthan, and Utter Pradesh it is known as *sarson.* The milder seeds are tiny, beadlike and reddish-brown to black in color. Yellow mustard seeds are more pungent. The recipes in this book use only the reddish-black seeds.

The seeds are used in many pickles. They are also very popular as a *baghar, chonk,* or *tarka* (see Glossary), lightly fried and added to lentils just before serving.

Mustard leaves are a very popular green in India. They are available here at most grocery stores and are especially delicious when cooked with mustard oil. (Mustard oil is available at most Indian stores.)

Mustard oil slightly warmed (with or without garlic cloves) is a favorite massage to soothe aching bones or painful muscles and is regularly rubbed onto infants before their daily baths.

Nutmeg *(Jaiphal)*

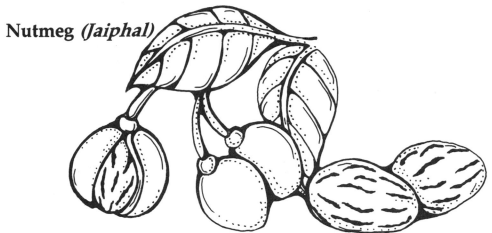

This nutlike spice, the fruit kernel of the nutmeg tree, acts as an appetite stimulant and improves digestion. The sweet flavor of nutmeg, with a warm spicy undertone, makes it a highly prized cooking tool. Mughal meat and rice dishes, along with some desserts, achieve a distinction with its sparing use.

Onion Seeds *(Kelonji)*

These small black seeds, with their very distinctive flavor, are similar to anise in shape. They're used in pickles and for flavoring some vegetable dishes and breads.

Oregano Seeds *(Ajwain)*

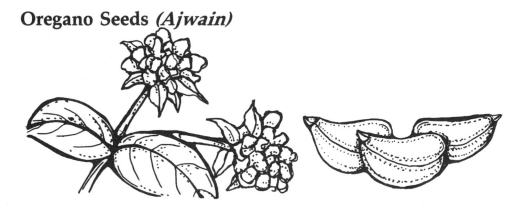

The small tear-shaped seeds of the oregano plant are a delightfully aromatic spice. They are an excellent aid to digestion and are helpful in combatting the common cold and the symptoms associated with it.

These seeds are very popular in Punjab, Utter Pradesh and some other parts of north India. Their strong, pleasant flavor is used to great advantage in bread and vegetable recipes.

Papaya *(Papita)*

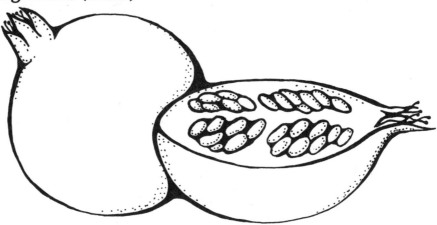

A common sight outside Indian homes is raw green papaya, thinly sliced and strung up like a necklace to dry in the sun. The dried fruit is stored either in slices or pounded to a fine powder for use as a meat or fowl tenderizer, especially in Moghul recipes, which also make use of unripened papaya pulp. Ripe papaya is very popular as a breakfast food or as a dessert. It grows plentifully and needs little nurturing.

Papaya is an excellent digestive aid, and is also believed to relieve allergies and combat intestinal worms. People in villages in India often wrap papaya leaves around a wound to help the healing process. The juice is also good for removing skin blemishes.

Pomegranate *(Anar)*

Pomegranate has been used in India for centuries. Poets rhapsodized on the beauty of the orange pomegranate flowers set against the deep green leaves. These two colors (orange and green) were favorites of the Moghul court. My grandmother had a gorgeous *gharara* (costume) set in shades of these colors. The seeds of the pomegranate are dried and stored for use as a spice whenever a tangy flavor and a dark color are needed in a dish.

Taken daily mixed with *pudina* (mint), pomegranate acts as a natural antacid. Because of its astringent qualities, the rind is helpful as a gargle for throat irritations.

Poppy Seeds *(Khas Khas)*

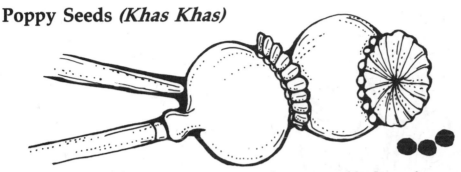

Babuji used to go into raptures over the sweet, nutlike flavor of poppy seeds. There are two kinds of poppy seed, one white and the other blue-black. We use the white poppy seed most often, for it works well in seasoning and thickening curries.

These seeds, pounded and boiled with milk, relieve colds and act as a tranquilizer.

Rose Hips *(Gulab Kay Beech)*

Rose hips have a full bodied "rosy" flavor and are delicious in jams and syrups. They are also wonderful when brewed as a light, delicate tea. If you want to collect rose hips to make tea or jam, freeze a few at a time until you have enough. Freezing will keep most of their essential vitamins (particularly vitamin C) intact. For treating common colds, rose hips are excellent medicines, for, taken regularly, they help to build up the necessary resistance.

Rose Water *(Gulab Ka Pani)*

Rose water is a clear liquid, distilled from fresh rose petals. It is used in small amounts for flavoring. Pink rose petals are occasionally used to add an exquisite touch to certain desserts, and my family adds it as a festive decoration on *Raan,* Spicy Leg of Lamb (see Index).

Rose petals mashed with sugar (or honey) are used as a mild purgative and as a cure for intestinal ailments.

Saffron *(Zafraan)*

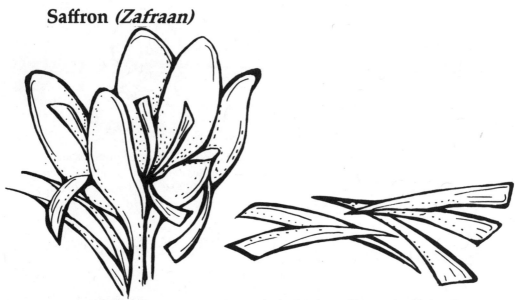

Saffron is very expensive to buy, for the only portion of the plant that is used are the flower's dried stigmas and part of the style. Therefore, over 35,000 flowers are needed to produce one pound of the spice.

Often used to color food a golden yellow, saffron also imparts an exquisite flavor. It comes in two forms, threads and powder. You need only half the amount of powdered saffron when using it instead of the saffron threads.

Sesame Seed *(Til)*

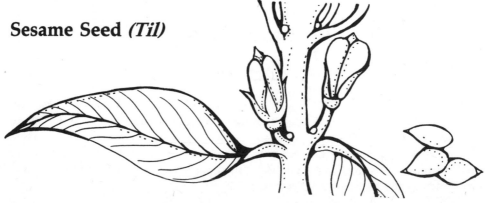

These small, cream-colored seeds, besides having a lovely nutty flavor, were purported in ancient times to have magical properties. They still carry a mystical aura, as they have been used for centuries as offerings to gods and as an aphrodisiac, mixed with simple ingredients, like rice, milk, and honey, or with extravagant ones, like sparrow's eggs and crow's gall! These popularly used seeds are quite rich in nutrients.

Tamarind *(Imli)*

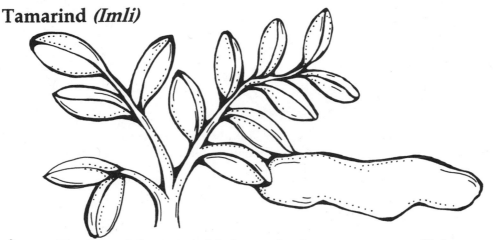

The fruit of the tamarind is known for its sweet-sour taste. Under every village tamarind tree in India, you're sure to see a group of children trying to knock down the fruit with sticks and stones.

The dark brown tamarind pulp is dried and stored for use in a large variety of dishes. A very refreshing and popular tart drink (known also for reducing fever) is made from this pulp. Sometimes, the leaves are used externally as a poultice.

Turmeric *(Haldi)*

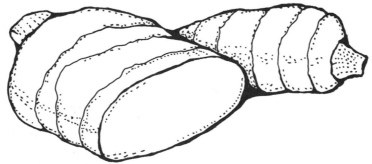

Turmeric, a yellow root, dried and powdered, is found in every kitchen in India. Apart from imparting color to food, it is used so widely because of its marvelous preservative and health-giving properties. Turmeric purifies the blood, acts as an antiseptic, and when applied as a paste, is good for itches, some skin diseases, and minor cuts and bruises.

Wood Sorrel *(Khatta Patta)*

This delightful herb grows as plentifully in India as it does here in the United States. The beautiful leaves are rich in vitamin C and make a refreshing change used as a garnish.

some recipes basic to indian cooking

The varied Indian cuisine derives much of its unique flavor from a combination of spices, the use of homemade dairy products, and exotic ingredients such as coconut milk, tamarind juice, and jaggery. We would like to share some of these recipes with you.

Clarified Butter — *Ghee*

3 pounds unsalted butter

In a large skillet with a heavy base, melt the butter on low heat. Reduce the heat to the lowest point possible and cook until the milk solids separate from the clear yellow oil which will form. This takes between 45 minutes to a little over an hour.

Being careful not to shake the contents of the skillet, strain through damp cheese-cloth. Collect the clear liquid which is the *ghee* and discard the residue.

Pour into a jar with a tight-fitting lid and close when cool. In winter, *ghee* can be left at room temperature but keeps better when refrigerated. *Ghee* will become solid at low temperatures.

Yields 4 cups

Coconut Milk — *Nariyal Ka Dudh*

Choose a coconut full of liquid, with dry "eyes" (the smooth dark parts). To open easily, puncture the two eyes. Save the liquid and refrigerate it to use as a cool, refreshing drink. Bake the drained coconut in a preheated oven for 15 minutes at 400°F. Remove it immediately from the oven and while the coconut is still hot, split with several sharp blows. The coconut meat should fall away easily from the hard outer shell. You do not need to remove the outer dark brown part of the coconut meat unless a recipe specially calls for doing this.

Chop the coconut meat and blend with hot water. (If you prefer, grate the coconut meat, soak in hot water, and squeeze out the liquid which is your coconut milk.)

The process is described in detail in recipes where it is required.

Jaggery — *Gur*

Jaggery is available at Indian stores. However, if you do not have it on hand, you can make 1 tablespoon of jaggery substitute by combining:

½ tablespoon unsulfured molasses

½ tablespoon honey

_____ *Chenna* _____ Homemade
Cottage Cheese

2 quarts milk

2 tablespoons lemon juice

½ cup Homemade Yogurt (see page 41)

Bring milk to a boil. Reduce heat to low and stir in lemon juice and yogurt. Stir until milk curdles. Remove from heat immediately.

Strain through cheesecloth, collecting the drained liquid in a pan, and the cheese, which will be in small lumps, in the cloth.

Yields 2 quarts

Remarks

If you like, add some thick cream for smoothness, and flavor it with your favorite spices.

_____ *Dahi* _____ Homemade
Yogurt

3 cups nonfat dry milk powder

6 to 8½ cups cold water

¾ tablespoon plain yogurt (for culture)

Place the milk powder in a 4-quart pot. Pour in the water and mix thoroughly with a whisk.

Set the pot on moderately high heat for 12 to 15 minutes. Stir occasionally to prevent sticking. After 15 minutes the milk should be scalded. Remove from heat and allow the milk to cool to lukewarm (about 109°F—not less than 106°F). This normally takes between 35 to 45 minutes, if the milk is left to cool on its own.

Smear the yogurt along the base and side of a large, thick ceramic or glass bowl. Pour the milk in, stir once and immediately cover the bowl with a flat lid to enclose the top.

Drape 2 layers of thick cloth over the lid and then tuck under the bowl of milk. Set a kettle of boiling water on top of the cloth-covered lid of the bowl of milk and leave overnight. Next morning, uncover the yogurt and refrigerate.

Yields 2 quarts

Remarks

Usually the packet directions on the powdered milk container suggest you mix 3¾ cups water and 1⅓ cups milk powder. We use less water than indicated to make thick yogurt. If you use 6 cups of water to 3 cups milk powder, you will get very thick yogurt. If you do not require very thick yogurt, use 8 to 8½ cups water.

Yogurt is well loved and used extensively in Indian cooking. It is said to promote longevity because of its marvelous qualities. One of its most beneficial effects is improved digestion.

Sometimes yogurt will curdle if cooked for too long or at high temperatures. While this may not look particularly attractive, it does no harm to the intrinsic flavor of the dish.

A Blend of ———————————————— *Garam Masalla* ————————————————
  Freshly Ground Spices

2 teaspoons freshly ground
  cardamom (about 40 to 48 seeds)

4 teaspoons cinnamon sticks,
  broken into small pieces (about 4
  medium-size sticks)

8 teaspoons whole cloves
  (1 teaspoon when ground)

4 teaspoons peppercorns
  (1 teaspoon when ground)

4 teaspoons black cumin seeds
  (1 teaspoon when ground) or
  4 teaspoons cumin seeds

¼ teaspoon nutmeg powder

⅛ teaspoon mace powder

To make the powder, take the seeds out of the cardamoms and grind them in a coffee or spice grinder. If you do not have such a grinder, use an electric blender. You should have 2 teaspoons of freshly ground cardamom seeds. Set aside.

Grind the cinnamon, cloves, peppercorns, and black cumin seeds, one by one.

In an airtight container, mix together the freshly ground spices with the nutmeg powder and mace powder. Shake the container to mix the spices thoroughly.

Yields about 2 tablespoons

Remarks

Different combinations can be used to make garam masalla, *but we give you our favorite.*

To save time, you can grind all the spices together. However, using the above method assures your having the exact amounts needed, as peppercorns, cloves, and cardamoms tend to vary slightly in size.

Garam masalla is also available at Indian stores. But the store-bought spice mixture will not have the fresh flavor you will get from your own freshly made batch. Also, the marketed garam masalla *includes spices not used in most homemade recipes, many of which need a longer cooking period to enable their flavors to mellow and blend. Allspice can be used, in a pinch, as a substitute. In fact, we prefer it to the commercially available brands of* garam masalla.

I enjoy making garam masalla, *as the kitchen air is full of the aroma of these freshly ground spices!*

Tamarind ———————————————— *Imli Ras* ————————————————
  Juice

Soak tamarind pulp in hot water for at least 15 minutes. Squeeze the pulp hard to extract all the juices and strain the liquid through a sieve. Discard the pulp and any seeds, and use the liquid. The exact amount you will need is given in each recipe.

For a thick juice: 1 tablespoon tamarind pulp

3 to 4 tablespoons hot water

For a thin juice: 1 tablespoon tamarind pulp

½ cup hot water

_____ *Panir* _____ Homemade
Plain Cheese

2 quarts milk

2 tablespoons lemon juice

½ cup Homemade Yogurt (see page 41)

Make *chenna* as described above.

Wrap the cheese in the cheesecloth, spreading it to form a flat square or circle, and place a heavy weight on it. Leave for 2 or 3 hours, or until cheese is uniformly flattened and forms one solid mass. Carefully remove from the cloth and cut into ¾-inch squares. These cheese pieces are called *panir*.

Yields 2 quarts

Remarks

You can lightly fry these cheese cubes if you like.

We have used chenna *or* panir *in* Matar Panir I *(Lightly Curried Homemade Cheese and Peas),* Matar Panir II *(Curried Homemade Cheese and Peas), and* Chenna Aur Tinday Ki Halki Sabzi *(Lightly Curried Homemade Cheese and Frizzle Squash). See Index for these recipes.*

When a recipe calls for water, we often use the strained liquid (whey) from the chenna *instead.*

suggested menus for family meals

To represent even a portion of our diverse cuisine is no easy task! The menus that an Indian family might devise are endless. We have chosen menus to reflect this range—from the simple to the more elaborate—and to accommodate those who are vegetarians as well as those who are not. **See Index for page numbers of the recipes.**

I

Matar Bhaji (Spicy Green Peas)

Tehri (Lightly Spiced Rice with Hard-Cooked Eggs)
or
Asaan Pullau (Easy Rice/Lamb Pilaf with Saffron)

Kheeray Ka Raita (Spicy Yogurt with Cucumber)

Pudina Chutney (Mint Chutney)
or
Dhania Chutney (Fresh Coriander Chutney)

Fresh Fruit

II

Khitchri I (A Light Dish Made with Rice and Orange Lentils)
or
Khitchri II (Split Lentils and Rice)

Dahi (Homemade Yogurt)
or
Kheeray Ka Raita (Spicy Yogurt with Cucumber)

Tazay Tamatar Ki Chutney (Fresh Tomato Chutney)
or
Pudina Chutney (Mint Chutney)

Suji Ka Halva I (*Halva* of Cream of Wheat, Nuts, and Raisins)

III

Korma I (Curried Lamb Cubes with Saffron)
or
Mughlai Murgh Ka Saalan (*Mughlai* Chicken Curry)

Gobi Gajar (Lightly Curried Cauliflower with Carrot Slivers)

Dahi (Homemade Yogurt)

Pudina Chutney (Mint Chutney)

(Menu III continued on next page)

Chapati (Whole Wheat, Flat Round Bread)
or
Sada Chaval (Plain Boiled Rice)

Fresh Fruit

IV

Macher Jhol (Fish Curry with Tamarind)

Baingun Bhaja (Savory, Shallow-Fried Eggplant Slices)

Sada Chaval (Plain Boiled Rice)

Ghana Dada Ki Meethi Dahi (Ghana Dada's Sweet Yogurt with Fresh Dates)

Tazay Tamatar Ki Chutney (Fresh Tomato Chutney)

V

Alu, Dosay Kay Liyay (Curried Potato with Fresh Coconut, to Accompany Dosa)

Gajar Bean Bhaji (Lightly Curried Carrots and Beans with Coconut)

Sambar (Lentils with Vegetables)

Sada Chaval (Plain Boiled Rice)
or
Dosa (Thin, Ground Rice and Lentil Bread)

Nariyal Chutney I (Coconut Chutney with Yogurt)

Payasam (Milk Pudding with Sago and Vermicelli)

VI

Saag (Spicy Mixed Greens, Pureed)

Sukha Kala Chana (Dry Curried Dark Chick-Peas)
or
Sabut Masur Aur Tamatar (A Spiced Lentil Dish with Tomatoes)

Makkay Ki Roti (Cornmeal Bread)
or
Naan (Leavened, Baked, Whole Wheat Bread)

Tazay Tamatar Ki Chutney (Fresh Tomato Chutney)

Yogurt with Honey

VII

Keema Matar (Curried Minced Meat with Peas)

Khat Mithi Simla Mirch (Sweet and Sour Green Peppers)

Pudina Aur Dhania Chutney (Mint and Coriander Chutney)

Paratha (A Shallow-Fried Bread)

Fresh Fruit

VIII

Murgi Ka Saalan (Chicken Curry)

Khat Mithi Kaddu (Sweet and Sour Pumpkin or Acorn Squash)

Dahi (Homemade Yogurt)
or
Kheeray Ka Raita (Spicy Yogurt with Cucumber)

Pudina Chutney (Mint Chutney)

Paratha (A Shallow-Fried Bread)

Puri I (A Deep-Fried Round Bread)

Fresh Fruit

suggested menus for parties

The conventional "party" spread in India is comprised of meat, fowl, and fish along with two or three curried vegetables, lentils, yogurt salad, rice, chutney, bread (Indian) and one or two rich desserts. As you see from the following party menus, the number of items has been modified to accommodate the Western lifestyle. **See Index for page numbers of the recipes.**

I

Malai Kofta (Cream-Stuffed Meatball Curry)
or
Murgh Mussallam (Spiced Whole Chicken)

Asho Ko Rye Saag (Asho's Lightly Curried Whole Mustard Leaves)

Gobi Gajar (Lightly Curried Cauliflower with Carrot Slivers)

Kali Sabut Urad Daal (Small Whole Black Lentils)

Shahi Biryani (A Royal Rice and Lamb Dish)

Tamatar Raita (Yogurt with Tomatoes)

Paratha (A Shallow-Fried Bread)

Gajar Ka Halva (A Rich Carrot Nut Pudding)

II

Paturi (Fish with Mustard Oil and Mustard Seeds)

Korma I (Curried Lamb Cubes with Saffron)
or
Tandoori Murgh I (Whole *Tandoori* chickens)

Saag (Spicy Mixed Greens, Pureed)

Nariyal Chaval (Rice Cooked in Coconut Milk)

Kheeray Ka Raita (Spicy Yogurt with Cucumber)

Puri I (A Deep-Fried Round Bread)

Payasam (Milk Pudding with Sago and Vermicelli)

(Menus continued on next page)

III

Raan (Spicy Leg of Lamb)

Haaq (Whole Spinach Greens)

Tok (Sweet and Sour Tomatoes)

Murgh Pullau (Rice and Chicken Pilaf)

Kailay Ka Raita (Yogurt with Banana and Nuts)

Baingun Ki Chutney (Eggplant Chutney)

Khamiri Roti (Whole Wheat, Leavened, Quick-Baked Bread)
or
Naan (Leavened, Baked, Whole Wheat Bread)

Beheshti Golay (Heavenly Chick-Pea Flour Balls with Almonds)

IV

Mughlai Murgh Ka Saalan (*Mughlai* Chicken Curry)
or
Rogan Josh (Mutton or Lamb Curry)

Seekh Kabab (Broiled Kabobs of Minced Meat and Spices)

Bhara Kerela (Stuffed Bitter Gourd)

Dhuli Maash Ki Daal (Split White Lentils with Onion Crisps)

Masalla Pullau (A Spicy Rice Dish)

Nariyal Chutney I (Coconut Chutney with Yogurt)

Naan (Leavened, Baked, Whole Wheat Bread)
or
Puri II (Light-Colored, Deep-Fried Whole Wheat Bread)

Sivain (A Dessert of Thin Vermicelli Cooked in Milk)

V

Kaju Badaam Bharay Pasanday (Meat Rolls Stuffed with Nuts)

Mughlai Murgh Ka Saalan (*Mughlai* Chicken Curry)

Same Bhaji II (Diamond-Cut Fava or Green Beans with Mustard Seeds)

Bhuna Chaval (Rice Fried to a Golden Brown)

Dahi Bara (with *sonth*) (Deep-Fried Rissoles Made from Lentils, in Yogurt)

Asho Ko Tamatar Chutney (Asho's Tomato Chutney)

Puri I (a Deep-Fried Round Bread)
or
Paratha (a Shallow-Fried Bread)

Srikand (Light Dessert with Yogurt, Saffron, and Almonds)

VI

Korma I (Curried Lamb Cubes with Saffron)
or
Korma II (Succulent Lamb or Beef Curry)

Asho Kay Tandoori Tukray (Asho's *Tandoori* Chicken Breast Pieces)

Khat Mithi Kaddu (Sweet and Sour Pumpkin or Acorn Squash)
or
Puri Phulgobi (Whole Cauliflower with Carrots and Potatoes)

Biryani E Mahi (Rice Pilaf with Fish)
or
Matar Pullau (Rice Pilaf with Peas)

Puri II (Light-Colored, Deep-Fried Whole Wheat Bread)

Shahi Tukray (Princely Delicacy of Fried Toast Cooked in Milk)

(Menus continued on next page)

VII

Hussaini Kabab (Three-Inch-Long Kabobs with Almonds)
or
Murgh Massalam (Spiced Whole Chicken)

Jhinga Curry (Curried Prawns with Coconut)

Baingun Bharta (Eggplant Crush)
or
Turai Bhaji (Curried Zucchini)

Matar, Soya Pullau (A Delicate Rice Dish with Green Peas and Fresh Dill Leaves)

Tamatar Raita (Yogurt with Tomatoes)

Dhania Chutney (Fresh Coriander Chutney)
or
Pudina Aur Dhania Chutney (Mint and Coriander Chutney)

Bhatura (A Leavened, Deep-Fried Bread)
or
Naan (Leavened, Baked, Whole Wheat Bread)

Phal Ka Salaad, Rabri Kay Saath (Fruit Salad with Thickened Milk)

all recipes listed by category

VEGETABLES

the trip to aligarh

My brother, Rashid (known to all as Baba), and I were fortunate to grow up in Shillong, a small, green town nestled in northeast India's Khasi Hills near the foothills of the Himalayas. We were lucky also, in that we had two families. Our "immediate" family—M. B. (a nickname endearingly given to my father), my mother, Rashid, and I—was encircled in the warmth of another larger family. My grandfather, aunts, uncles, cousins, family friends and loyal, trusted family servants were part of this big, close family.

Shillong was a meeting place of different cultures. The region is known as the Khasi and Jaintia Hills, after the two predominant tribes. Other hill tribes from neighboring areas, including the Garos, Mizos, and Nagas, as well as many plains people—Assamese, Bengalis, and others—had also made their homes there.

In those days Shillong was the capital of Assam. It was also a large air force and army center, which brought together government servants and service personnel from all parts of India. It offered a unique opportunity for us to learn and grow. Through our friends from different regions, we were able to feel the pulse of the country, even in this far-off corner of India.

Each year when school was closed for the winter in Shillong, Baba, my mother, and I would make the pilgrimage to Papa's (her father's) home in Aligarh in the north of India. It began with a train journey that was two days and three nights long. The traveling party always included Asho, Baba's *ayah* or nurse. Actually, Asho was more like a second mother to Baba and me, and she brought warmth and an irrepressible sense of humor to all our lives. Her two children, Madhu (which means "honey") and Lama came along, of course. The party was completed with Hansraj, a gentle, steadfast family servant, who was a constant source of support to us all.

My father, a senior civil servant, could not leave his work for the 2½ months that we would be away. Yet, having lost his own parents at an early age, he was always very supportive of my mother's wish to see her family each year and always, toward the end of our Aligarh visit, he would find time to join us there for a few days. M. B., who loved my grandfather, Papa, as if he were his own father, was always greeted with much affection by him, my aunts, and our old family friends and retainers.

The Journey Begins

In the earlier days, there was no airstrip in Shillong. The only link with the outside world, with the rest of India, was through a narrow, winding road, hewn out of the wooded hillsides. This road wound sixty-three miles through the hills to the nearest city, Gauhati, from where we would start our much-awaited, exciting train journey.

We would pass orchards of citrus fruit, with oranges and lemons of many sizes and hues. Entire hillsides were covered with potato, banana, plum, peach, rose, and pineapple plantations. The pineapple of the Khasi Hills is surely the sweetest in the world.

As you can imagine, having these luscious pineapples so readily available inspired the people of the region to create many irresistible recipes that feature this lovely fruit.

"The juice would run down our fingers as we stopped at our favorite stall (run by a rosy-cheeked child with the business acumen of a seasoned banker) to sample a pineapple or two."

A Pineapple, ——————— *Annanas Srikand* ———————
Homemade Cream Cheese Dessert

4½	cups Homemade Yogurt or thick Homemade Yogurt (see page 41)	1	teaspoon warm milk
2	cups chopped pineapple	8	small pale green cardamom pods
¼	teaspoon *zafraan,* saffron powder	8 to 11	tablespoons honey
		1	tablespoon pistachio nuts

Place the yogurt in the middle of a large piece of doubled cheesecloth, or in a large cloth napkin. Gather up the ends carefully and tie them together. Hang the wrapped yogurt with a container below to collect the draining whey—a sink faucet is excellent for this purpose—until the texture is thick like cream cheese (about 14 to 24 hours).

In an electric blender, process the pineapple until it is a thick puree.

Allow the saffron powder to soak in the milk until completely dissolved.

Peel the skin from the cardamon pods. Wrap the seeds in thick paper toweling and pound until the seeds are reduced to a coarse powder.

Scoop the solid yogurt, which we call our homemade cream cheese, from the cheesecloth and place in a bowl. It will "peel" off easily. There should be about 1½ cups.

Mix together the cream cheese, 1 cup crushed pineapple, the milk with the saffron powder, cardamom powder, and 8 tablespoons honey. Stir thoroughly. Add more honey if desired.

Ladle into small individual serving bowls and chill. Garnish with finely sliced pistachio nuts before serving.

Serves 6

Remarks

Srikand *is a delicacy from Maharastra. We have added pineapple and honey, both of which are abundantly available in Shillong.*

——————————————— *Annanas Salaad* ——————————————— Pineapple
Fruit Salad

¾ cup pineapple juice

1 tablespoon arrowroot

4 to 6 tablespoons honey

¾ teaspoon orange extract

⅛ teaspoon *kewra* water

1 pineapple

2 apples (about ½ pound)

2 bananas

2 tablespoons raisins

2 tablespoons chopped pine nuts or pistachio nuts

1 to 2 tablespoons lemon juice

½ cup ripe strawberries

½ cup sour cream

Bring pineapple juice to a boil. In a separate bowl, combine arrowroot, honey, and orange extract. Stir mixture into pineapple juice. Simmer 15 minutes. Add the *kewra* water and simmer an additional 3 minutes. Pour the syrup into a 2-quart serving bowl.

Cut the pineapple into ¾-inch slices (about 6 slices). Place each slice on a board and with a small sharp knife, cut away the skin and eyes. Immerse the pineapple slices in the syrup.

Wash and core the apples. Lay the apples sideways, cut into ½-inch slices, and add to the syrup.

Peel and slice the bananas finely. Add to the pineapple and apple.

Gently stir in the raisins, pine nuts, and lemon juice. Refrigerate, covered, for about 2 hours. Shake the contents of the bowl once or twice to make sure the syrup reaches all the fruit.

Wash the strawberries, drain, cut in half, and stir into the bowl.

Serve with a dollop of sour cream.

Serves 10 to 12

Remarks

We usually serve this salad as a dessert, to round off a heavy meal.

———

It was customary for the farming villagers of the vicinity to set up makeshift stalls often manned by a rosy-cheeked little child with the business acumen of a seasoned banker. Each individual pineapple is huge, smelling strongly of nature's fragrance. The fruit, when cut, is soft and succulent, yet crisp. The juice would run down our fingers as we stopped at our favorite stall to sample a pineapple or two or a jar of honey on our way down the hill. Almost every Khasi home had a beehive in its carefully tended garden.

Gauhati is located on the banks of the mighty Brahmaputra (meaning Son of Brahma) River. Here, we were seen onto the train by M. B., Babuji (who was much, much more than our family cook) and a large number of close family friends. Among them was Ghana Dada, as he was popularly called, a village elder who had worked closely with my father. He had virtually become a family member, as had many of our close friends.

We would await Ghana Dada's arrival with much anticipation, for we knew that word of our journey would have reached him through the village grapevine. He would appear, rotund and jolly, accompanied by a retinue of followers, laden with packages of food for our journey. We had long given up asking him not to bring anything, as we saw that it was no use.

The Joy of Unwrapping the Bundles

In the packages there would be *Ghana Dada Ki Meethi Dahi,* Ghana Dada's Sweet Yogurt with Fresh Dates (see Index), thick and tempting, in a large earthen container. There would be hundreds of small *puris,* a favorite bread, cooked in the purest homemade *ghee.* They were wrapped in soft banana leaves, in bundles of 10 or 20. It was always such a thrill to carefully unfold each separate package, and peep in expectantly, even though we already knew what was inside!

Ghana Dada's ——————————— *Ghana Dada Ki Meethi Dahi* ———————————
Sweet Yogurt with Fresh Dates

24 to 30 ripe dates

5 cups milk

1 tablespoon plus ¾ teaspoon thick Homemade Yogurt (see page 41)

Place the dates in a colander and wash under cold running water. Drain thoroughly. Place them on a board and cut the flesh away from the seeds. Chop, then mash to a pulp.

In a pan with a heavy base, mix the milk and date pulp. Slowly bring the milk to a full boil. Remove from the heat, stir well, and strain through a fine sieve, pressing the dates to extract all the juices. Discard the strained pulp. Allow the milk to become lukewarm (106° to 109°F). In winter, the milk should be a little warmer than lukewarm before you set it.

Smear yogurt along the sides and all over the inner base of a large ceramic or earthen bowl. Pour the lukewarm milk in slowly and stir thoroughly. Quickly cover with a *thali* or lid that will overlap the edges of the bowl. Drape two or three layers of kitchen cloth over the lid and bowl and tuck in the cloth so that the bowl is kept warm. Keep the bowl in a warm place or place a kettle of boiling water on top. Uncover after 8 to 10 hours. If well set, refrigerate before serving. Otherwise, cover again and set a kettle of hot water on top until well set.

Serves 6

Remarks

This dish makes a lovely light dessert. It was one of my father's favorites.

To go with the *puris* we would find a number of different chutneys and pickles, of mangoes, chilies, lemons, each in an individual little red earthen pot. We Indians are great believers in the marvelous digestive properties of lemon. *Nibu Pani* is a popular drink, and there is hardly a home that doesn't have a jar of lemon pickle maturing in the sun. We also think that it is very good for the complexion, mixed with cream and applied as a facial pack. The food parcels always included, of course, *alu bhaji* (curried potatoes), a dish which is popular throughout India. We could eat the yogurt either as a dessert or as an accompaniment to the meal. For the real dessert, there was a typical Assamese coconut preparation, *pitha,* which is a must at the yearly harvest festival.

Naturally, Babuji, our cook, was not pleased with these goings on. He took it as a personal affront that we should accept any food other than that which he had so lovingly prepared for us. He would have packed some of our favorite dishes for us in *tiffin* (lunch) carriers—three or four separate steel or aluminum containers that are fitted, one on top of another, and held securely in place by a sort of folding frame, with a handle on top. This way, each dish can be kept neatly separate. These *tiffin* carriers are marvelous for picnics or journeys and are a common sight in India. My mother would protest that he was giving us enough food for an army, but Babuji was determined, and he prevailed. It is typical in India for family and friends to send off the traveler laden with homemade goodies.

An Indian boy carries a tiffin *loaded with treats.*

Babuji's Menu

Babuji's *kababs* were famous, as he well knew. He guarded the recipes so jealously that even my mother had a difficult time learning his secrets. He made sure that we had both *Seekh* and *Shami* kabobs. We all love *kerela* (bitter gourd), so he would include a dish of this. As the name implies, it has a slightly bitter taste. The art of cooking this vegetable lies in taking advantage of this bitterness, to enhance its flavor, and preserve its medicinal properties. *Kerela* is believed to purify the blood.

To complete the main meal, there would be Babuji's crisp fried fish, *urad daal* and his *rumali rotis,* unbelievably paper thin, a preparation secret known to very few chefs. *Rumal* means handkerchief, and the *roti* really lives up to its name, soft and delicately thin as fine muslin. Two or three sweets would be included, often *Gajar Ka Halva* (A Rich Carrot Nut Pudding) and Babuji's special *Gur Ki Taffee* (Soft Jaggery and Peanut Toffee). See Index for these two recipes.

A Deep-Fried _____ *Puri I* _____
Round Bread

2 cups whole wheat flour

¾ cup water

1 tablespoon *ghee* (see page 40) or vegetable oil

3 or more cups vegetable oil for deep frying

Place the flour in a large bowl. Slowly add water and the *ghee* while mixing. If a mass forms, begin kneading. If the flour does not adhere, add 1 tablespoon of water at a time until you have a mass of dough.

Turn onto a board and knead until the dough becomes soft and pliable (about 7 to 12 minutes). Cover with a wet cloth and set aside for 30 minutes.

Heat oil in a *karhai* or wok. If you use an ordinary pan, you will need more oil. The oil should be hot enough so that a tiny piece of dough dropped in will immediately rise to the surface.

Divide the dough into 12 portions. Shape each portion in a ball, flatten, and roll out until 4½ to 5 inches in diameter.

Gently slide the *puri* into the *karhai* from the edge. When it rises to the surface of the oil, press down with a large slotted spoon and hold the *puri* in the oil until the lower surface is a light golden brown. This takes only a few seconds. Turn the *puri* over and cook until golden brown. It takes about a minute to cook a *puri* if the oil is hot enough. Continue to adjust the heat between high and moderately high. When you lift a cooked *puri* out of the oil, increase the heat to high and as you put in a new puri, reduce the heat to moderately high. Set on paper toweling.

Serves 6

Remarks

Puris *go very well with* Dum Alu *(Small Potatoes with Mustard Oil and Spices),* Khatta Chana (Cholay), *Curried Dark Chick-Peas with a Sour Tang, or* Khat Mithi Kaddu, *Sweet and Sour Pumpkin or Acorn Squash (see Index).*

Everyone loves puris. *They are a common sight at wedding feasts or religious festivals. They also keep well wrapped in foil or plastic and refrigerated.*

_____ *Nariyal Chutney I* _____ Coconut
Chutney with Yogurt

1 coconut

1½ teaspoons vegetable oil

½ teaspoon mustard seeds

½ teaspoon *safed urad daal,* a lentil, or minced peanuts

1 dried red chili

1½ teaspoons minced garlic

8 tablespoons thick Homemade Yogurt (see Index)

2 tablespoons minced coriander leaves or your favorite herb

Break the coconut. (For procedure, see page 40.) Chop half the coconut into small pieces. Place in a blender and process until finely shredded. You should have 1½ cups.

Heat the oil in a skillet and fry the mustard seeds. As soon as they begin to sputter, add the *urad daal* and chili and fry until the *daal* is lightly browned. Remove the skillet from the heat and stir in the garlic.

Grind the fried spices. In a clean blender, blend together the ground spices and yogurt for a few seconds.

Combine the yogurt mixture and coconut. Spoon into a serving bowl and garnish with coriander leaves. Serve chilled or at room temperature.

Serves 6

Remarks

Coconut chutney is a traditional south Indian delicacy that is served with idlis *or* dosas.

We love to serve this delicious chutney with any kind of meal. It also goes beautifully with a Western meal. You might like to try it as a topping for baked potatoes.

_____ *Pudina Aur Dhania Chutney* _____ Mint and
Coriander Chutney

1 tablespoon tamarind pulp

½ cup hot water

2 cups mint leaves

2 cups coriander leaves with stems

1½ cups chopped onions

2 or 3 small green chilies, chopped

2 tablespoons scraped and grated ginger

1 teaspoon honey

Soak the tamarind pulp in the hot water for at least 15 minutes. Squeeze the tamarind pulp thoroughly, strain, and collect the juice. Discard the pulp and any seeds.

Wash the mint and coriander leaves thoroughly in a colander.

Mix all the ingredients together in a bowl. Place a few tablespoons of the mixture in a blender and blend about 3 seconds. Scrape down the sides of the container and then add another few tablespoons of the mixture. Repeat the process until all the mixture is blended. Place the chutney into a bowl, cover, and chill.

Yields about 2¼ cups

Kabobs ————————————— *Shami Kabab* ——————————————
Cooked with Lentil and Spices

¾ cup *chana daal,* a lentil

2¾ cups water

1 tablespoon plus ¾ teaspoon scraped and finely sliced ginger

1 tablespoon plus ¾ teaspoon chopped garlic

3 large cardamom pods

1½ pounds leg or shoulder of lamb or beef, minced

1 cup chopped onions

25 to 30 peppercorns

6 whole cloves

1-inch cinnamon stick, broken into pieces

3 bay leaves

2 or 3 dried red chilies

2 eggs

3 tablespoons chopped coriander leaves

½ tablespoon scraped and minced ginger (optional)

1 tablespoon lemon juice

2 small green chilies

3 tablespoons *ghee* (see page 40) or vegetable oil

2 tablespoons *besan,* chick-pea flour

Remove any sticks or stones from the *daal.* Wash the lentils thoroughly several times and soak in a small bowl with 2 cups of water for a few hours, preferably overnight. Drain.

Place the ginger and garlic in a heavy 4-quart pot. Pound the cardamom pods lightly and add them to the pot. Add the meat, onions, peppercorns, cloves, *daal,* cinnamon, bay leaves, red chilies, and ¾ cup water. Bring the water to a boil, stir thoroughly, reduce heat to low, and simmer, covered, for about 50 minutes. Stir occasionally.

Uncover and cook over moderate heat until the water is absorbed. Stir occasionally.

Spoon the cooked meat into a large mixing bowl and remove the cardamom skins and bay leaves. Beat the eggs lightly and add them to the bowl. Add the coriander leaves, minced ginger (if used), and lemon juice. Slit the green chilies in half and remove the seeds under cold running water. Mince the chilies and add them to the bowl.

Using your fingers, mix all the ingredients in the bowl thoroughly. Divide into 18 portions or 12 larger portions.

Heat the *ghee* in a large nonstick or cast-iron skillet. (I divide the *ghee* and use 2 skillets.)

Sprinkle the chick-pea flour on a plate. Form each meat portion into a flat, round patty-shaped *kabab.* Lightly coat each *kabab* with the flour and place the *kababs,* side by side, in the skillet. Leave enough room to be able to turn the *kababs* with a flat metal spatula. Reduce the heat to low and cook until the *kababs* are brown (about 10 minutes). Turn the *kababs* over and fry until the second side is brown. Add a teaspoon of oil if needed.

Serves 6

Remarks

This traditional Muslim dish, one of Babuji's specialties, is served with Chapati *(Whole Wheat, Flat Round Bread), or other breads, such as* phulka, *or* rumali roti. *On special occasions it is served with meat* pullau.

——————————————— *Seekh Kabab* ——————————————— Broiled
Kabobs of Minced Meat and Spices

1½ pounds lean round of lamb or
    beef

1 tablespoon peeled and ground
    unripened papaya or lemon juice

1 tablespoon *ghee* (see page 40) or
    vegetable oil

20 peppercorns

2 teaspoons *khas khas,* white poppy
    seeds

10 whole cloves

1 tablespoon plus ¾ teaspoon
    coriander seeds

2 teaspoons black cumin seeds

2 large dark brown cardamom pods

6 tablespoons *besan,* chick-pea flour

1 tablespoon scraped and grated
    ginger

¼ teaspoon nutmeg powder

¼ teaspoon cinnamon powder

    pinch of mace powder

½ teaspoon chili powder

1½ tablespoons thick Homemade
    Yogurt (see page 41)

2 tablespoons plus ¾ teaspoon
    water

2 tablespoons chopped coriander
    leaves or parsley

3 to 4 tablespoons vegetable oil

Wash the meat and dry it. Cut it into pieces and pass through a mincing machine using a fine plate, or a meat grinder. Mix well with the papaya and *ghee* and set aside, covered, for 1 to 2 hours.

Heat a *tava* or griddle, and roast the peppercorns, poppy seeds, cloves, coriander seeds, cumin seeds, and cardamom pods, while stirring, until the coriander seeds are lightly browned. Grind these spices to a powder and set aside. Then roast the chick-pea flour until lightly browned (about 1 minute).

Mix the roasted ground spices, roasted chick-pea flour, ginger, nutmeg, cinnamon, mace, chili, yogurt, and water with the meat and knead for 1 to 2 minutes. Add the coriander leaves to the meat and mix. Divide the meat into 24 to 30 portions.

Roll each portion into a ball, then flatten it into a roll and pass a flat skewer through it. Dip your hands into water and begin to gently press the meat, to form a roll about 4 inches long. You can form as many *kababs* as will fit on a skewer. Moisten your hands as you work. Lightly brush oil over the *kababs.* Roast on a charcoal grill or broil for a few minutes on each side.

Meanwhile, prepare the *salaad* (see Index) to accompany the *seekh kabab.* Arrange the *kababs* on a bed of the salad and serve immediately.

Serves 6

Remarks

If you find the kababs *are too dry, fry them very lightly in oil before serving. Babuji always lightly fried his* kababs *after cooking them over charcoal.*

A Rich Carrot Nut Pudding — *Gajar Ka Halva*

6 carrots (about 1 pound)	2 tablespoons plus ¾ teaspoon *ghee* (see page 40) or butter
4 cups milk	2½ tablespoons gold raisins
½ cup light cream	3½ tablespoons slivered almonds
4 drops *kewra* water	2 or 3 sheets edible silver leaf
1 teaspoon pale green cardamom seeds	
6 to 8 tablespoons honey	

Wash the carrots and grate. Set aside.

Bring the milk to a boil. Add the carrots and any juice that may have accumulated, cream, and *kewra* water. Cook over low heat until thickened (about 1½ to 1¾ hours). Stir frequently to prevent sticking to the pan.

Wrap the cardamom seeds in a double layer of paper toweling and pound with a mallet until the seeds are crushed.

Add the cardamom seeds, honey, *ghee,* and raisins. Cook over low heat while stirring until the mixture forms a solid mass and is a deep orange-pink color. Transfer to serving dish.

On a heated *tava* or griddle, stir the slivered almonds over moderate heat until lightly brown (about 1 minute). Allow to cool and then use to garnish the *halva.*

As a final festive touch, lightly place the silver leaf over the *halva.*

Serves 6

Remarks

We love our Gajar Ka Halva *hot, but you may serve it chilled if you prefer.*

Auntie Joy is like a member of our family. Her husband, Ian Hunter, was a tea planter in Assam and our families have spent many happy times together. She is a cordon bleu chef, and her halva *is as good as you'd get anywhere!*

We were thus well fortified for our long cross-country journey. Laden with Babuji's goodies, and Ghana Dada's affectionate contributions, we arrived at the railway station. After our tearful farewells, we would be off, waving until we could no longer see M. B. and Babuji on the platform. My mother, Baba, Asho, Madhu, Lama, and I settled down in our reserved compartment. It was accepted that men servants traveled "third class."

At the first train stop, we would crowd near the windows and beckon to one of the many tea vendors, who rushed up and down calling out their wares. *"Chai garam"*—"Hot tea"—they shouted, in the typical drawn-out, familiar, singsong voice. This was the call we were most interested in. The tea was always piping hot, and the vendor would pour it into a little earthen cup straight from his enormous kettle. The flavor of the earthen container mingled with the hot tea, and created a drink beyond compare. If the stop was a longish one, we would blow feverishly on our tea to cool it quickly, so we could get another cup.

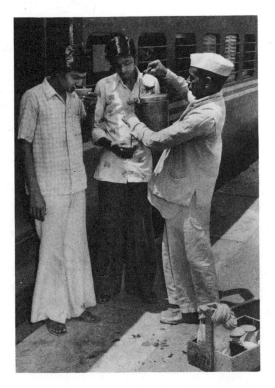

Two travelers stretch their legs and patronize the ever-present tea vendor.

The train always started with a lurch, and no matter how we braced ourselves for the shock, we always spilled a drop or two of our precious drink! We'd go to the window and toss the *culhar* (earthen cup) out with a flourish. It would break with a sharp crack, scattering clay splinters, much to our satisfaction. My mother always liked to see that we broke each cup, to make sure that no one else would be offered tea in the same one! This tea is especially good in winter when anyone has a cold or is feeling a bit under the weather. The ginger and cloves in the tea are excellent for combatting the sore throat and congestion that go with a cold or flu. They also give a lovely warm feeling on a frosty day.

Excitement at Every Stop

The lull of the journey was broken by a sudden onslaught of noise, bustle, and activity at each stop. The platform would be filled with people, some jostling each other at the ticket counter, others fast asleep in the middle of the platform, huddled under sheets or shawls. Baggage of assorted shapes and sizes was everywhere. Porters carrying many tiers of luggage on their heads were running ahead of passengers rushing to board the trains. Wandering cats, dogs, goats, and cows mingled with the crowd, sure of picking up a morsel or two.

Stalls of fresh fruit dotted the platform: mango, papaya, and winter fruits such as oranges, guava, and sugarcane. Sweetmeats and savories of all kinds were also temptingly arranged.

The stall owners knew very well what most people liked to eat. Many varieties of sweets were prominently displayed. Mounds of walnut-size yellow *laddus,* glistening white, diamond-shaped *barfi, halvas,* and sweet rounds of syrup-soaked *rosogullas* tempted everyone with a sweet tooth. Sizzling in huge *karhais* were savories such as *pakoras, samosas,* and *puris.* The ever-popular *cholay* (a chick-pea preparation) garnished with onions and long, thin, hot green chilies was very popular.

The recipes for some of these universal favorites are given elsewhere in this book. The recipe for *laddu,* a well-loved sweetmeat used for most celebrations and festive occasions, appears below. Every time I have done well at an exam or been successful at something, my friends have asked, *"Laddu nahen khilaogi?,"* meaning, "Aren't you going to feed us *laddus?"* Laddus are also distributed to family and friends at the birth of a child. A *laddu* has always been a symbol of happy times. The recipe below, invented by my mother, was pieced together from what she remembered of her aunt's cooking.

Cream of ───────────────── *Laddu* ─────────────────
Wheat, Chick-Pea Honeyed Balls

8 tablespoons *ghee* (see page 40) or butter	3 tablespoons slivered almonds
1 cup Cream of Wheat	3 tablespoons desiccated coconut
1 cup *besan,* chick-pea flour	4 tablespoons honey
8 small green cardamom pods	

In a *karhai* or skillet, melt 4 tablespoons of butter and fry the Cream of Wheat over moderate heat until it is light brown and emits an aroma (about 15 to 18 minutes in a *karhai* and 10 to 12 minutes in a skillet). Stir frequently. Keep the Cream of Wheat warm.

In the same *karhai,* or in another skillet, melt the remaining butter and fry the chick-pea flour over moderate heat until light brown (about 12 to 15 minutes). Stir frequently. Keep the chick-pea flour warm.

Remove the cardamom seeds from the pods, wrap them in several layers of paper toweling, and pound with a mallet until finely ground.

In a large bowl, quickly mix together the warm Cream of Wheat, chick-pea flour, cardamom, almonds, coconut, and honey. Form into 18 walnut-size balls, working quickly before the mixture becomes cool. Toss each ball gently around in your palms. Use this method to form the *laddu* instead of pressing or squeezing firmly. Serve when slightly cool.

Serves 6

Remarks

When thoroughly cooled, the laddus *can be stored in an airtight container for weeks.*
Serve as a coffee snack or a dessert.

Gossiping Is Fun

While Baba and I explored the sights, sounds, and smells of the platform, my mother chatted with neighbors in adjoining compartments. When women get together in India, they talk freely and intimately among themselves, discussing family details, such as the impending marriage of a daughter. Young women, on a few minutes acquaintance, would begin complaining about their mothers-in-law! Other women would cluck sympathetically, not at all offended by these revelations.

The mother-in-law is all powerful in an extended family. Her word is law at home, and she takes the responsibility of family honor very seriously. Newcomers to the family pass under her training automatically, and it is a rare daughter-in-law who measures up to expectations! Generally, mothers-in-law, guardians of family honor, do not complain in public about their daughters-in-law. They do, however, indulge in oblique hints and knowing looks, to show the sorry state of affairs they have to put up with.

Domestic servant problems would be discussed, and of course, the subject of cooking would inevitably come up. Asho would visibly brighten and in her charming, humorous way, would try to find out a few culinary secrets. She was generous too, in sharing hers, but I noticed that she always left out some key ingredients in recounting a recipe! Asho's tomato chutney was loved by everyone. She would readily give the recipe but would omit crucial ingredients such as mustard oil and fenugreek seeds! However, here is Asho's recipe, intact!

Asho Ko Tamatar Chutney — Asho's Tomato Chutney

8 large tomatoes	1¾ tablespoons minced ginger
5 tablespoons mustard oil	3 small green chilies
¼ teaspoon fenugreek seeds	1 teaspoon turmeric powder
¾ cup chopped onions	1½ teaspoons paprika
1½ tablespoons minced garlic	

Cut tomatoes into 1-inch cubes and set aside.

In a 4-quart heavy-bottomed pot, heat the mustard oil until it is almost smoking. Drop in the fenugreek seeds and when they are almost black, add the onions and fry over medium heat until golden brown (about 10 minutes). Add 1 tablespoon garlic and 1 teaspoon ginger and fry over moderately high heat for 2 minutes.

Add the tomatoes, ½ tablespoon garlic, 1½ tablespoons ginger, chilies, turmeric powder, and paprika and bring to a boil. Lower the heat to moderate, cover, and cook 15 minutes. Stir occasionally. Uncover and cook over moderately high heat until the liquid thickens and resembles a thick sauce (about 30 minutes). Stir frequently during the last stages of cooking.

Serves 6

Remarks

This dish is a delicious addition to most meals. It freezes well and can be reheated many weeks later with no loss of flavor.

Asho was always very secretive about this recipe. She gave it to me very reluctantly.

Back in our own compartment we would read, play cards, or just dream, gazing out of the window. I loved to watch the miles and miles of undulating, gleaming fields of mustard, bright with yellow flowers at this time of the year. *Rye saag* (mustard green) is a very popular dish throughout India, and this very tasty and nutritious vegetable is prepared in many different ways. Pink, yellow, and white water lilies, and water chestnuts abounded in every stretch of still water. The roots and tender stems of water lilies are used in pickles and vegetable dishes. In India, an exquisite form of bread is made from dried, powdered water chestnuts.

My mother is very good at storytelling. Throughout the journey, I would ask her questions about her childhood in Aligarh. From her I learned many things. She told me how my grandparents had dedicated their lives to the education of Muslim women, at a time when even education for boys was not common. They persisted in their goal against great resistance, criticism, and skepticism, and succeeded in establishing a school, and later a college, which are now very well known in India. My grandparents also maintained a huge, open, generous household which included unmarried aunts, relatives, friends in financial straits, and young orphan girls whom they were educating.

My great aunt (my grandmother's sister) shared the burdens and joys of running this bustling household with my grandmother. She was a cook, seamstress, artist, counselor, and housekeeper par excellence. Many of her recipes have been faithfully followed by family cooks since, and we were often reminded when enjoying a meal together, that a particular dish was Amma Begam's recipe. (*Amma* means mother and *Begum* is a Moghul title for a noble lady.) Since she observed *purdah,* her interviews with any nonfamily male were conducted from behind a curtain, light and beautiful, but properly opague.

Adventure on the Platform

I could go on listening to mother's stories forever, but Baba would get restless and tired of sitting. So he and I would get down at a stop with Asho and take a walk on the platform to stretch our legs. My mother would be anxiously watching to make sure we got back in time before the guard blew his whistle as a final warning. At a long stop, at a large station, we occasionally went with Hansraj, who came often to inquire if we needed anything. We were always very interested to see what was going on in his third class compartment, and we would gaze with unabashed, childish curiosity at his traveling companions.

There were people of all sorts here. A bearded Sardar from the Punjab, with a fascinating moustache! A Rajasthani peasant with his colorful smock and impressive turban, smoking his small hand *hukka* (a kind of pipe where the smoke is filtered through water). I remember a Bihari woman, heavily draped, with her *sari* pulled over her head, thus protected from prying eyes. Only her arms, covered with lovely red glass bangles, were visible. Perhaps a sedate south Indian couple would be traveling, the man in cotton shirt and checked *lungi* (cloth wrapped around the waist, like a sarong), the woman wearing a brilliantly colored, pure silk Madrasi *sari,* a large vermilion mark on her forehead, and a diamond in her nose. The train trip was a much-awaited opportunity for village women who traveled third class to wear their finery. Village life does not allow much opportunity for women to dress up and show off their few precious belongings.

Apart from the larger trunks and boxes, each person would be carrying bundles of all sorts of shapes and hues. We were always fascinated to see what was inside. Their families had packed the best of homemade, traditional snacks to eat on the journey. Family ties are strong everywhere, and if a family member is leaving for even a few days, much is made of the occasion. Simple, yet nutritious food is thoughtfully provided for the traveler, with much love and care. We Indians consider it a privilege to prepare food for our loved ones.

The south Indian couple would unwrap their bright Madras cotton-wrapped parcel. Pretending not to notice, we would look from the corners of our eyes to see what was inside. There might be *dosas,* with special potato stuffing, and *idlis.* In little stainless steel containers there would be mango pickle and coconut chutney. To complete the meal, there might be a sweet preparation made from the coconut that grows so abundantly in coastal regions.

Everyone was always very friendly. The men would discuss the latest harvest among themselves and the women would talk about their families. The Bihari woman I had noticed earlier told me all about her life, and how happy she was to be going to her parents, a few stops away, whom she rarely had an opportunity to visit. She was accompanied by her uncle, who, she said, had been sent especially to chaperone her. We spoke in hushed voices. A radiant smile appeared on her face when I gave her children some of our Western style sweets, a kind of rock candy, wrapped in thin, colored cellophane paper, relatively expensive in India.

She opened her worn, old, but clean bundle and offered me some of her home-cooked *chana* and *roti.* I think I rather gained from the barter!

Coming from a rather secluded corner of India, it was always fun for Baba and me to see the "many faces of India." The different regional dresses, the sounds of different languages, and the exchange of ideas and stories was fascinating. Each person had brought the delicacies of his particular area. Typical recipes from different regions of India exemplify the range and diversity of our Indian cuisine. Some of these recipes have been collected by my family members from our large circle of friends. We have often included them in our family meals, and greatly enjoyed them, as I hope you will.

From the window we saw the panorama of our vast country unfold before us. We watched the states of Assam, Bengal, and Bihar merge one into the other, until finally we were speeding through Utter Pradesh, nearing Aligarh.

At each stop there was a commotion as a number of people got down to go home and others came in. Always, a large number of family members would come to see the traveler off or to greet him and escort him home. We were fast nearing our own destination, passing now the last sugarcane plantations, shady mango groves, the yellow fields of mustard flowers, and the purple hyacinths that blossomed in every pool of still water, along the way.

As we approached Aligarh station, we craned our necks eagerly to see the

Dry Curried ——————————— *Sukha Kala Chana* ———————————
Dark Chick-Peas

2 cups *kala chana,* small, dark chick-peas	5 or 6 small green chilies or ½ to 1 teaspoon chili powder
5 cups cold water	½ teaspoon turmeric powder
2 tablespoons vegetable oil	1½ teaspoons *amchoor,* powdered mango or 1½ tablespoons lemon juice
1 cup minced onions	
⅛ teaspoon *heeng,* asafetida	1 teaspoon crushed *anar dana,* pomegranate seeds
1 tablespoon minced garlic	¼ cup thinly sliced onion rings
1 tablespoon plus ¾ teaspoon freshly ground cumin powder	
1 tablespoon scraped and minced ginger	

Remove any sticks and stones from the chick-peas. Wash thoroughly 3 or 4 times and soak in water for 24 hours. After soaking, the chick-peas swell to about 3½ to 4 cups.

In a 5-quart heavy-based pot, heat the oil and fry the onions over high heat for 3 to 4 minutes. Stir occasionally. Add the asafetida and garlic and fry until the garlic is golden brown. Stir in the chick-peas, their soaking water, cumin powder, ginger, 2 or 3 green chilies, and turmeric and bring to a boil. Reduce heat to low and simmer, covered, for 1¼ hours.

Stir in the powdered mango and pomegranate seeds and continue to simmer, covered, for another 2 to 2½ hours.

Uncover and stir thoroughly. If the chick-peas are tender, continue to simmer, uncovered, just until the water is absorbed. If the chick-peas do not disintegrate when pressed between your fingers, then continue to simmer, covered, until tender.

Before serving, garnish with chilies, whole or slit into halves, and onion rings.

Serves 6 to 8

Remarks

This simple, inexpensive dish cooked with different combinations of spices is enjoyed by most Indians. Dry cooked chana *is also eaten as a snack and is a great favorite with vegetarians.*

———————————————————————————————

familiar faces of Shahid and Havai, our grandfather's trusted male servants. We were never allowed to call them by their names; to us they were Shahid and Havai *Mamu,* meaning uncle. They had already arranged a *tonga,* an old-fashioned horse carriage, to take us home. Rickshaws (three-wheeled cycles) also waited to carry our excess baggage.

Whether we left home for a week or a month, we were always loaded with trunks, a trait we have in common with many Americans! Of course, the usual last minute food packages were a regular feature of our traveling kit. (I miss the sight of these multicolored, odd-shaped bundles in the United States. Traveling seems so streamlined here!) Finally, bone-weary from our long journey, we were home!

Aligarh at Last!

Picture a huge mansion, red brick, with turrets, terraces, staircases and court-yards. It was typical of the upper middle class homes built in the 1920s. The spacious kitchens, the well, the pomegranate, lemon, mango, papaya, and guava groves, and servants quarters were a short distance from the main building. The path to the mansion, winding along the back courtyard, enclosed by huge brick walls to ensure privacy, was an intricate mosaic of inlaid bricks.

Papa (the name by which he was lovingly called by family members and close friends; others respectfully knew him as "Papa Mian") was there, sitting on his huge cane armchair on the front, paved veranda of Abdullah Lodge, waiting for us. I remember well how his face would light up to see his youngest daughter, my mother, and his smallest grandchildren, Baba and me. Amma and Nimmi Ala, my two wonderful aunts, were also there to welcome us, taking time off from their busy work schedules to encircle us in the family bond of warmth and acceptance.

Mamujan ("Uncle close to the heart") and our cousins were all there and when Appi, my exuberant and beautiful aunt happened to be visiting from Pakistan with her daughters, our family was complete.

Apabi, my mother's beloved eldest sister, was an extraordinary person. She was a doctor, and an author of plays and novels that dramatized the need for change regarding the social rights of women. Long before it became well-known or even fashionable, she emphasized the importance of good nutrition. Whole wheat, liver, yogurt, fresh fruit, and vegetables were all part of the daily diet at Abdullah Lodge, together with the regular abundant fare.

Feasting and Fun

Lunch and dinner were a time for fun, and for taking pleasure in fine food. The family would be seated along the huge, white-cloth-covered dining table, with Papa at the head. Family portraits smiled down at us. Appi, a raconteur par excellence would regale us with stories. We had happy times together.

A typical meal consisted of *Seekh Kabab,* long, elegant rolls of ground meat, *daal,* or lentil, *korma,* a traditional curried meat preparation, *paratha,* a layered, whole wheat, shallow-fried bread and *raita,* a yogurt dish with fruit or vegetable.

In the afternoon, Papa would stroll through his papaya, guava, and mango groves, with Baba holding onto his finger. I remember Papa proudly pointing out a particularly large and well-formed papaya, planted by himself, to "Khalid," as he called Baba. We had naturally sweet garden fresh *papitas* (papaya) for breakfast every day.

We make use of both the immature and ripe fruit. Raw papaya is finely sliced, dried in the sun, pounded, and then stored as a powder, to be used as a tenderizer. Or, where it is readily available, we marinate the unripe, mashed fruit with meat, to make the meat juicy and tender. Unripe papaya is also cooked as a vegetable in many parts of India.

A Shallow- _____ *Paratha* _____
Fried Bread

2 cups whole wheat flour	12 tablespoons melted *ghee* (see page 40) or butter
1 cup water	

Sift the flour into a bowl. Gradually add up to ¾ cup water, while constantly mixing. Gather into a ball. If the particles won't adhere, add a little water to make a dough that is not sticky.

On a lightly floured surface, knead the dough until it is smooth and pliable (about 6 minutes). Place in a bowl, cover with a dampened cloth, and set aside for at least 30 minutes. Divide the dough into 12 portions and shape into balls.

Roll each ball into a flat round about 6 inches in diameter. (Sprinkle a little flour on the surface as you roll if necessary.) Lightly brush the top of the round with about 1 teaspoon of the melted *ghee.* Fold the *paratha* in half. Brush the top with a little *ghee* and fold again. Now you will have a quarter circle with 4 layers. Roll out the *paratha,* keeping the triangular shape you now have or shaping it into a circle, about 4½ to 6 inches in diameter. Cover the *paratha* with a lightly dampened cloth while you roll the others. Do not place the rolled *parathas* on top of each other; they will stick together.

Heat a large heavy cast-iron or nonstick skillet until hot. Adjust heat to moderate and place 1 to 2 teaspoons *ghee* in the skillet. Cook each *paratha* for 2 to 3 minutes, moving once or twice with fingertips to make sure the *ghee* reaches the entire surface. When the *paratha* is a golden brown underneath, pour 1 to 2 teaspoons of *ghee* on top, spread it over the surface, and turn over. Cook until the second side is golden brown (about 2 to 3 minutes). Keep covered or wrapped in foil until all the *parathas* are cooked.

Yields 12 *parathas*

Remarks

Parathas *are one of our most popular breads. Traditionally, they are served warm with a yogurt dish or with plain yogurt.*

These rotis *keep very well when made ahead of time. Wrap them tightly in foil and warm in a medium oven for about 4 to 5 minutes before serving.*

The Amazing *Anvla*

Baer, a date-shaped juicy berry, grew practically wild, along the hedges. This is a delicious fruit, very nutritious, and accessible to everyone in India. The family servants and their children and, of course, all of us cousins would pluck a *baer* or two each time we passed those bushes! Then there was the huge *anvla* tree, reaching up to and spilling the round sour fruit onto the terraces of the second and third stories of Abdullah Lodge. The fruit of this tree has an amazing quality. Though it is sour, if you drink some water immediately after eating *anvla,* the water will taste honey sweet!

We cousins would collect buckets full of *anvla* and take it to the kitchen. Here, in huge iron cooking pots, the fruit would be boiled to a pulp. We would massage this pulp into our scalps before a hair wash. It makes a perfect hair conditioner. It is one of nature's forms of competition for the hairdressing salon! Baba and

I would then accompany the servants to the well in a corner of the compound to watch the buffaloes making their slow circles around the well to activate the Persian wheel. We would then follow the *bihishti,* the water carrier, who brought gallons of water to the bathrooms in large sacks made of goat skins.

One entire side of the estate was devoted to mangoes. There are many kinds, and everyone has his own favorite variety of mango. Among the popular varieties are *chaunsa, langra,* and *dasehri.* We find the just-ripe *samar behisht* (which means "fruit of heaven") beyond compare.

In India, slices of raw mango are cut, dried in the sun, and pounded to be stored for future use as a tangy spice. This powdered form is known as *amchoor.* Unripe mango is also cooked as a vegetable or prepared as a pickle or chutney. Luckily, even in the Shillong hills, where they do not ripen to their full flavor, we can prepare mango dishes from our own unripened garden mangoes. Here is a mango recipe that my mother learned from a friend, Mrs. Saraogi, who cooks wonderful Rajasthani dishes.

Kachay Aam Ki Sabzi — Curried Unripened Mango

5	unripened mangoes	1¼	teaspoons *kelonji,* onion seeds
8 to 10	tablespoons mustard oil	1	teaspoon chili powder
1	teaspoon fenugreek seeds	2	tablespoons grated jaggery
1¼	teaspoons fennel seeds		

Wash and dry the mangoes. Cut the unpeeled mangoes into 1½ by ¾-inch pieces. Discard the seeds.

In a *karhai* or wok, heat the mustard oil until it smokes. Reduce the heat to low and after 1 minute add the mango pieces. Increase the heat to moderate, add the fenugreek seeds, fennel seeds, and onion seeds and fry for 1½ minutes, while stirring. Add the chili powder and cook for another 2 minutes. Stir in the jaggery thoroughly, remove the *karhai* from the heat, and continue stirring for 1 minute before serving.

Serves 6

Remarks

Serve hot with rice or roti. *This delightful dish also tastes delicious cold.*

Mrs. Saraogi, an excellent cook of Rajasthani dishes, taught my mother this recipe years ago. Since we had a mango tree in our garden in Shillong, this dish was always a favorite.

Some of the finest kinds of mangoes, including the *samar behisht,* are grown in my father's mango groves in Lucknow. Unfortunately, they were never "in season" in winter, either in Lucknow or Aligarh, when we visited Papa. Still, the mango trees made excellent hiding places for our games of hide and seek!

In the summer, my aunt often sent us a packing-case full of mangoes. So, even in far-off Shillong, we would be reminded of the happy times we had spent as part of the "Abdullah clan."

meat

———————— *Ala Bi Kay Kachay Keemay Kay Kabab* ————————

Ala Bi's Minced Meat Kabobs with Mango and Spices

1½ pounds lean round of beef, minced

¾   tablespoon minced garlic

1   tablespoon plus ¾ teaspoon scraped and grated ginger

3   tablespoons plus ¾ teaspoon vegetable oil

1⅓ cups finely sliced onions

5   tablespoons peeled and finely grated raw mango

1½ teaspoons *garam masalla,* a spice mixture (see page 42)

1 to 3 small green chilies, minced

2   tablespoons minced coriander leaves, or any minced herb

Mix together the meat, garlic, and ginger and set aside.

Heat 2 tablespoons plus ¾ teaspoon oil in a skillet and fry the onions until they become a reddish brown. Stir constantly.

Using your fingers, mix the fried onions, mango, *garam masalla,* and green chilies with the meat until the mixture feels soft and pliable. Form into 12 round, patty-shaped *kababs,* about 3 to 4 inches in diameter.

In a large skillet, spread 1 tablespoon oil evenly over the surface. Place the *kababs* side by side and cook, covered, over moderate heat 15 minutes. Uncover and cook over moderately high heat 2 to 3 minutes. Drain any surplus liquid. Brown the *kababs* well on both sides, transfer to serving dish, and garnish with coriander leaves.

Yields 12 *kababs*

———————— *Kacha Keema Kabab* ————————

Patty-Shaped Minced Meat Kabobs

1½ pounds lean round of lamb or beef, minced

1   tablespoon grated unripened green papaya (optional)

4 to 6 whole cloves

2   large dark brown cardamom pods

30 to 35 peppercorns

2½ teaspoons *khas khas,* white poppy seeds

3½ tablespoons *besan,* chick-pea flour

1   tablespoon scraped and grated ginger

6 to 10 garlic cloves, minced

1½ cups finely minced onions

4 to 6 tablespoons mustard oil or vegetable oil

Mix the meat and the papaya (if used) thoroughly and set aside for 15 minutes.

Using a mortar and pestle or a coffee grinder, grind together the cloves, cardamom pods, peppercorns, and poppy seeds.

Heat a *tava* or griddle and roast the chick-pea flour over moderate heat 3 to 4 minutes. Stir frequently.

Mix the ground spices, chick-pea flour, ginger, garlic, and onions with the meat. Form the meat into 12 to 14 round flat patties.

In a large heavy-based skillet, heat half the oil to smoking point. Reduce heat to moderate and carefully place the *kababs,* side by side, in the skillet. Cook, covered, 10 to 15 minutes. Turn over, add remaining oil, and cook, covered, until the *kababs* are tender.

Yields 12 to 14 round *kababs*

—————————————————— *Dorothy Ka Roast* ——————————————————

Dorothy's Roast

tamarind pulp, the size of a lemon	4 large garlic cloves
¼ cup boiling water	½ teaspoon freshly ground black pepper
2 pounds roasting beef	1¾ to 2 teaspoons arrowroot
2 tablespoons molasses	1 sprig wood sorrel (20 to 30 leaves) or watercress
1½ tablespoons tamari soy sauce	
2 cups pineapple juice	

Soak the tamarind pulp in hot water for at least 20 minutes. Squeeze the pulp with your fingers to extract all the juices. Strain, squeezing the pulp as you strain. Collect the tamarind juice and discard the pulp.

Wash the meat and trim the excess fat. Leave only a very thin layer of fat. If preferred, trim all the fat. Poke holes in the meat with a sharp utensil, such as a fork.

Rub the tamarind juice, molasses, and tamari into the meat and then poke the meat again. Cover with foil and set aside for 8 to 12 hours. Turn the meat over, baste with juices, cover again, and set aside in a cool place. Do not refrigerate. Allow the meat to marinate for at least 24 to 30 hours.

Place the meat and its juices in a 3-quart, heavy-bottomed pan. Pour the pineapple juice over the meat. Add the garlic and black pepper. Quickly bring the meat to a boil, then immediately reduce the heat to low, and simmer, tightly covered, 50 to 60 minutes. Turn the meat over and continue to simmer, covered, until the meat is tender (about another 40 to 60 minutes).

Drain the liquid from the meat into a 2-quart pan. In a small bowl, mix the arrowroot with 2 tablespoons of the cooked liquid. Stir thoroughly to remove lumps. Then stir the dissolved arrowroot back into the pan of liquid. Cook over moderate heat, while stirring, until the pineapple juice thickens enough to use as a sauce.

Arrange the meat on a serving platter and garnish with sorrel leaves. Serve the thickened pineapple juice separately as a sauce.

Serves 6

Remarks

In the Khasi *(tribal) tradition, Dorothy cooks the roast in beer seasoned with salt. However, our recipe uses the same basic principle sans beer and salt and produces excellent results.*

Serve with baked potatoes topped with sour cream.

Saral Bean Bhaji *(Quick and Easy Lightly Curried Beans) or* Gobi Gajar *(Lightly Curried Cauliflower with Carrot Slivers) are two of the vegetable dishes that go very well with this roast. See Index for these recipes.*

Gosht Aur Chukandar Ka Korma

Meat Curry with Beets

1½	pounds lean lamb or beef	1¾	tablespoons coriander powder	
1	pound beets (about 5 or 6 medium-size beets)	1¾	teaspoons cumin powder	
		1	teaspoon turmeric powder	

5½ to 6 tablespoons vegetable oil

1½ cups finely sliced onions

1½ tablespoons scraped and minced ginger

1½ tablespoons minced garlic

1¾ tablespoons coriander powder

1¾ teaspoons cumin powder

1 teaspoon turmeric powder

3 to 3½ cups water

¼ to ½ teaspoon chili powder

1 teaspoon *garam masalla,* a spice mixture (see page 42)

Wash the meat and cut it into 1-inch cubes.

Wash the beets thoroughly. Trim the ends and scrub well. Scrape off any rough parts on the skin. Rinse again and dice.

In a large saucepan, heat 5½ tablespoons of the oil. Fry the onions in the oil until they become a golden brown. Add the ginger and garlic and fry until the garlic is lightly browned. Then put in the coriander powder, cumin powder, and turmeric powder and fry, while stirring, 3 or 4 minutes on moderate heat.

Add the meat and fry until the meat is lightly browned (about 15 minutes). Remove the meat from the pan and set aside.

Stir in the beets and fry for about 2 minutes, while stirring. Add ½ tablespoon of oil if needed.

Add water and bring to a boil. Reduce heat to moderately high and cook 20 to 25 minutes.

Return the meat to the pan, add chili powder, and simmer, covered, until the meat is tender (about 1 hour).

If the water is completely absorbed, add an additional ¼ cup. Stir in the *garam masalla* and simmer, uncovered, about 10 to 15 minutes. Cook until there is no liquid left in the pan before serving.

Serves 6

Remarks

This delightful meat curry (one of Babuji's specialties) takes on a lovely burgundy-colored appearance from the juices of the beets.

We serve it with any one of our rotis. *Since it is a dry curry, it can be served with a roti and a lentil with some gravy.*

An alternative method of cooking this korma *is faster, but loses some of the juices of the beets when boiled.*

Wash the meat and cut it into 1-inch cubes.

Wash the beets thoroughly. Trim the ends and scrape off any rough parts on the skin. Dice and then boil the beets 30 minutes.

In a large saucepan, heat the oil. Fry the onions in the oil until they become a golden brown. Add the ginger and garlic and fry until the garlic is lightly browned. Then stir in the coriander powder, cumin powder, and turmeric powder and fry, while stirring, 3 or 4 minutes over moderate heat.

Add the meat and fry until lightly browned (about 15 minutes). Stir in the boiled beets, 2¾ cups water, and chili powder and simmer, covered, 1 hour.

If the liquid has evaporated, add an additional ¼ cup water. Stir in the garam masalla *and simmer, uncovered, about 10 to 15 minutes. Cook until there is no liquid left in the pan.*

Kaju Badaam Bharay Pasanday

Meat Rolls Stuffed with Nuts

2 pounds lean round of lamb, lean round of beef, or lean, thin steak

1½ tablespoons scraped and grated ginger

1½ tablespoons minced garlic

¼ to ½ teaspoon freshly ground black pepper

9 tablespoons vegetable oil

1 cup minced onions

16 whole cashew nuts

2 tablespoons pistachio nuts

1 teaspoon cumin powder

1 tablespoon desiccated coconut

1 tablespoon lemon juice

1¾ cups finely sliced onions

10 tablespoons thick Homemade Yogurt (see page 41)

¾ teaspoon *garam masalla,* a spice mixture (see page 42)

1 to 2 tablespoons chopped green coriander leaves or parsley

1 to 3 small green chilies, chopped (optional)

Trim any fat off the meat. Cut the meat into 1½-inch cubes. Rub the ginger, garlic, and black pepper thoroughly into the meat and set aside for at least 30 minutes. It is best if you leave the meat refrigerated overnight, covered.

Flatten each piece of meat by gently but firmly pounding with a small mallet on a wooden board. Continue to gradually flatten the meat until each piece is about 3½ × 2 inches in size and is as thin as possible without tearing it. If you use thin steak, cut into pieces 3¼ × 2 inches and flatten and enlarge further by gently pounding. You should have over 30 pieces.

In a large skillet, heat 1½ tablespoons oil and fry the minced onions until they are brown (about 6 to 8 minutes).

Pound the cashew nuts and pistachio nuts. Add these to the onion with the cumin powder and coconut. Fry, while stirring, over moderate heat 1 minute. Remove from heat. Stir in the lemon juice and allow to cool slightly.

Lay the strips of meat on a board. Spoon ½ to 1 teaspoon of the onion and nut mixture onto the middle of one strip. Roll one side over the mixture tightly, then the other side over the rolled portion. Press gently but firmly, holding the roll in the palm of your hand so that the stuffing is securely enclosed from all sides. You can tie each roll lightly with string (I do not) to keep the stuffing inside the roll.

In another large skillet, heat 4 tablespoons oil. Put the meat rolls in, one at a time, and fry until the rolls become brown (about 6 to 7 minutes). Alternate heat between moderate and moderately high. Turn the rolls over carefully, lifting with a tablespoon and gently dropping over. Cook until the moisture evaporates and the rolls are a golden brown (about 10 to 12 minutes).

While the rolls are cooking, heat 3½ tablespoons oil in a skillet and fry the sliced onions over moderate heat until they are a reddish brown (about 10 to 12 minutes). Beat yogurt lightly, and stir in, with *garam masalla,* coriander leaves, and chilies (if used) and simmer 3 to 4 minutes, while stirring.

Pour the contents of the skillet over the browned meat, stir gently, cover, and simmer 6 to 10 minutes before serving.

Serves 6

Remarks

This is a lavish dish fit for festive occasions. Yet, it is not difficult to prepare, and is a special family favorite that we serve with Naan *(Leavened, Baked Whole Wheat Bread),* Khamiri Roti *(Whole Wheat, Leavened, Quick-Baked Bread), or* Chapati *(Whole Wheat, Flat Round Bread). See Index for these breads.*

Hussaini Kabab

Three-Inch-Long Kabobs with Almonds

2 pounds lean shoulder or leg of lamb or beef, minced

1 tablespoon scraped and grated ginger

1 tablespoon minced garlic

4 to 5 tablespoons vegetable oil

½ tablespoon cumin seeds

1 tablespoon coriander seeds

15 whole almonds

6 cloves

2 large dark brown cardamom pods

½-inch cinnamon stick

20 peppercorns

small piece of nutmeg, the size of a peppercorn

4 heaping tablespoons thick Homemade Yogurt (see page 41)

2 tablespoons lemon juice

Mix the meat with the ginger and garlic thoroughly. Cover and set aside for 30 minutes.

In a large skillet, heat 2 tablespoons oil and fry the cumin seeds, coriander seeds, almonds, cloves, cardamom pods, cinnamon, peppercorns, and nutmeg over moderately high heat until the cumin seeds become lightly browned (about 2 to 3 minutes). With a slotted spoon, scoop the fried spices and almonds out immediately, leaving the surplus oil behind. Discard the skin from the cardamom pods. Grind all the fried spices.

Lightly pound the almonds just until broken. Place the almonds and spices in the jar of a blender, add the yogurt, and blend until the mixture is reduced to a thin paste.

Mix the blended spices with the meat. Add the lemon juice. Knead with your hands to mix well and soften the meat. Set aside, covered, for 30 minutes.

Form the meat into 20 or 21 rolls, 3 inches long and 1 inch wide, to resemble sausages.

To the reserved surplus oil in the skillet, add 2 additional tablespoons oil and heat. Place the *kababs* side by side and fry on moderate heat until nicely browned (about 5 minutes). If the *kababs* emit excess liquid, scoop out with a spoon and discard. Turn the *kababs* over and cook until they are well browned.

Serves 6 to 8

Remarks

Serve with rice pullau *or* rotis.

If you prefer your kababs *very tender, cook for a longer period of time, covered, on low heat and then brown on moderately high heat for about 1 minute.*

Halka Gosht Aur Alu Ka Saalan

Light Meat and Potato Curry

1¼ pounds lean round of steak, lamb, or beef	¼ to ½ teaspoon turmeric powder
5 tablespoons vegetable oil	1 cup finely chopped tomatoes
2¼ cups finely sliced onions	6 *kardi patta,* curry leaves
1 tablespoon minced garlic	3 cups cold water
1 tablespoon plus ¾ teaspoon scraped and minced ginger	1 pound potatoes (1 large and 1 medium-size)
1 tablespoon coriander powder	2 tablespoons chopped coriander leaves or other favorite herb
1 teaspoon cumin powder	

Lightly wash the meat and pat dry. Cut into 1-inch cubes.

In a large skillet, heat the oil over moderate heat. Fry the onions until they are a light golden brown (about 10 to 15 minutes). Stir occasionally. Meanwhile, prepare your other spices.

Add the garlic and ginger to the pan and fry over moderately high heat, while stirring, until the garlic is lightly browned (about 3 to 5 minutes). Stir in the coriander powder, cumin powder, and turmeric powder and fry 1 minute, while stirring. Add the tomatoes and fry until the mixture resembles a lumpy puree and oil appears around the sides of the pan. Then put in the meat pieces and curry leaves and fry until the meat is browned. Stir occasionally. Pour in the water, stir, and bring to a boil.

Reduce heat immediately to moderate and cook, covered tightly, 20 minutes. Stir once. Reduce heat to low and cook another 20 to 25 minutes.

Wash and scrub the potatoes and cut into ¾-inch cubes. Add the potatoes to the meat and stir thoroughly. Simmer, tightly covered, until the meat is tender (about 40 to 45 minutes).

Sprinkle coriander leaves on top, simmer 1 minute, then serve.

Serves 6

Remarks

This light curry is made very often in my Aunt Nimmi Ala's (Khatoon's) home. I remember enjoying the light, yet tasty gravy and scooping it up with hot, thin Chapatis, Whole Wheat, Flat Round Bread *(see Index).*

Since this dish yields an excess of gravy, it can also be served with rice. However, we have always enjoyed saalans, *as some of our curries are called, with some form of Indian bread, mostly* Chapatis.

Kashmiri Koftay

Small, Sausagelike Minced Meat Rolls

1½ pounds lean ground lamb or beef

1½ tablespoons minced green coriander leaves

¾ teaspoon coriander powder

1 teaspoon ginger powder

⅛ teaspoon *heeng,* asafetida

½ teaspoon *garam masalla,* a spice mixture (see page 42)

1 teaspoon *kashmiri mirch,* a chili; paprika or chili powder may be used

2¼ teaspoons fennel seeds

1 medium-size tomato

3 cups boiling water

5 whole cloves

2 tablespoons mustard oil

3 tablespoons vegetable oil

4 bay leaves

6 dried red chilies

3½ tablespoons thick, Homemade Yogurt (see page 41)

4 small green cardamom pods

¼ teaspoon black cumin seeds or cumin seeds

In a large bowl, mix together the meat, coriander leaves, coriander powder, ½ teaspoon ginger powder, half of the asafetida, *garam masalla,* and *kashmiri mirch.*

Pound the fennel seeds a few times in a mortar and pestle until they are broken but not ground to a fine powder. Or, wrap the seeds in a double layer of paper towels and pound lightly with a mallet. Add 1¼ teaspoons of the coarsely ground seeds to the meat and mix thoroughly, using your hands in a pressing and kneading motion.

Divide the meat mixture into 36 portions. Shape each portion into a 2½ to 3-inch sausagelike roll, slightly tapering at the ends instead of rounded. Be sure the ends are not too sharp or pointed or they might break off during the cooking.

Drop the tomato in boiling water for a few seconds. Drain, peel, and chop very finely, being careful to save the juice.

Wrap the cloves in a double layer of paper towels and pound a few times with a mallet.

In a 5-quart pot, heat the mustard oil for about 1 minute over moderate heat. Add the vegetable oil and when it becomes hot, drop in the remainder of the asafetida. Immediately add 6 *koftas* (meat rolls) and the coarsely ground cloves and fry 1½ to 2 minutes over moderate heat. Add the rest of the *koftas* and the bay leaves. Some water will come out of the *koftas.* After 1 to 2 minutes turn the *koftas* over, being careful not to break them. Cover tightly and cook 5 minutes on moderate heat. Uncover and continue cooking until all the water has evaporated (about 10 to 15 minutes). Then add the chilies and fry 1 minute. Beat yogurt lightly. Add ½ teaspoon ginger powder, 1 teaspoon fennel seeds, ¼ cup chopped tomato, yogurt, cardamom pods, cumin seeds and fry 1 minute. Shake the pan gently to mix the ingredients instead of stirring the *koftas.*

Add the remaining tomato, shake the pan gently, cover tightly, reduce heat to low, and simmer 40 to 60 minutes. Shake the pan gently on occasion. Serve hot.

Yields 36 *koftas*

Remarks

Mrs. Sheila Dhar taught me this Kashmiri speciality. It is one of my very favorite dishes for two main reasons—my husband, children, family members, and friends all love it; and nothing ever goes wrong with it. And it's easy to make!

Serve with rice, or puris *and* Haaq, *Whole Spinach Greens (see Index).*

Keema

Lightly Curried Minced Lamb

3¾ tablespoons vegetable oil

2 cups minced onions

1 tablespoon scraped and grated ginger

1 tablespoon minced garlic

1½ tablespoons coriander powder

1 teaspoon cumin powder

⅛ teaspoon turmeric powder

2 medium-size tomatoes

3 cups boiling water

1¼ pounds lean round of lamb or 1½ pounds beef, minced

3 cups water

¼ to ½ teaspoon *garam masalla,* a spice mixture (see page 42)

2 tablespoons chopped coriander leaves

1 to 3 small green chilies, slit in halves

Heat oil in a 4-quart pot and fry ½ cup onions until they are a deep reddish brown. Remove onions with a slotted spoon and set aside.

In the same pot and using the same oil, fry the rest of the onions over moderate heat until they are well browned (about 15 minutes). Add the ginger and garlic and fry until they become a light brown (about 3 to 4 minutes). Stir in the coriander powder, cumin powder, and turmeric powder. Fry and stir 1 to 2 minutes.

Meanwhile, drop the tomatoes in boiling water for less than a minute. Drain, then peel, chop, and add to the onion-spice mixture. Continue frying until the tomatoes are well mashed (about 3 to 5 minutes).

Add the minced meat and fry until browned (about 8 to 10 minutes).

Stir in 1 cup water and reserved onions. Reduce heat to low and simmer, covered, 30 to 35 minutes.

Uncover and add 1½ to 2 cups hot water, the *garam masalla,* and coriander leaves. Stir well and simmer a few minutes, uncovered, before serving. Transfer to serving bowl and garnish with chilies.

Serves 6

Remarks

Keema *can be served with some gravy as we have done here. It can also be served as a "dry" curry. In that case, do not add the 2 cups of hot water, but stir the* keema *until the water evaporates and the meat is well browned.*

Keema Bhari Simla Mirch

Green Peppers Stuffed with Cooked Minced Meat

Keema (see Remarks in recipe in this section)

6 small green peppers

5 to 6 cups oil for deep-frying

First make "dry" *Keema* for stuffing. (See recipe in this section.)

Wash and dry the green peppers. Neatly slice across the top of the pepper, just under the stem section. Set aside for use as a cap. Remove membrane from inside the pepper to make room for the stuffing.

Mix some of the pepper seeds with the *Keema*. Stuff each pepper with the cooled meat mixture and place the cap on top. Tie each one securely with string.

Heat oil in a large *karhai,* wok, or deep-frying pan. When the oil is nearly at smoking point, reduce heat to moderate and gently slide in the peppers. Fry about 5 minutes. Increase heat to moderately high and turn the peppers over. Fry until cooked on all sides (about 10 to 15 minutes).

Serves 6

Keema Matar

Curried Minced Meat with Peas

1¼ pounds lean round of lamb or beef, minced

3 tablespoons well-mixed Homemade Yogurt (see page 41)

1 to 3 small green chilies

1½-inch piece of ginger, scraped and chopped

2 teaspoons *khas khas,* white poppy seeds

10 to 15 small garlic cloves

1 teaspoon cumin seeds

3 to 6 dried red chilies (optional)

1 teaspoon turmeric powder

¾ cup water

4 tablespoons vegetable oil

⅛ teaspoon *heeng,* asafetida

2 cups finely sliced onions

2 cups green peas

1½ cups chopped ripe tomatoes

2 cups boiling water

1 tablespoon *ghee* (see page 40)

1 tablespoon chopped coriander leaves

Mix the meat with yogurt and set aside.

In a blender, blend together the green chilies, ginger, poppy seeds, garlic, cumin seeds, red chilies (if used), and turmeric powder. Scoop the *masalla* (blended spices) out of the blender and set aside. Pour the ¾ cup water into the blender, blend 1 to 2 seconds, and set aside.

Heat the oil in a heavy 4-quart pot, drop in the asafetida, and then immediately add the onions. Fry until they are golden brown. Stir in the blended *masalla* and 2 tablespoons of the reserved spicy water. Fry 3 to 4 minutes over moderate heat while stirring. Add the meat and fry 2 minutes. Stir in the rest of the spicy water, reduce heat to low, cover, and simmer until the meat is cooked. You should see oil at the sides of the pan.

Add peas, tomatoes, boiling water, *ghee,* and coriander leaves. Bring to a boil, reduce heat, and simmer, covered, a few minutes, until the peas are done.

Serves 6

Keema Alu

Curried Minced Meat with Potatoes

4 tablespoons vegetable oil	1 cup well-mixed Homemade Yogurt (see page 41)
1¼ cups chopped onions	
1 tablespoon scraped and grated ginger	1 cup water
1 tablespoon minced garlic	2 to 3 small green chilies
1 tablespoon coriander powder	¼ teaspoon freshly ground black pepper
1 teaspoon cumin powder	½ to ¾ teaspoon *garam masalla,* a spice mixture (see page 42)
1 pound lean round of lamb or beef, minced	1 teaspoon lemon juice
1 pound potatoes (1 medium size and 1 small)	3 tablespoons chopped coriander leaves
¼ teaspoon chili powder	

In a medium-size skillet, heat the oil and fry the onions until they are golden brown. Add the ginger and garlic and fry until they are brown (about 4 to 5 minutes). Stir in the coriander powder and cumin powder and fry, while stirring constantly, 2 minutes over moderate heat. Add the meat and fry 15 minutes. Stir occasionally.

Meanwhile, wash the potatoes thoroughly and cut into ½-inch cubes. Add them to the meat and fry 5 minutes. Stir occasionally. Add the chili powder and fry an additional minute. Slowly stir in the yogurt. Add the water, chilies, and black pepper and bring the *keema* to a boil. Immediately reduce the heat to low, stir, cover, and simmer until meat is cooked (30 to 35 minutes).

Uncover, add the *garam masalla,* and simmer 5 minutes. Stir in the lemon juice and coriander leaves. Simmer 1 to 2 minutes and serve.

Serves 6

Remarks

Whenever possible I like to leave the potatoes unpeeled. In India, they would be peeled and then cut. This dish can be served with either rice or roti. *My children enjoy* Keema Alu; *I'm sure yours will too!*

Mutton Shakuti

Lamb Cooked in Coconut Milk

1 small coconut	¾ tablespoon minced garlic
5 cups plus 9 tablespoons water	1 tablespoon scraped and chopped ginger
1½ pounds lean round of lamb or beef	seeds of 2 large dark brown cardamom pods
2 tablespoons tamarind pulp	1-inch cinnamon stick, cut into pieces
½ cup hot water	15 to 20 peppercorns
9½ tablespoons vegetable oil	3 whole cloves
¾ teaspoon cumin seeds	1 piece of nutmeg, the size of a peppercorn
1 tablespoon plus ¾ teaspoon coriander seeds	2 to 3 tablespoons chopped coriander leaves
2 cups sliced onions	

Break the coconut. (For procedure, see page 40.) Grate 9 tablespoons coconut and set aside.

Cut the rest of the coconut into small pieces. You will need 1½ cups of chopped coconut. Place in a blender container. Add 3 cups water and blend for a few seconds. Scrape down the sides of the blender and add another 1¼ cups of water and blend again. You should have about 3 cups of coconut milk.

Trim any excess fat from the meat, wash, and cut into 1-inch cubes.

Soak the tamarind pulp in the hot water for 15 minutes. Squeeze the pulp thoroughly and strain. Collect the juice and discard the pulp.

In a large skillet with a lid, heat 4½ tablespoons oil. Fry the grated coconut, cumin seeds, and coriander seeds until the coconut is a pale golden brown. Remove from the skillet and place in a clean jar of a blender.

Add 3 tablespoons oil to the skillet and fry ¾ cup sliced onions until reddish brown in color. Remove the onions with a slotted spoon and add to the spices in the blender jar. Add the garlic, ginger, cardamom, cinnamon, peppercorns, cloves, and nutmeg. Pour 9 tablespoons water into the blender jar and blend all the spices until they are reduced to a puree.

In the same skillet with the surplus oil, heat an additional 2 tablespoons oil and fry 1¼ cups of the onion until golden brown. Add the meat and fry until brown over moderate-high heat (about 10 to 15 minutes).

Scoop the blended spices out of the blender jar into another container. Pour ¾ cup water into the blender jar and shake so as not to waste any of the spices. Pour this water over the meat, stir, and cook over moderate heat until the water evaporates; stir occasionally.

Add the prepared coconut milk, tamarind juice, and blended spices, reduce the heat to low, and cook, covered, for about 1 hour. If the gravy becomes too thick, gradually add up to 1 cup of hot water. Continue cooking, covered, until oil appears at the sides of the skillet and the meat is very tender.

Sprinkle the meat with coriander leaves and simmer a few minutes before serving.

Serves 6 to 9

Remarks

Serve this rich, tasty dish with rice or roti.

Korma I

Curried Lamb Cubes with Saffron

2 pounds lean round of lamb

2 large garlic cloves

¼ teaspoon ginger powder

½ teaspoon cumin powder

¼ teaspoon chili powder

¼ teaspoon freshly ground black pepper

⅛ teaspoon freshly ground cinnamon

6 tablespoons peanut oil or vegetable oil

⅛ teaspoon *zafraan,* saffron powder

1 cup warm water

2 cups finely sliced onions

1½ teaspoons coriander powder

1 tablespoon chopped coriander leaves or parsley

3 tablespoons lemon juice

1 lemon, sliced

Wash and drain the meat. Cut it into 1-inch cubes and place in a large bowl. Rub the garlic cloves thoroughly into the meat. Rub in the ginger powder, cumin powder, chili powder, and black pepper. Stir the cinnamon powder into the oil and pour over the meat. Add saffron powder, stir, and marinate for 1 hour. Stir thoroughly and marinate for another 2 hours.

Pour the meat and any liquid into a 4-quart, heavy-bottomed pot (preferably an iron base). Add the warm water and bring to a boil. Lower heat to medium, cover, and cook until the meat is tender (about 20 to 35 minutes).

Remove the meat with a slotted spoon, reduce heat to low, add onions and coriander powder, and simmer until the onions are soft and the liquid is slightly thickened. Put the meat back into the pot, a few pieces at a time. Sprinkle the coriander leaves over the meat and bring to a boil again. Reduce heat, cover, and cook 15 minutes over low heat. Stir in lemon juice and simmer 1 minute before serving.

Serve hot, garnished with lemon slices.

Serves 6

Remarks

My aunt adapted this lamb korma *from a Turkish recipe.*

Rogan Josh

Mutton or Lamb Curry

2½	pounds meat from shoulder or leg of lamb or mutton
5 or 6	red chilies (without seeds) or 2 to 2½ teaspoons paprika
½	cup hot water
1¾	tablespoons coriander powder
1½	teaspoons chopped almonds
1½	teaspoons chopped peanuts
1¾	teaspoons cumin seeds
1¾	teaspoons *khas khas,* white poppy seeds
3	large brown cardamom pods
8 to 10	whole cloves
14 to 16	peppercorns
	pinch of mace powder
	pinch of nutmeg powder
1	tablespoon plus ¾ teaspoon desiccated coconut

	2-inch piece of ginger
12 to 15	medium garlic cloves
8	small pale green cardamom pods
3½ to 4	tablespoons *ghee* (see page 40) or vegetable oil
2¼	cups finely chopped onions
¼	teaspoon turmeric powder
1¼	cups plus 1 tablespoon well-mixed Homemade Yogurt (see page 41)
3	fresh ripe tomatoes
2½	cups boiling water
1	teaspoon *garam masalla,* a spice mixture (see page 42)
3	tablespoons green coriander leaves or parsley

Wash the meat, pat dry, and cut into 1-inch cubes.

Soak the chilies in hot water for 20 minutes.

Place a *tava* or griddle over moderate heat and roast the coriander powder for about 20 seconds and then remove. Stir in the almonds, peanuts, cumin seeds, poppy seeds, cardamom pods, cloves, peppercorns, mace powder, nutmeg powder, and coconut and continue stirring until you smell the aroma of roasting spices (about 1½ minutes).

Scrape the ginger and chop it into 5 or 6 pieces. In a blender, blend together the chilies and their soaking water, coriander and roasted spices, ginger, and garlic until they are reduced to a puree.

Wrap the small cardamom pods in kitchen cloth and pound with a small mallet until slightly crushed.

Heat the *ghee* in a large, heavy-bottomed skillet with a tight-fitting lid. Fry the crushed cardamom pods and onion until they become a deep golden brown. Add the blended spices and turmeric powder and fry over low heat 4 to 5 minutes. Stir in one-fourth of the yogurt and continue adding another one-fourth, while stirring, until the yogurt dries up.

In the meantime, drop the tomatoes into the boiling water and after 1 minute, remove, peel, and chop. Add the tomatoes to the skillet, increase the heat to moderate, and fry 4 to 5 minutes, while stirring. The mixture should resemble a thick puree at this stage.

Add the meat and fry until the pieces become slightly brown. Stir in the boiling water, cover, and cook over low heat until the meat becomes tender (about 1½ hours). If needed, add up to 1 cup of hot water so that there is a thick gravy with the meat. When the meat is tender, sprinkle the *garam masalla* and coriander leaves over the top. Cook, uncovered, an additional minute and serve.

Serves 6

Malai Kofta

Cream-Stuffed Meatball Curry

1½   pounds lean round of lamb or beef, minced

1½   teaspoons finely ground fennel seeds

  1   teaspoon *garam masalla,* a spice mixture (see page 42)

1½   tablespoons scraped and grated ginger

1½ to 2   heaping tablespoons sour cream

  2   tablespoons vegetable oil

½   cup coarsely chopped tomatoes

2   tablespoons thick Homemade Yogurt (see page 41)

¼   teaspoon chili powder

2   teaspoons cumin seeds

4 to 6   small green chilies, halved

Mix together the meat, fennel seeds, *garam masalla,* and ginger. Knead together for 1 minute. Separate meat into 18 portions. Flatten each portion into a round patty. Place about ¼ to ½ teaspoon sour cream in the middle. Fold up the sides to form a ball. You should have a walnut-size ball with the sour cream securely stuffed in the center. Judge how much sour cream you can use without its oozing out when shaping the ball, and proceed accordingly.

In a 5-quart pot, heat the oil. Put the *koftas* in, one at a time, and fry 3 to 4 minutes over moderate heat. Turn each *kofta* carefully, reduce heat to low, and cook, covered, 8 to 10 minutes. The meat will release water. Uncover and cook over moderate heat until the water evaporates (about 10 to 15 minutes). Do not stir, but shake the pan to move the *koftas.*

Blend the tomatoes in a blender. Then mix well with the yogurt and chili powder. Pour this paste over the *koftas,* reduce heat to low and simmer, covered, 10 minutes.

Heat a *tava* or griddle and roast the cumin seeds for 1 minute over moderate heat. Wrap the seeds in a kitchen cloth or a double thickness of paper towels and coarsely crush with a mallet or rolling pin. Sprinkle the cumin over the *koftas* and add the chilies. Shake the pan gently to allow the ingredients to mix and continue to simmer until *koftas* are soft (about 15 to 20 minutes).

Serves 6

Remarks

This very delicious, but easy-to-make dish is a great family favorite. I have adapted this from a Kashmiri recipe of a friend, Mrs. Dhar. I find it very satisfying to serve since everyone seems to love it! Serve with rotis *or rice.*

Saag Keema Kofta

Curried Meatballs with Spinach

1½ pounds lean leg or shoulder of lamb or beef, minced

1 tablespoon scraped and grated ginger

1½ teaspoons minced garlic

½ pound spinach leaves

1¼ teaspoons *amchoor,* powdered mango or 1½ tablespoons lemon juice

2 tablespoons minced coriander leaves

½ teaspoon *garam masalla,* a spice mixture (see page 42)

1 egg

4 tablespoons mustard oil or vegetable oil

⅛ teaspoon *heeng,* asafetida

3 tablespoons wheat germ

4 to 6 dried red chilies

3 medium-size tomatoes

2½ cups boiling water

Mix together the meat, ginger, and garlic and set aside.

Wash and drain the spinach leaves. Mince leaves and most of the stems.

Add the minced spinach leaves, powdered mango, coriander leaves, ¼ teaspoon *garam masalla,* and the egg to the meat. Mix well, kneading lightly for 1 minute, and form into 24 walnut-size balls *(koftas)* or 38 small ones.

In a large 5-quart pot, heat the oil. Drop in the asafetida and remove the pot from the heat. Stir in the wheat germ and return the pot to moderate heat. Add the *koftas* and cook until lightly browned (about 7 to 8 minutes). Carefully turn each *kofta* over and cook about 5 to 6 minutes. As the liquid begins to evaporate, add the chilies, increase the heat to moderately high, and fry 2 to 3 minutes. Gently shake the pot from time to time to prevent the *koftas* from burning.

Meanwhile, immerse the tomatoes in the boiling water for about 1 minute and then drain, peel, and mince.

Sprinkle the remaining ¼ teaspoon *garam masalla* over the *koftas,* add tomatoes, and stir. Reduce heat to low, and simmer, covered, 15 to 20 minutes. Gently shake the pot once or twice during this time. Serve immediately.

Serves 6

Remarks

You can serve the koftas *with rice or* rotis.

poultry

Bhara Murgh

Roast Stuffed Chicken

2 small chickens (about 2¼ pounds each) or 1 large chicken (4 to 5 pounds)

3 tablespoons orange juice

¾ teaspoon honey

¾ teaspoon *garam masalla,* a spice mixture (see page 42)

½ teaspoon paprika

3 tart apples or Golden Delicious apples

½ cup dates

6 tablespoons chopped mixed nuts

1½ teaspoons minced small green chilies

1 tablespoon minced spring onions

¼ teaspoon black pepper

1 tablespoon plus ¾ teaspoon lemon juice

¼ to ½ teaspoon allspice powder

3½ tablespoons melted butter

¼ to ½ teaspoon cornstarch (optional)

Trim the skin and all the fat from the chickens. Wash and allow to drain for 15 minutes in a colander.

Mix together the orange juice, honey, *garam masalla,* and paprika. Prick the chickens lightly with a fork. Rub the mixture thoroughly into the chickens and set aside for 30 minutes. Turn once or twice.

Wash, dry, and core the apples. Cut each in half and grate coarsely. Deseed and chop the dates.

In a bowl, mix together the apples, dates, nuts, chilies, onions, pepper, lemon juice, and allspice powder.

Stuff the chickens with the apple mixture and lay them side by side in a baking dish. Dribble half the melted butter over the chickens. Bake at 350°F for 1 hour, basting once during that time. Then, baste again and bake at 400°F for 15 minutes.

Turn the chickens over, baste thoroughly, and dribble with the remaining melted butter. Bake another 15 to 20 minutes. Scoop out any liquid in excess of 4 tablespoons and reserve. Baste the chickens again and broil 1 to 2 minutes before serving.

The surplus liquid may be stored for future use as a rich stock or thickened with the cornstarch for use as a sauce to accompany the chickens.

Serves 6 to 8

Remarks

This dish is rich and delicious, yet very easy to prepare. Serve it with a rice pullau; *I like to serve it with* Haaq, *Whole Spinach Greens (see Index).*

The stuffing is not "typically" Indian. My mother chanced on this combination while trying to recall an example of her adventurous aunt's cuisine.

Bhuni Murgi

Chicken, Curried, Dry

 4½ pounds chicken pieces

  6 tablespoons vegetable oil

 2¼ cups minced onions

  2 tablespoons scraped and minced ginger

 1½ tablespoons minced garlic

  ¼ teaspoon turmeric powder

  ½ teaspoon black pepper

 2¼ teaspoons cumin powder

  2 cups chopped tomatoes

  1 cup well-mixed Homemade Yogurt (see page 41)

  6 *kardi patta,* curry leaves

  ½ teaspoon *garam masalla,* a spice mixture (see page 42)

  2 teaspoons *kashmiri mirch,* a chili, or paprika

Remove the skin and fat from the chicken. Wash, pat dry, and let drain 15 minutes in a colander.

In a large skillet, heat oil and fry the onions 3½ minutes over moderately high heat. Add the ginger and garlic and fry until the spices turn light brown (about 3 to 4 minutes).

Reduce heat to moderate and fry the turmeric powder, pepper, and cumin powder with the onions 4 to 5 minutes. Stir occasionally. Add the tomatoes, yogurt, and curry leaves. Stir for 1 minute, then reduce heat to low, and simmer 20 minutes. Stir occasionally.

While the onions and spices are cooking, heat 6 tablespoons oil in a large skillet and fry the chicken pieces over moderately high heat for 10 minutes. Then turn heat to medium and continue frying until the chicken is browned (about 5 to 10 minutes). Stir gently.

Pour the onion mixture over the chicken, stir, reduce heat to low, and cook, covered, for 20 to 30 minutes. Stir once or twice during that time.

Stir in the *garam masalla* and chili and cook, uncovered, until the liquid evaporates.

Serves 6 to 8

Remarks

This is a delicious "dry" curry which Babuji used to serve hot with one of our breads and a vegetable dish.

Masalla Murgh (Tukray)

Spicy Baked Chicken Pieces

4¾ to 5 pounds chicken pieces

  4 teaspoons scraped and grated ginger

  1 tablespoon minced garlic

  3 tablespoons freshly ground coriander seeds

1½ tablespoons freshly ground cumin seeds

  1 cup thick Homemade Yogurt (see page 41)

½ teaspoon *garam masalla,* a spice mixture (see page 42)

¼ to ½ teaspoon chili powder

½ teaspoon *amchoor,* powdered mango (optional)

  3 tablespoons vegetable oil

Remove the skin and fat from the chicken pieces. Rinse under cold running water and pat dry with paper towels. Rub the ginger and garlic into the chicken thoroughly and set aside, covered.

Place a *tava* or griddle over moderately high heat and roast the coriander seeds and cumin seeds, while stirring constantly, until the aroma of the spices becomes apparent (about 10 seconds).

Beat yogurt lightly. Rub the roasted coriander seeds, cumin seeds, *garam masalla,* chili powder, powdered mango (if used), and yogurt into the chicken and refrigerate, covered, for 24 hours.

When ready to cook, place the chicken pieces close together on a large baking dish. Pour any surplus liquid evenly over the chicken and then brush 1½ tablespoons of the oil over the pieces. Bake at 350° F for 50 to 60 minutes.

Remove all the liquid from the chicken. Set 4 tablespoons aside and reserve the rest for future use as a rich stock.

Turn the chicken pieces over. Pour the 4 tablespoons stock over the chicken. Brush with the remaining 1½ tablespoons oil and broil until the chicken is browned (about 6 to 9 minutes).

Serves 6

Remarks

Serve hot with rice or roti. *This delicious dry "curry" is always a favorite with guests. It is very easy to prepare, since most of the work is done the day before cooking it.*

I often use the surplus stock as part of the liquid in cooking rice. It gives plain rice a nice flavor.

Mughlai Murgh Ka Saalan

Mughlai Chicken Curry

2 chickens (2½ to 3 pounds each) or 5½ to 6 pounds of chicken pieces

3 tablespoons vegetable oil

1 cup finely sliced onions

1¼ cups grated onions

2 tablespoons scraped and minced ginger

2 tablespoons minced garlic

¼ teaspoon turmeric powder

6 dried red chilies

3 large dark brown cardamom pods

2-inch cinnamon stick

4 bay leaves

1 cup well-mixed Homemade Yogurt (see page 41)

2 tablespoons *khas khas,* white poppy seeds

4 tablespoons halved cashew nuts

¼ teaspoon *garam masalla,* a spice mixture (see page 42)

1 tablespoon lemon juice (optional)

3 tablespoons chopped coriander leaves or parsley

Cut the chickens into convenient size pieces. Remove skin and fat, wash thoroughly, and let drain in a colander for 30 minutes.

In a 5-quart pot, heat the oil over moderate heat and fry the sliced and grated onions until they are well browned (about 15 to 20 minutes).

Stir in the ginger and garlic and fry about 3 minutes over moderately high heat. Add the chicken pieces, turmeric powder, chilies, cardamom pods, cinnamon, and bay leaves. Fry, while stirring, until the chicken is lightly browned.

Stir in ½ cup yogurt and cook, covered, over moderate heat until the chicken is cooked. Stir occasionally.

Meanwhile, heat a *tava* or griddle and roast the poppy seeds and cashew nuts until very lightly browned (about 30 to 40 seconds). Blend the poppy seeds and 3 tablespoons cashew nuts with 3 tablespoons yogurt. Set 1 tablespoon cashew nuts aside.

Stir the blended yogurt, *garam masalla,* and lemon juice (if used) into the chicken and simmer, uncovered, 4 to 5 minutes before serving. Transfer the chicken to a serving dish and garnish with coriander leaves and the reserved roasted cashew nuts.

Serves 6 to 8

Remarks

This is a lovely dish to serve at parties with Naan, Leavened, Baked, Whole Wheat Bread *(see Index), a rice* pullau, *and vegetables.*

If you prefer, you may remove the cardamom pods, bay leaves, and other whole spices before serving.

Murgh Kay Tukray

Baked Chicken with Tamarind and Jaggery

3 pounds chicken pieces, breasts and legs

3 tablespoons tamarind pulp

6 tablespoons hot water

1¾ to 2 tablespoons grated jaggery or 1¾ tablespoons molasses

¼ to ½ teaspoon chili powder

1 tablespoon scraped and finely grated ginger

¼ teaspoon ginger powder

½ teaspoon *garam masalla,* a spice mixture (see page 42)

1 tablespoon vegetable oil

1 tablespoon tamari soy sauce

3 spring onions

Remove skin and excess fat from the chicken pieces. Wash and let drain 15 minutes in a colander.

Soak the tamarind pulp in hot water for 10 minutes. Add the jaggery to the tamarind water and continue soaking for 10 minutes. Squeeze the tamarind pulp thoroughly and strain. Discard the pulp and set the tamarind/jaggery juice aside.

In a baking dish, mix together the chicken pieces, tamarind/jaggery juice, chili powder, grated ginger, ginger powder, and *garam masalla.* Rub the spices into the chicken pieces and marinate for 4 hours, covered.

Rub the oil and tamari into the chicken pieces. Bake at 350°F for 30 minutes. Turn the chicken pieces over, baste thoroughly with the accumulated juices, and bake another 25 to 30 minutes.

Wash and mince the green part of the spring onions and use as a garnish.

Serves 6

Remarks

If you prefer the chicken crisp, broil the pieces for 1 to 2 minutes on each side.

I find the recipe excellent for serving at cocktail parties. Then I use 1½-inch square pieces of chicken breasts and slightly reduce the baking time.

Murgh Ki Tikki

Deep-Fried Chicken Cutlets

2 pounds chicken pieces	1¼ to 1½ teaspoons minced green chilies
1¼ cups oats	1 egg plus 1 egg yolk
⅓ cup barley	1½ tablespoons lemon juice
1 cup minced onion	2 tablespoons minced mint
¾ tablespoon scraped and grated ginger	1½ teaspoons white sesame seeds
1½ teaspoons minced garlic	vegetable oil for deep frying
1 teaspoon *garam masalla,* a spice mixture (see page 42)	

Remove skin, bones, and fat from chicken. Mince or chop into tiny pieces.

Grind the oats and barley to a powder.

In a bowl, mix together the chicken, ground oats and barley, onion, ginger, garlic, *garam masalla,* chilies, eggs, lemon juice, mint, and sesame seeds. Mix with your hands, pressing and kneading, to make the mixture as pliable as possible.

Divide the mixture into 16 to 18 sections. Shape each section into a small, round, flat patty, about 2 inches in diameter and 1 inch thick.

Heat the oil in a *karhai.* When the oil is almost at smoking point, lower the heat and after 1 minute fry 5 or 6 patties over moderate heat about 7 minutes. Turn them over, reduce heat to low, and fry another 6 to 9 minutes. Remove with a slotted spoon and place on a dish lined with paper towels. Repeat this process until all the *tikkis* are fried. Serve immediately or keep warm until ready to serve.

Serves 6

Remarks

Murgh Ki Tikki *makes a lovely snack served with* Papitay Aur Khajur Ki Meethi Chutney *(Sweet Chutney with Papaya and Dates),* Dhania Chutney *(Fresh Coriander Chutney), or* Pudina Aur Dhania Chutney *(Mint and Coriander Chutney). See Index for these chutneys.*

Murgh Vindaloo

Chicken *Vindaloo*

2½ pounds chicken pieces

3 tablespoons minced garlic

3 tablespoons scraped and chopped ginger

3 tablespoons white vinegar

1½ tablespoons jaggery or 1 tablespoon molasses

1 teaspoon turmeric powder

1 to 2 small green chilies, chopped

¼ teaspoon fenugreek seeds

1 teaspoon mustard seeds

1 tablespoon coriander seeds

1 teaspoon cumin seeds

⅛ teaspoon *heeng,* asafetida

¼ to ½ teaspoon red chili powder

1 pound small potatoes

7 tablespoons mustard oil or vegetable oil

1 cup minced onions

2 cups finely chopped tomatoes

2 to 3 tablespoons chopped coriander leaves or watercress

Remove the skin and fat from the chicken pieces, wash, and let drain 15 minutes in a colander.

Blend together the garlic, ginger, vinegar, jaggery, turmeric powder, and chilies.

Grind the fenugreek seeds, mustard seeds, coriander seeds, and cumin seeds together in an electric or coffee grinder.

Rub the blended spices, ground spices, asafetida, and chili powder thoroughly into the chicken pieces and set aside, covered, for 2 hours.

Boil the potatoes. Peel, cut into halves, and set aside.

Heat the oil in a heavy 5-quart pot and fry the onions until they become golden brown. Add the tomatoes and fry, while stirring and pressing with the back of the spoon until the tomatoes are well mashed and oil appears at the sides of the pan.

Add the marinated chicken pieces and cook over moderately high heat 10 minutes. Stir occasionally. Reduce the heat to moderate and cook another 10 minutes. Stir occasionally. Add the potatoes, reduce heat to low, and simmer, covered, until the chicken is done. Transfer to a large serving bowl and garnish with coriander leaves.

Serves 6 to 8

Remarks

This is a variation of pork vindaloo, a typical south Indian dish, and is lovely served with rice.
Generally, a vindaloo is made very hot with chilies.

Murgi Ka Saalan

Chicken Curry

3½ pounds chicken pieces	4 whole cloves
5 tablespoons vegetable oil	4 small pale green cardamom pods
1 cup finely sliced onions	1 teaspoon cumin seeds
1½ cups grated onions	1 tablespoon coriander seeds
2 tablespoons *khas khas,* white poppy seeds	12 peppercorns
2 tablespoons grated coconut	1½ cups chopped tomatoes
5 tablespoons thick Homemade Yogurt (see page 41)	⅛ teaspoon nutmeg powder
1 tablespoon minced garlic	⅛ teaspoon cinnamon powder
1 tablespoon plus ¾ teaspoon scraped and finely grated ginger	1½ teaspoons paprika
	2 to 3 tablespoons chopped coriander leaves

¼ to ½ teaspoon chili powder

Remove the skin and fat from the chicken pieces, wash, and let drain in a colander for at least 15 minutes.

In a 5-quart pot, heat 4 tablespoons oil and fry the sliced and grated onions until they are well browned. Remove with a slotted spoon and set aside.

In the same oil, fry the poppy seeds and coconut until lightly browned. Remove with a slotted spoon and grind to a thick paste, adding a teaspoon of yogurt if needed.

Rub the onions, poppy seed/coconut paste, garlic, ginger, and chili powder into the chicken pieces and fry over moderately high heat, while stirring, until the chicken is lightly browned (about 20 to 30 minutes). Add a little oil if needed.

Meanwhile, grind the cloves, cardamom pods, cumin seeds, coriander seeds, and peppercorns to a powder. Sift the powder and set aside.

Stir 2 tablespoons yogurt into the pot and cook with the chicken 2 to 3 minutes.

Add the remaining yogurt, tomatoes, ground spices, nutmeg powder, cinnamon powder, and paprika to the chicken. Stir thoroughly, reduce heat to low, and simmer until the chicken is tender.

Sprinkle coriander leaves on top, stir once, simmer 1 minute and serve.

Serves 6 to 8

Remarks

This simple chicken curry makes a lovely family meal served with either rice or rotis.

For a party, you can serve the chicken curry with a pullau *along with* kababs, *a barbecued fish, a leg of lamb, or another meat dish. Serve* rotis, *vegetables, and a* raita *or* chutney *to complete the meal.*

————————————— *Murgi Ka Stew* —————————————

Chicken Stewed in Coconut Milk with Vegetables

1¾ pounds chicken pieces

1 tablespoon coriander seeds

¼ teaspoon fenugreek seeds

2 teaspoons *chana daal,* a lentil

½ teaspoon whole wheat flour

1 fresh coconut

6 cups water

½ pound potatoes

½ pound carrots

¼ pound turnips

½ pound peas, fresh or frozen

3 tablespoons ground nut oil or vegetable oil

2 teaspoons scraped and grated ginger

2 teaspoons minced garlic

¾ teaspoon freshly ground black pepper

1¼ cups chopped onions

½ to 1 teaspoon chili powder

8 to 10 *kardi patta,* curry leaves

4 to 5 small green chilies, sliced in halves

2 slightly ripened mangoes

¼ cup chopped coriander leaves or parsley

1 tablespoon white vinegar (optional)

Remove the skin and fat from the chicken pieces. Wash thoroughly and allow to drain well.

Heat a *tava* or griddle. Stir in the coriander seeds, fenugreek seeds, *chana daal,* and whole wheat flour and roast over moderate heat until the flour is browned. Then, grind to a fine powder and set aside.

Break the coconut (for procedure, see page 40) and cut into small pieces. Put ¼ cup chopped coconut into a blender container and add 2 cups water. Blend until the coconut becomes a thick milk. Remove and set aside. Put 1 cup chopped coconut into the blender, add 2 cups water, and blend. Add another 2 cups water and blend until you have a thin coconut milk. Remove ½ cup of the milk and leave the rest in the blender.

Scrub the potatoes thoroughly. Remove the eyes and any rough or broken skin. Cut into ¾-inch cubes.

Scrub the carrots and chop into ¼-inch rounds.

Scrub the turnips and cut into ¾-inch cubes.

Remove the peas from the shells or defrost if using frozen peas.

In a 5-quart pot, heat the oil. Fry the chicken, ginger, garlic, and pepper until the chicken is lightly browned. Add the roasted powdered spices, ½ cup thin coconut milk, onions, chili powder, and curry leaves and cook, uncovered, until the liquid evaporates. Stir occasionally.

Blend the thin coconut milk in the blender for 1 second. Add the potatoes, carrots, turnips, chilies and the thin coconut milk to the pot. Stir and bring to a boil. Reduce heat to low and cook, covered, for about 1 hour.

Peel the mangoes and cut into long thin slivers. Discard the seeds. Add the mangoes and the peas to the pot and simmer 4 to 5 minutes. Stir in the thick coconut milk, coriander leaves, and vinegar (if used) and simmer a few minutes before serving.

Serves 6 to 9

Remarks

This recipe is adapted from a popular dish from Kerala, in south India, which is made with boneless fish instead of chicken. I have also added a few extra spices.

Serve with plain boiled rice and a salad or chutney.

Tandoori Murgh I

Whole *Tandoori* Chickens

2 chickens (about 2½ pounds each)

3 tablespoons lemon juice

⅛ teaspoon *zafraan,* saffron threads

1 teaspoon hot water

1½ teaspoons cumin seeds

3 teaspoons coriander seeds

4 tablespoons Homemade Yogurt (see page 41)

1 tablespoon minced garlic

1 tablespoon scraped and grated ginger

3 tablespoons grated onion

¼ to ½ teaspoon chili powder

½ teaspoon turmeric powder

½ teaspoon *garam masalla,* a spice mixture (see page 42)

2 tablespoons *ghee* (see page 40) or oil

Pyaz Ka Salaad, Onion Salad to Accompany *Tandoori Murgh I* (see Index)

Remove skin and excess fat from chickens. Wash and allow to drain in a colander for at least 15 minutes. Pat dry and cut 6 slits, 2 to 3 inches long and ¼ inch deep into the breast, legs, and thighs. Rub lemon juice over the chickens, rubbing it into the slits as well, and set aside. After 10 minutes, turn the chickens, baste with the lemon juice, and set aside for another 15 to 20 minutes. Baste once again during that time.

Soak the saffron threads in the water until dissolved.

Heat a *tava* or griddle. Stir in the cumin seeds and coriander seeds and roast for 1 minute over moderately high heat. Remove immediately and grind to a powder.

Beat the yogurt and blend it with the saffron threads, ground spices, garlic, ginger, onion, chili powder, turmeric powder, and *garam masalla,*

Pour the excess lemon juice off the chickens. Place the chickens in a baking dish and rub the blended yogurt mixture over them. Rub the yogurt inside the slits as well. Cover securely and set aside for 8 hours at room temperature or 18 hours in the refrigerator.

Place the chickens on their backs in the baking dish. Baste them with the blended marinade. Brush 1 tablespoon *ghee* over the chickens and broil for 10 to 12 minutes. Turn the chickens over, baste, brush remaining *ghee* on top and broil about 10 minutes. Then broil at 400°F for about 10 to 15 minutes. Turn the chickens onto their backs, baste, and broil at 400°F until golden brown. If you cannot regulate the broiling temperature, then turn the oven to 350°F and bake until golden brown.

Meanwhile, prepare the *Pyaz Ka Salaad.*

Place the chickens, whole, in the middle of a large, flat serving dish. Arrange the salad in a ring around the chickens and serve. Or, cut the chickens into convenient pieces, place in the middle of the serving dish, and arrange the salad around the chicken.

Serves 6

Remarks

This is a very well known and typical north Indian dish. We generally serve it with Naan *(Leavened, Baked, Whole Wheat Bread), or* Khamiri Roti *(Whole Wheat, Leavened, Quick-Baked Bread). See Index for these breads.*

Tandoori Murgh II

Whole *Tandoori* Chickens

2 chickens (about 2½ pounds each)

2 tablespoons plus ¾ teaspoon lemon juice

1¾ teaspoons cumin powder

1 tablespoon plus ¾ teaspoon coriander powder

1 tablespoon scraped and grated ginger

1 tablespoon minced garlic

¼ teaspoon chili powder

¾ teaspoon turmeric powder

3½ tablespoons thick Homemade Yogurt (see page 41)

1 tablespoon grated unripened papaya pulp

3 tablespoons melted *ghee* (see page 40) or vegetable oil

1 teaspoon paprika

3½ tablespoons *besan,* chick-pea flour

Remove skin and excess fat from the chickens. Wash and let drain in a colander for a few minutes.

Cut 8 to 10 slits, about 2 inches long and ½ inch deep, into the breast, thighs, and legs of each chicken. Rub the lemon juice over the chickens and into the slits, and set aside for 30 minutes.

In a hot *tava* or small pan, roast the cumin powder and coriander powder, while stirring, until the aroma is apparent (about 20 to 30 seconds).

Mix the roasted cumin and coriander, ginger, garlic, chili powder, turmeric powder, yogurt, and papaya pulp together and rub over the chickens and into the slits. Cover securely and refrigerate for 24 hours or marinate in a cool place for 6 hours.

Preheat oven to 375°F. Rub 2½ tablespoons *ghee,* the paprika and chick-pea flour over the chickens and lay them on their backs side by side in a baking dish. Bake for 20 minutes.

Lower the oven temperature to 350°F and bake another 30 minutes. Brush remaining ½ tablespoon *ghee* on top of the chickens and continue to bake another 15 to 20 minutes. The chickens should now be a reddish brown color. Turn the chickens over and baste with the accumulated liquid. Bake another 10 to 20 minutes, then broil until the second side becomes a reddish brown (about 2 minutes).

Serve with *Pyaz Ka Salaad* (see Index).

Serves 6 to 8

Remarks

Tandoori chickens in India have a wonderful reddish brown color because food coloring is added. In our recipe, we have used turmeric and paprika to achieve the colored effect.

Chick-pea flour is not normally used in preparing this dish, but my mother and I found that using a little of it gave the chickens an appearance similar to the one achieved by cooking the chickens in a real tandoor *(clay oven).*

fish

Jhinga Curry

Curried Prawns with Coconut

24 medium-size prawns (about 2 pounds)	5 tablespoons *ghee* (see page 40) or vegetable oil
1 small coconut	
2 cups water	1 to 1½ cups minced onions
1 teaspoon tamarind pulp	1 tablespoon minced garlic
2 tablespoons hot water or white vinegar	½ teaspoon turmeric powder
¾ tablespoon coriander seeds	¼ to ½ teaspoon chili powder
1 teaspoon cumin seeds	3 to 4 small green chilies
1 to 1½ teaspoons black or red mustard seeds	3 tablespoons chopped coriander or parsley

Shell and devein the prawns. If you have difficulty, dip the prawns in boiling water for less than a minute, drain, and then shell and devein. Set aside.

Break the shell of the coconut. (For procedure, see page 40.) Chop 1 cup of fresh coconut and place in a blender container. Add ½ cup water and blend. Scrape down the sides of the blender jar and add another cup of water and blend again. You should now have 2 cups of coconut milk. If not, add enough water to equal 2 cups and blend again.

Soak the tamarind pulp in hot water 15 to 20 minutes. Squeeze the pulp thoroughly and strain. Collect the juice; discard the pulp and seeds, if any.

In a *tava* or griddle, roast the coriander seeds and cumin seeds over moderate heat, while stirring, until lightly browned (about 1 minute). Using an electric grinder or a mortar and pestle, grind the roasted seeds and then the mustard seeds until they are reduced to a powder.

In a large skillet, heat the *ghee* and fry the onions over high heat, while stirring, 2 to 3 minutes. Add the garlic and stir over moderate heat 3 to 4 minutes. Stir in the tamarind juice, coriander and cumin powder, ground mustard seeds, turmeric powder, and chili powder, and simmer 3 to 4 minutes. Stir occasionally.

Add the coconut milk and chilies. Cook until heated through, while stirring constantly, but do not allow the coconut milk to boil.

Stir in the prawns and cook, uncovered, over moderate heat until the prawns are cooked (about 4 to 6 minutes). Add the coriander leaves, stir thoroughly, reduce heat to low, and simmer 1 to 2 minutes before serving.

Serves 6

Remarks

Jhinga Curry is almost always served with rice.

The preparation takes some time, but this is offset by the very short time it takes to actually cook this delicious curry.

Macher Jhol

Fish Curry with Tamarind

2 pounds river trout or sea trout	1½ teaspoons *safed urad daal,* a lentil
1 piece of tamarind, the size of 2 limes	2 large onions, finely sliced
¾ cup hot water	6 *kardi patta,* curry leaves
1½ cups grated coconut	1½ tablespoons freshly ground coriander
1¾ teaspoons cumin seeds	
2½ to 2¾ cups water	1 to 2 teaspoons chili powder
	1 teaspoon turmeric powder
4 tablespoons mustard oil or vegetable oil	2 to 4 small green chilies, quartered lengthwise
1½ teaspoons black or red mustard seeds	1 teaspoon grated jaggery

Wash and clean the fish. Pat dry and cut into 1½-inch pieces. Set aside.

Soak the tamarind in the hot water and set aside.

Place the coconut and cumin seeds in the jar of a blender with ¼ cup water and blend. Scrape down the sides of the blender, add ¼ cup water, and blend until reduced to a puree. Set aside. Add ¼ cup water if needed.

In a 5-quart pot, heat the oil until it smokes. Add the mustard seeds; when they begin to sputter, add the *safed urad daal* and stir until the *daal* turns a light brown. Add the onions and curry leaves and fry until onions are golden brown. Stir in the coriander, chili powder, and turmeric powder and fry over medium heat. Then add the chilies and fry 2 to 3 minutes.

Squeeze the tamarind to extract all the juices. Strain and discard the pulp. Add the tamarind juice to the pot along with the coconut and cumin seeds. Bring slowly to a boil and simmer 5 minutes. Add the fish and 2 cups water and bring slowly to a boil again. Reduce heat, sprinkle jaggery over top and cook, covered, over low heat, shaking the pot gently once or twice, until the fish is done and the gravy is thick.

Serves 6

Remarks

This fish delicacy is traditionally served with rice and a chutney.

Machli Kabab

Broiled Fish Kabobs with *Kardi Patta*

2 pounds fillet of trout or any firm fish

12 cherry tomatoes

12 pearl onions

4 medium onions

8 tablespoons lemon juice

12 *kardi patta,* curry leaves

2 teaspoons freshly ground black pepper

2 teaspoons freshly ground cumin powder

6 small green chilies, halved

¼ to ½ teaspoon chili powder

4 tablespoons mustard oil

2 cups chopped mint leaves or watercress

2 to 3 lemons, cut into wedges

Cut the fish into 1½-inch pieces. Place in a large bowl with tomatoes and pearl onions.

Finely chop the medium onions or blend in a blender for a few seconds. Place the onions in a muslin cloth and gather the edges of the cloth together. Hold the cloth containing the onions over the fish and squeeze thoroughly to extract as much onion juice as possible.

Pour the lemon juice into the bowl containing the fish. Add the curry leaves, black pepper, cumin powder, chilies, chili powder, and 1 tablespoon mustard oil and stir very gently. Marinate for at least 1 hour in a cool spot. Stir gently once or twice.

Arrange alternately on flat skewers the fish, tomatoes, onions, curry leaves, and green chilies. Brush the entire *kababs* with the remaining oil and place on a hot grill 10 to 15 minutes. Turn the skewers as each side cooks. (In oven, broil kabobs 5 to 6 minutes on each side.)

Arrange the fish on a platter prepared with a bed of mint leaves and garnish with lemon wedges.

Serves 6 to 8

Paturi

Fish with Mustard Oil and Mustard Seeds

1½ pounds firm white fish fillets

1½ tablespoons black or red mustard seeds

6 small chilies

3¾ tablespoons mustard oil

3 tablespoons vegetable oil

¾ teaspoon turmeric powder

1 tablespoon water

2 teaspoons lemon juice

Wash the fish, pat dry, and cut into 3-inch pieces.

Place the mustard seeds in a blender and blend just until coarsely crushed (about 2 to 3 seconds).

Wash the chilies and cut in half. If you wish, you may remove the seeds. This will make the chilies less "hot."

Mix together the fish, crushed mustard seeds, chilies, mustard oil, vegetable oil, turmeric powder, and water.

Preheat the oven to 350°F. Place the fish pieces side by side in a baking dish. Pour the liquid over it, bake 30 minutes, and then turn the oven off.

Sprinkle lemon juice over the fish and leave in the oven a few minutes before serving.

Serves 6

Machli Ka Korma

Fish Curry with Coconut Milk

1½	pounds flounder, halibut, or any firm white fish	1½	tablespoons *khas khas,* white poppy seeds
1	coconut	3	tablespoons peanut oil or vegetable oil
3½	cups water	1½	cups finely sliced onions
1½	tablespoons tamarind pulp or 2 to 3 tablespoons lemon juice	2 to 3	small green chilies, sliced in halves lengthwise
4	tablespoons hot water	8	*kardi patta,* curry leaves
1½	tablespoons coriander seeds	1½	tablespoons minced garlic
¼	tablespoon peppercorns	¾	teaspoon turmeric powder
1	tablespoon *chana daal,* a lentil, or peanuts	¼ to ½	teaspoon red chili powder
¼	tablespoon whole wheat flour	4	tablespoons chopped coriander leaves
½	teaspoon fenugreek seeds		

Wash and clean the fish. Cut into 1-inch pieces.

Open the coconut. (For procedure, see page 40.) Chop enough of the coconut to make 1½ cups. Place ½ cup of the chopped coconut in a blender container, add 1 cup water, and blend. Scrape down the sides of the blender and pour this thick coconut milk into another container and set aside. Put the remaining chopped coconut in the jar of the blender, and 1½ cups water, and blend. Scrape down the sides of the blender, add another cup of water, and blend again. Pour this thinner coconut milk into another container and set aside.

Soak the tamarind pulp in the hot water for at least 15 minutes. Squeeze the pulp thoroughly and strain. Collect the tamarind juice and discard the pulp.

Heat a *tava* or griddle. Mix together the coriander seeds, peppercorns, *chana daal,* flour, fenugreek seeds, and poppy seeds. Stir the mixture on the *tava* until the flour is browned. Remove and grind to a fine powder. Set 3¼ teaspoons aside to use in the curry and store the rest in an airtight container for future use.

In a large skillet, heat the oil. Fry the onions, chilies, and curry leaves over moderate heat 4 to 5 minutes. Add the garlic and fry 1 to 2 minutes.

Stir in the fish, the thinner coconut milk, tamarind juice, the prepared ground spices, turmeric powder, and chili powder, and bring to a boil. Reduce the heat to low and cook, covered, about 35 minutes. Alternate the heat between low and moderate so that the liquid is always very hot but not boiling. Stir once during that time.

Add the thicker coconut milk and coriander leaves and cook, uncovered, a few minutes before serving.

Serves 6

Remarks

This delicious curry, adapted from a south Indian recipe, is best served with plain boiled rice and a chutney.

Machli Ka Saalan

Fish Curry with Coconut Milk

2 tablespoons tamarind pulp	1 coconut
¼ cup hot water or 2 to 3 tablespoons lemon juice	5 cups water
	3½ tablespoons vegetable oil
1½ pounds any boneless white fish	1¾ cups finely sliced onions
3 tablespoons coriander seeds	1¾ tablespoons minced garlic
½ tablespoon peppercorns	10 to 12 *kardi patta,* curry leaves
1 tablespoon *chana daal,* a lentil, or peanuts	1 teaspoon turmeric powder
1 teaspoon fenugreek seeds	3 to 4 tablespoons chopped coriander leaves
1 tablespoon whole wheat flour	3 to 4 small green chilies
2 to 3 dried red chilies	

Soak the tamarind pulp in the hot water for 15 minutes. Squeeze the pulp thoroughly and strain the juice. Discard the pulp and seeds, if any. Wash fish fillets, cut them into 1-inch pieces, cover, and set aside.

Place a *tava* or griddle over moderate heat 1 minute. Roast the coriander seeds, peppercorns, *chana daal,* fenugreek seeds, and flour, while stirring, until the flour becomes brown. Set aside. Roast the red chilies a few seconds on all sides. Grind all the roasted spices to a fine powder.

Break the coconut. (For procedure, see page 40.) Chop enough of the coconut meat to make 2 cups. Grate the coconut meat by hand or in an electric blender. Place the grated coconut in a blender jar, add 1 cup of water, and blend. Scrape down the sides, add another ½ cup water, and blend again. Strain this coconut milk; press and squeeze as much of the thick milk as possible through the strainer. Reserve 1 cup of this thick coconut milk. Add 3½ cups water to the remaining milk and pulp and blend again until you have about 3¾ to 4½ cups of thin coconut milk.

In a 5-quart pot, heat the oil and fry the onions, garlic, and curry leaves over moderate heat about 5 to 6 minutes. Add the turmeric powder and 5 teaspoons of the roasted ground spices. Fry and stir 3 to 4 minutes.

Add the tamarind juice, fish, and 4 cups of thin coconut milk. Stir gently. Slowly bring to a boil and then immediately reduce heat to low and simmer, covered, until the fish is cooked (about 25 minutes).

Stir in the thick coconut milk, coriander leaves, and green chilies and simmer a few minutes before serving.

Serves 6 to 8

Remarks

This fish curry from south India is best served with plain boiled rice and Pakay Aam Ki Chutney *(Quick Sweet and Sour Mango Chutney),* Pudina Chutney *(Mint Chutney), or* Dhania Chutney *(Fresh Coriander Chutney). See Index for these chutneys.*

Store surplus roasted ground spices in an airtight container for future use.

Masalla Bhari Machli

Stuffed Broiled Fish

½ cup long grain brown rice	4 spring onions, minced
1 cup water	½ teaspoon grated jaggery or molasses
5½ tablespoons mustard oil or vegetable oil	3 tablespoons raisins
2 eggs, beaten	1 medium onion, finely chopped
1 to 2 small green chilies, minced	1½-inch piece of ginger, scraped and grated
2 pomfret, Dover sole, or halibut, whole (1½ to 2 pounds each)	1 teaspoon freshly ground coriander seeds
3 tablespoons lemon juice	1 teaspoon crushed mustard seeds
1 teaspoon black pepper	½ teaspoon *garam masalla,* a spice mixture (see page 42)
2 cups water	1 teaspoon turmeric powder
½ cup whole cashew nuts	2 medium, firm tomatoes, chopped
1 tablespoon whole almonds	

Wash the rice. Place in a 2-quart saucepan with water and bring to a boil. Lower heat and simmer, covered, until the rice is cooked. Set aside.

Heat 1 tablespoon oil in a large skillet. Make a thin omelette with the eggs and ¼ teaspoon chilies. Cut the omelette into little squares and set aside, covered, with the rice in a large bowl.

Clean the fish, remove the eyes, trim the fins and tail but leave the head in place. Wash under cold running water, pat dry inside and out, and rub the surface and inside with 1 tablespoon lemon juice and ½ teaspoon pepper.

Boil water in a 2-quart saucepan, remove from heat, drop the cashews and almonds in the water, and soak for 15 to 20 minutes.

In a deep bowl, combine the rice, remaining 2 tablespoons lemon juice, ½ teaspoon pepper, spring onions, jaggery, and raisins.

In a large, heavy skillet, heat 3 tablespoons oil until it smokes. Reduce heat to moderate, stir in the chopped onion, and fry 4 to 5 minutes. Add the ginger, coriander seeds, mustard seeds, and *garam masalla.* Fry and stir until the onions are a golden brown. Add the turmeric powder and fry, while stirring constantly, 3 minutes. Sprinkle a few drops of water into the skillet if needed. Stir in the remaining chilies, and tomatoes and fry until the tomatoes are pureed.

Empty the contents of the skillet into the bowl with the rice and omelette. Lightly toss until all the ingredients are well mixed.

Drain the nuts, peel the skins from the almonds, place them on a board and finely chop the cashews and almonds. Stir them into the rice mixture. Stuff the fish with the rice mixture and tie lightly with thread. Lightly brush one side of the fish with half of the remaining mustard oil. Place in a shallow baking pan, oiled side up, and broil until crisp (about 20 to 30 minutes). Turn, brush with oil, and broil until done.

Serves 6

Remarks

You will be pleased with this deceivingly simple dish!

Tali Machli

Deep-Fried Fish Fillets with Batter

1½ pounds firm white fish fillets	vegetable oil for deep frying
1 cup *besan,* chick-pea flour	2 large onions, sliced into rings
½ cup rice flour	1 tablespoon lemon juice
1 tablespoon *amchoor,* powdered mango	2 to 3 lemons, cut into wedges
¼ to ½ teaspoon chili powder	1 to 2 tablespoons green coriander leaves
¼ to 1 teaspoon black pepper	1 teaspoon cumin powder
¼ cup water	

Rinse the fillets, pat dry, cut each in half lengthwise, and then cut into 3-inch pieces.

In a bowl, mix together the chick-pea flour, rice flour, powdered mango, chili powder, and black pepper. Stir in the water in small amounts and mix, preferably with your fingers, until a thick batter is formed.

Warm a baking dish in a 200° to 300°F oven. Line the dish with a few layers of thick paper toweling.

Heat the oil in a *karhai* or wok until a haze forms on top and a drop of batter dropped in rises immediately to the surface.

Dip the fish pieces into the batter, thoroughly coat each piece, then hold sideways to allow excess batter to drain. Deep fry 5 or 6 pieces at a time until they are golden brown (about 4 to 6 minutes). Remove with a slotted spoon to the paper-lined dish and keep warm in the oven. Continue until all pieces are fried.

Arrange the onion rings on a large flat serving platter and sprinkle with the lemon juice. Arrange the fish pieces on the platter and decorate with lemon wedges. Sprinkle the coriander leaves over the fish.

Heat a *tava* or griddle and roast the cumin powder 1 minute over moderate heat. Sprinkle the cumin powder evenly over the fish and serve immediately.

Serves 6

Remarks

Serve with a rice dish.

little pleasures

Sometimes it takes an enthusiastic visitor to make one look anew at the simple things of home that one takes for granted. When Pamie, my friend from Canadian college days, was visiting me in India, she found everything fascinating, and it was fun to share in her excitement. When we sat down to even a simple meal together, she would exclaim with delight over our yogurt dishes, our vegetables, and our breads, especially the plain whole wheat *chapati.* Pamie was happy to learn our ways and soon began eating with her fingers, as we do in India. She would smile and say in her soft Canadian accent, *"Aacha hai"*—"It is good!"—and declare that food tastes better eaten this way. Of course, we have always known this.

The *chapati,* our Indian bread, is very popular and in fact is a staple in the diet of north Indians. In many poorer homes, *chapatis* are made for both the evening

Chapati

Whole Wheat,
Flat Round Bread

2 cups whole wheat flour

1 cup plus 2 tablespoons water

3 tablespoons melted *ghee* (see page 40) or vegetable oil

Sift the flour into a bowl. Make a dent in the center and pour in ¾ cup water. Mix to form a mass of dough. If necessary, slowly add up to ¼ cup more water until you can form the flour into one mass.

Knead for 6 to 12 minutes until the dough is soft and pliable. Gather the dough into a ball and place in a bowl. Sprinkle about 2 tablespoons of water over the dough, then flatten the ball slightly. Cover with a bowl inverted over the dough for at least 30 minutes.

Divide the dough into 10 to 12 portions. Shape each portion into a ball, then roll it out on a lightly floured surface until flattened into a thin round 5 to 6 inches in diameter.

Heat a *tava* or griddle over moderately high heat. Sprinkle with some flour. If it gets dark brown in seconds, lower heat before you begin to cook a *chapati.* Place a *chapati* on the *tava* for 1 minute. Turn it over and cook the second side another minute. Keep several layers of paper toweling in your hand and lift the *chapati* carefully. Press down lightly over any spot that looks raw on either side. This pressing motion will also make the *chapati* puff up with air between the layers. Lift off the *tava* and place in a bowl lined with foil. Brush about ¼ teaspoon *ghee* over the *chapati* and fold the foil over it to keep the *chapati* warm while you cook the rest.

Yields 10 to 12 *chapatis*

Remarks

The chapati *is our most basic and popular bread. While it is supposed to be simple to make, it really is not. It is difficult to make a* chapati *soft yet properly browned. Once cooked, it should be light brown in appearance with a few dark brown patches. It takes a little practice before developing this technique.*

There is no need to grease the chapatis *if serving them immediately as we normally do in India. It is only necessary when preparing them in advance in order to prevent drying when reheated.*

At mealtime, the chapati *is kept in a small side plate or at the edge of the* thali *or plate. Small bits are broken off and used to scoop up the meat, vegetables, or lentils.*

meal and for breakfast the next morning at the same time. This is often done to save cooking fuel, but it also adds an extra bit of nutritive value to the *roti*. Kept overnight, the yeast in the *chapati* has a chance to become activated, and the vitamin B value of the *chapati* increases.

Of course, the wealthier Indians were always reluctant to eat what they considered stale food. However, my mother-in-law and I have always loved having our "stale" *chapati* in the morning with a glass of *masalla* tea. Sometimes we add a dab of pure *ghee* and a spoon of melted jaggery to the *roti*, roll it up, and it becomes a delicious sweet roll. You can use honey or sorghum syrup instead of the jaggery.

Spiced Tea ————————————— *Masalla Tea* ————————————

2-inch piece of ginger

9 cups cold water

1½-inch cinnamon stick

6 to 8 small pale green cardamom pods

6 to 8 whole cloves

1 tablespoon tea leaves, preferably a blend of Indian teas, or 2 or 3 tea bags

honey

Scrape the ginger. Place it on a board and give it a few gentle blows with a mallet so that it breaks into several pieces.

Pour the water into a medium-size pot. Add the ginger, cinnamon, cardamom pods, and cloves and bring to a boil. Reduce heat to low and simmer, covered, about 45 minutes to 1 hour.

Add tea leaves and boil 2 to 4 minutes. Strain and serve the tea with honey to taste.

Serves 6

Remarks

I make this tea for friends who have colds or coughs. Sometimes when I am not well, they sweetly remind me to take a dose of my own medicine!

Pamie got along immediately with everyone in the family, especially my father, who delighted in her sharp mind and loving ways. She fast formed an easy companionship with Irene, my Khasi *ayah*. The two of them got along together famously. At first, Pamie found it hard to accept the idea of a "servant," with all the implications of the word. It was natural for her to treat the girl as a complete equal and Irene responded.

Irene is a vibrant, lively person from a tiny village tucked away in the hills of Shillong. For her, too, the big city of Delhi was a thrilling aspect of India that she was newly discovering. She and Pamie loved to shop together. They would go off in the morning, carrying big jute shopping bags to bring home the fresh vegetables for the day's meal. They never made good bargains! But Pamie found the variety of fresh fruits and vegetables thrilling.

The variety of fresh fruits and vegetables at the bazaar was always thrilling, especially for a visitor.

The Subtle Art of Bargaining

Irene was so excited about the outings, having spent an hour getting ready, wearing her best clothes, that bargaining would be the last thing on her mind! I was indulgent of this because, to tell the truth, I haven't mastered the subtle techniques of good bargaining myself!

However, the process of haggling and bargaining is a part of the fun (or business) of shopping in India. It is an important rule never to express too much delight on seeing the proffered wares. Thus, a pleasant, but noncommittal, semicritical facial expression is cultivated for shopping. One goes from stall to stall checking prices, sometimes touching, but always looking less happy than one might feel. It is all a part of the accepted shopping game. The shopkeeper expects this and would be secretly scornful of anyone who constantly exclaimed with delight on seeing a particularly large cauliflower, a juicy-looking peach, or a fragrant mango!

Another unspoken rule is to reduce the suggested price by about half. The shopkeeper will then indignantly protest and suggest another price. We then shake our heads solemnly. Sometimes we say, "But so-and-so is selling this for only one *rupee.*" Or, "Your fruit doesn't look too fresh." Or, "But yesterday I bought this for only 80 *paisa.*" And so on.

Imagine—a wholesale market stall just for oranges!

After a few minutes of this kind of (totally illogical) reasoning, a price is agreed upon to the satisfaction of both parties. If we cannot agree, another gambit is open to us. We can walk away, pretending we are not interested, while looking back out of the corners of our eyes. Then, if the shopkeeper is keen to sell, she will quickly call out, "Come back!" We return and we might buy the vegetable at the price we both feel is reasonable. Otherwise, fresh haggling begins!

A "Chorus" for Shoppers

Prita, my sister-in-law, is a notoriously bad bargainer. One day she, Pam, and I went off to Crawford market, a huge shopping center in Bombay, to buy a crate of mangoes, which were then gloriously in season. A cacophony of sounds greeted our ears. "Mem Sahib, I will give you a good bargain." "Mem Sahib, I have the best mangoes from Lucknow." "Which kind do you like? I have them all!" "Mem Sahib, come with me, I will take you to a good shop." This last from one of the many little boys who make a living carrying the day's purchases for as many shoppers as they can attract.

These small boys are part of the market scene in larger marketing centers. They carry woven baskets and scurry around frantically trying to latch on to a shopper to earn a few *paisa.* If a shopper agrees to "employ" him, the boy will then follow the person around, placing each new purchase into his basket. Some of these little boys are "agents" of various shopkeepers and try very hard to persuade their current employer to visit a particular shop. So, as you enter a large market, four or five little boys clamor at the same time for your attention, each hoping you will choose him. It is annoying to some and pathetic to others, but it is all part of the color and feel of a large market in India.

A Westerner may have several reactions to all of the activity in the marketplace. He or she may be fascinated and amused, as Pamie was, or it may seem very tiresome and time-consuming in comparison with the quick and efficient supermarket shopping with everything neatly mechanized. The visitor is most probably bewildered in any case! Whatever the reaction, it is impossible to escape the human element. Shopping in the West is certainly fascinating, with the mind-boggling array of merchandise so well displayed. But I sometimes find it rather depressing. I find myself missing that most elusive ingredient, the human touch. This is what Pamie particularly noticed. She would begin long conversations at each stall where her smiles and gestures more than compensated for her limited knowledge of Hindi. Then, at the end of our shopping, she gave our little boy a large tip, so everyone was happy.

Prita came home proudly that day with what she thought was a good bargain. We discovered later that under the first two rows of shiny, ripe mangoes were two layers of tiny, unformed fruit. We had not bothered to check underneath. More seasoned shoppers would never have made this mistake! However, all was well as we used the raw fruit to make mango pickles and that delightful drink, *Mango Fool.*

Mango Fool — A Mango-Based Cool Drink

1¼ pounds unripened mangoes	4½ cups milk
1 cup water	honey (optional)
4½ to 5 tablespoons honey	

Wash the mangoes and wipe thoroughly. Remove the skins and cut the flesh away from the seeds. Chop the mango flesh into small pieces.

In a saucepan with a heavy base, bring the chopped mangoes and water to a boil. Reduce temperature to moderate and cook, covered, 15 minutes. Add honey, stir, and cook, covered, an additional 15 minutes. Uncover, stir, and cook over low heat until the mangoes are soft and the water evaporates (about 30 minutes). Do not let the mangoes burn.

Pass the mangoes through a sieve or mash thoroughly with a fork until you have a soft puree. Store in a tight container in the refrigerator until needed.

When ready to make *Mango Fool,* divide the mango pulp into 6 parts. For each glass, blend one part of mango pulp (about 1 heaping tablespoon) and ¾ cup milk until a milkshake consistency. Pour into a glass and add ice cubes and honey to taste, if needed.

Yields 6 glasses

In Shillong, shopping was different. We personally knew all the shopkeepers and had our own favorites. Sometimes, as children, Zhava, my dearest childhood friend and I would accompany one of our *ayahs* on their weekly shopping days. Zhava's Lithuanian parents, the Traubs, had settled in Shillong, as had a number of British people. It was always a real treat to be allowed to accompany Asho on her vegetable-shopping expeditions. We would go to the *Bara Bazaar* (big market), which was built on a slope with platforms dug into the hillside at intervals. From the foot of the bazaar, it was a sight to see the layered mounds upon mounds of fresh produce on all sides. The staggering variety of vegetables and fruit, always fresh and glistening, was newly plucked from nearby farms or small home gardens. There is something very satisfying about handling and choosing your vegetables while having a chat with the seller, sometimes bargaining in a friendly way, sometimes engaging in a more personal conversation.

Ma Rose's Vegetable Stall

Ma Rose, a robust Khasi lady, was a great favorite with many shoppers, as she was with Asho. Ma Rose's vegetable stall, typical of the Khasi lifestyle, was clean and sparkling. The Khasis and Garos, like the other hill tribes, are very democratic

Shoppers take pleasure in viewing the endless varieties of fruits and vegetables and in the personal contact between buyer and seller.

people. In most other places in India, shopkeepers belong to a "middle class" group of people. Here, in the Khasi hills, it is not uncommon to see a rich man's wife or daughter sitting next to a poor villager, both carrying on the business of selling.

With a smile, Ma Rose would call out, *'Bibi,* Asho *didi,* come and see my fresh *saag* (greens), my tender bhindi (okra), and my Dorris plums. You can't get better ones anywhere." Part of the fun was in going from stall to stall, comparing, choosing, or stopping to say hello to an old, old friend, who it seemed, had spent her entire life seated cross-legged behind her baskets of fruits. She was an aged Nepali lady who had settled in India but always told us how much better Nepal was. "You should just see our markets there," she would say. Asho would nod knowingly and they would spend a few conspiratorial minutes together. (Asho is a Nepali.)

This scene is fairly typical of most Indian vegetable markets, whether in villages or cities. In the smaller towns, as in Shillong, the atmosphere is relaxed and easy. The pleasure of viewing endless varieties of fresh fruit and vegetables is matched by the personal contact between seller and buyer, neither of whom is in a hurry.

Asho Ko Rye Saag — Asho's Lightly Curried Whole Mustard Leaves

1¼ pounds mustard leaves	¾ tablespoon crushed fennel seeds
5 tablespoons mustard oil	2 small green chilies, cut into halves lengthwise
⅛ teaspoon *heeng,* asafetida	4 whole cloves
1 tablespoon scraped and grated ginger	
1 tablespoon crushed black or red mustard seeds	

Wash the mustard leaves thoroughly under cold running water. Trim the ends of the stems. Keep the leaves and stems intact.

In a large skillet, heat the oil until a haze forms on top. Reduce heat to moderate. Drop the asafetida into the oil and then immediately add the ginger. Fry until the ginger is a pale brown. Stir in the crushed mustard seeds, crushed fennel seeds and chilies and fry ½ minute.

Place all the mustard leaves into the skillet.

Wrap the cloves in thick paper toweling and pound until the cloves are coarsely ground. Sprinkle the cloves over the mustard greens and stir thoroughly. Cover and cook about 8 minutes.

Uncover and stir until only about ½ cup of liquid is left (about 4 to 5 minutes).

Serves 6

Remarks

This lovely, nutritious vegetable dish is a variation of mustard greens as cooked in Nepal. We always serve this dish with plain boiled rice and a meat, fish, or lentil dish. One of our favorite meals is Paturi, *Fish with Mustard Oil and Mustard Seeds (see Index) with rice and Asho's* Saag.

Spicy Mixed ———————————— *Saag* ————————————
Greens, Pureed

12 ounces spinach, fresh or frozen	¾ teaspoon turmeric powder
8 ounces mustard greens, fresh or frozen	¾ cup chopped onions
10 ounces broccoli, fresh or frozen	2 tablespoons mustard oil plus 2 tablespoons vegetable oil, or 4 tablespoons vegetable oil
10 ounces kale leaves, fresh or frozen	1 cup finely sliced onions
¼ cup water	1 tablespoon minced garlic
2 tablespoons chopped ginger	6 dried red chilies
1⅓ tablespoons chopped garlic	½ tablespoon cumin seeds
1 tablespoon chopped small green chilies	

Wash the greens thoroughly and chop them coarsely. If using frozen greens, defrost and chop.

In a 5-quart pot with a heavy bottom, warm the water and put in all the greens, ginger, garlic, green chilies, turmeric powder, and chopped onions. Cook, covered, over moderate heat 15 minutes. Uncover and stir well, then reduce the heat to low, and simmer, covered, 50 minutes.

Remove the pot from the heat and place a quarter of the greens in a blender. Blend, adding a tablespoon of the liquid from the pot, until the greens are reduced to a puree. Remove and set aside. Continue this process until all the greens are pureed.

Return all the pureed greens to the pot and simmer until excess moisture evaporates and the puree becomes thick.

Meanwhile, in a skillet, heat the mustard oil over moderate heat 2 minutes, then add the vegetable oil and let it become hot. Fry the sliced onions until a reddish brown. Remove the onions and add them to the greens. In the same skillet and using the same oil, fry the minced garlic until it becomes a golden brown. Add the red chilies and cumin seeds and fry another 1 to 2 minutes. Do not let the cumin seeds burn. Pour the contents of the skillet into the pot with the greens. Stir and serve hot.

Serves 6

Remarks

This form of pureed greens is a great favorite with Punjabis. Rajni, my husband's cousin, gave me this lovely recipe.

Saag is wonderful served with Makkay Ki Roti, *Cornmeal Bread (see Index) or any* roti. *We place a dab of butter on each serving and recommend you do so also!*

This recipe makes 6 huge helpings. It can serve up to 10 or 11 people. Saag is so delicious served a day or two after it is made that I always make extra. My husband prefers it the next day, and the next.

—————————————— *Masalla Bhari Bhindi* ————————————— Spicy Stuffed
Okra

1½ pounds small okra	1 teaspoon turmeric powder
2½ tablespoons freshly ground coriander seeds	1 teaspoon chili powder (optional)
1 tablespoon freshly ground cumin seeds	1 tablespoon *amchoor,* powdered mango, or 2 tablespoons lemon juice
¾ teaspoon allspice powder (optional)	6 tablespoons vegetable oil
1½ teaspoons black pepper	

Wash the okra and pat dry. Then spread it out and allow it to dry completely. Make a lengthwise slit in each one but do not cut in half. The slit should be only large enough to allow the spices to be rubbed inside.

Mix together the coriander seeds, cumin seeds, allspice powder (if used), pepper, turmeric powder, chili powder (if used), and powdered mango. If lemon juice is used, you will have a paste instead of a dry mix.

Sprinkle a little of the mixture into each slit and rub it into the okra with your fingers. If using the paste, rub a little into each slit.

Heat the oil in a large skillet and fry the okra, uncovered, over moderate heat until lightly browned. Stir occasionally. When done, there should be no liquid left in the skillet.

Serves 6

Remarks

Bhindi *is delicious served with* Chapatis, *Whole Wheat, Flat Round Bread, or* Parathas, *A Shallow-Fried Bread (see Index).*

———————————————————————————————————————

Apart from the vegetables, you could buy practically anything you wanted at *Bara Bazaar.* There were cloth shops with bales and bales of material brought from larger centers like Calcutta. Meat was sold fresh from the hanging carcasses of sheep or other animals. The hill tribes are either animistic or Christian in their religious beliefs, so beef is readily available in Shillong and the adjoining hills. This is not true in other parts of India.

On the higher levels of the hill was the poultry section. You could choose and buy your chicken live from among the dozens of cackling, caged animals. I remember Babuji used to feed these chickens well, giving them a dose of raw garlic and green chilies every day along with their feed. Chicken is rather expensive in India, and it was a treat to have a chicken curry, especially Babuji's *Murgh Mussallam,* which we had on very special occasions.

Spiced Whole ————————————————— *Murgh Mussallam* ——————————————
Chicken

2 chickens (2½ to 3 pounds each)	6 whole cloves
1 tablespoon peeled and grated green, unripened papaya (optional)	12 to 20 peppercorns
	2 large cardamom pods
3 large onions	1 to 3 red chilies (optional)
6 to 8 tablespoons vegetable oil	2 tablespoons raw, unsalted peanuts
1-inch piece ginger	3 tablespoons plain Homemade Yogurt (see page 41)
12 medium garlic cloves	
1½ tablespoons coriander seeds	1 cup chopped green coriander leaves or mint or any green herb
1½ teaspoons cumin seeds	

Remove the skin from the chickens and trim off most of the fat. Poke lightly with a fork, rub with the grated papaya and set aside for 30 minutes.

Cut each onion into 4 pieces and finely slice 2 of the onions. Heat 2 tablespoons oil in a skillet and fry the 2 sliced onions until they become a dark reddish brown color (about 12 to 18 minutes). Remove from heat and set aside.

Scrape the ginger. Grate the ginger and garlic together with the remaining quartered onion in a machine or by hand.

In a coffee or spice grinder, grind the coriander seeds, cumin seeds, cloves, peppercorns, cardamom pods, red chilies (if used), and peanuts.

Mix the ginger mixture with the ground spices and rub all these spices into the chicken. Also rub in the yogurt.

Place the chickens with all the spices in a covered dish and refrigerate for 8 to 24 hours before cooking.

When ready to cook, heat 4 to 5 tablespoons oil in a large pan. Place the chickens in the pan and fry over moderate heat 10 to 15 minutes. If you do not have a large enough pan, do the initial 20 to 30 minutes of frying in two separate pans.

Turn the chickens and fry 10 to 15 minutes on the other side. Then lay both chickens close together side by side in the same pan, reduce heat to low, cover, and simmer until the chickens are tender (about 45 minutes).

Uncover and cook 5 to 15 minutes on each side to lightly brown the chickens. Serve on a bed of chopped coriander leaves.

Serves 6

Remarks

This is a grand dish, impressive looking and fit to serve at a banquet!

Apart from the fruits and vegetables, you could buy practically anything at the bazaar. Here is an entire stall devoted to spices.

Stalls Filled with Frivolities

In another section of the bazaar, there were rows of stalls full of the little frivolities that mean so much to most women. Thousands of bright glass bracelets were attractively displayed, sure to catch every woman's eye. Other pieces of costume jewelry and small inexpensive accessories were available so that every shopper could, after her "serious" shopping was over, indulge herself with a little trinket or two.

Much of the time though, we did not need to go to the market for fruit and vegetables because my mother grew them in our large back yard. I remember touring my mother's garden with her. She would be transformed, blooming, and glowing in the presence of her precious plants.

"Shahnaz," she would say, "There is no pleasure in the world like watching my plants grow."

When we built our family house in Shillong Meghalaya (the northeastern part of India, sharing borders with China, Burma, and Bangladesh), I was in charge of the supervision of the construction, as my father was posted in Calcutta at the time. My mother devoted her "green fingers" to nurturing a wonderful garden. When our friends would ask how the house was coming along, she would smile with satisfaction and point to the flourishing garden.

Mama and I spent many happy hours together, reminiscing about Papa's love for growing things. Together with his passion for education, my grandfather found time for astronomy, and the deep and simple pleasures of gardening which my mother appreciated and shared. We would be brought to earth by Babuji calling out, *"Aaray Babee, jara tamatar aur baingun lana bagechay say."*—"Baby (as he called me), bring me some tomatoes and eggplant from the garden." I would go with my mother, or

A Preparation ———————————————— *Baingun Kay Katlay* ————————————
of Semi-Crisp Shallow-Fried Eggplant

1 eggplant (about ¾ pound)	2 teaspoons dried parsley or any dried green herb
3½ tablespoons rice flour	
½ teaspoon turmeric powder	2 tablespoons white sesame seeds
¼ to ½ teaspoon chili powder	8 to 12 tablespoons vegetable oil
1 teaspoon *kashmiri mirch,* a chili, or paprika	

Wash the eggplant, pat dry, and cut into ½-inch slices.

Mix together the rice flour, turmeric powder, chili powder, *kashmiri mirch,* and parsley. Sprinkle the mixture over the surface of a plate. Then lightly coat the eggplant slices on both sides with the mixture and set aside.

Spread the sesame seeds on a board or counter top. Press the eggplant slices firmly into the sesame seeds. If you find the seeds are not sticking to the surface, then lightly score the slices. Press into the sesame seeds again until they stick to the slices.

In a large, heavy skillet, heat 4 tablespoons oil over moderate heat, and fry 5 or 6 eggplant slices, side by side, until the slices become pale brown (about 4 to 6 minutes). Add more oil when needed. Turn over and fry the other side.

Serves 6

Remarks

I usually cook Baingun Kay Katlay *in two skillets simultaneously. Keep the fried slices warm until all the eggplant slices are cooked.*

Serve with a rice pullau *or other rice dish and a meat or fish preparation.*

———

Asho, or Madhu and pick them fresh, along with dainty green coriander (that most delicate of garnishes), or chilies, or fresh dill leaves for flavoring.

Along the hedges, my mother had planted "passion fruit." It had the most beautiful, brilliant purple flowers and grew along with the profuse bamboo plants whose tender shoots are a prized delicacy. Near the edge of the stream that lazily flowed across our garden grew rushes, iris, and arom lilies, stately and white. Scattered near the lawn was a special kind of grass which we called *khatta patta*—sour leaf. This delicious wild plant grows in profusion in the Khasi Hills and Shillong. It has a succulent stem that can be eaten together with its slightly tart leaves. We loved to eat it freshly plucked but also used it to garnish our orange salad and other salads. I have seen *khatta patta* (wood sorrel) growing in many parts of the eastern United States. My children were delighted when I introduced them to it.

Creating Our Own Entertainment

One of the many advantages of growing up in a small relaxed town was that we had the time, and indeed, were forced to create our own interests and diversions.

————————— *Avocado Salaad* ————————— Avocado Salad

½ teaspoon coriander powder

2 medium avocados, chopped

½ cup diced tomatoes

¾ teaspoon ginger powder

1 tablespoon minced spring onions or white onions

⅛ teaspoon chili powder (optional)

½ teaspoon freshly ground black pepper

½ teaspoon lightly crushed garlic cloves

1 tablespoon olive oil or vegetable oil

4 tablespoons lemon juice

1 teaspoon paprika

2 teaspoons minced coriander leaves

1 tablespoon *khatta patta,* wood sorrel leaves

Heat a *tava* or griddle over moderate heat and roast the coriander powder until it turns a light brown (about ½ minute).

In a large bowl, mix together the avocados, tomatoes, ginger powder, spring onions, chili powder (if used), black pepper, garlic cloves, oil, and lemon juice and chill for at least 30 minutes.

Transfer the avocado mixture to a serving bowl, remove the garlic if desired, and garnish with paprika, coriander leaves, and wood sorrel leaves.

Serves 6

Remarks

This is not a "typical" Indian dish, since avocados are not readily available in India. We have merely added an Indian touch to a popular Western salad.

For a change of pace, mash the avocados and this dish becomes a marvelous dip for fresh vegetables.

There was little instant entertainment available. Our home was the regular meeting place for a number of friends. Dorothy, who was a Khadoh, was always full of fun and being a great mimic, kept everyone in splits. She reminded me of my Aunt Appi, who is very talented and bursting with life. Then there was Ansarul, who we had nicknamed Yankee because he always wore blue jeans and liked to eat hamburgers. He had developed a taste for burgers after a visit to Calcutta where he had eaten one at a Western restaurant!

He was a great friend of Asho's and loved to tease her, saying, "Asho, come, I will take you out to the Pinewood Hotel to eat." He knew very well Asho's opinion of Western food. She firmly believed that white people ate nothing but boiled meat, boiled potatoes, and boiled cabbage! It was amusing when the British-trained cook at the same Pinewood Hotel taught Asho how to make soups, a food uncommon in native Indian cuisine. She trusted him because he was a fellow Nepali. Thereafter, she took a great delight in preparing a few favorite soups for us, changing them with her inimitable touch from the bland fare offered at the hotel to something quite special.

Split Pea Soup ——————————— *Daal Ka Soup* ———————————

1¼ cups green split peas	½ cup peas, fresh or frozen
5½ cups water	½ cup cranberries, fresh or frozen (optional)
¾ teaspoon turmeric powder	2 tablespoons *ghee* (see page 40) or butter
1 teaspoon coriander powder	
¼ teaspoon ginger powder	1½ cups minced spring onions (onion greens or white onions may be used)
½ teaspoon garlic powder	
¼ teaspoon chili powder	
1 large tomato, minced	1 teaspoon cumin seeds
12 peppercorns	½ cup sour cream

Wash the split peas thoroughly and soak them overnight in the water.

The next day, place the split peas and soaking water in a 5-quart pot. Add the turmeric powder, coriander powder, ginger powder, garlic powder, chili powder, tomato, and peppercorns. Bring to a boil, then turn heat to low, and simmer, covered, until the peas are tender (about 1½ hours).

Add peas, and cranberries (if used) and simmer 3 minutes. Remove from heat.

In a skillet, heat the ghee, and then fry the onions for 5 minutes over moderately high heat until pale golden in color. Empty the contents of the skillet into the pot and stir.

Wrap the cumin seeds in 2 layers of thick paper towel. Pound a few times with a mallet to coarsely crush. Toss the cumin in a small skillet and fry over moderate heat, while stirring constantly, until lightly roasted (about 30 seconds). Add the cumin to the soup and simmer an additional 2 minutes.

Garnish each serving with a dollop of sour cream.

Serves 6

Remarks

The addition of cranberries gives this dish a zesty taste and a colorful appearance.

_____ *Masur Daal Soup* _____ Whole Lentil
Soup

1½ cups lentils	2 tomatoes, chopped
5 cups water for soaking	3½ tablespoons walnut oil or vegetable oil
6½ cups water	
2 green (or anaheim) chilies	1 onion, cut in half and finely sliced
3 garlic cloves, minced	
1 large onion, minced	2 garlic cloves, chopped
1 large bay leaf	1 teaspoon cumin powder
1 tablespoon coriander powder	2¾ tablespoons lemon juice
1 teaspoon scraped and grated · ginger or ginger powder	1 teaspoon paprika
1 teaspoon turmeric powder	2 tablespoons *ghee* (see page 40) or butter (optional)
¼ teaspoon ground pepper	

Wash the lentils and soak them in 5 cups water for 4 to 8 hours.

When ready to cook, drain lentils and place them in a 5-quart pot with 6½ cups fresh
water. Wash the green chilies under cold running water, remove seeds, quarter each one
lengthwise, and then add to the lentils. Stir in the garlic, onion, bay leaf, coriander
powder, ginger, turmeric powder, and ground pepper. Bring to a boil, reduce heat, and
simmer, covered, over medium low heat 1 hour. Stir occasionally.

To thicken the soup, mash some of the lentils by pressing down 20 times with *ghotni*
or potato masher. Stir in the tomatoes, cover, and let simmer.

Heat the oil in a skillet and brown the sliced onion and chopped garlic, while stirring,
until the onion is reddish brown in color, but not crisp (about 15 to 20 minutes). By now
the lentils should be cooked and tender. Empty the contents of the skillet into the lentils
and stir well.

Heat a griddle and toast the cumin powder for 10 to 15 seconds while stirring.
Remove from heat and stir into the lentils along with the lemon juice and paprika.

Ladle soup into individual bowls, placing a slice of chili in each serving, and garnish
with a teaspoon of *ghee* (if used).

Serves 6

Remarks

This daal *is a great favorite with everyone in the family. The taste improves with storing, and we
often serve leftover lentil soup on the second or third day after it is cooked. It gets thicker and can then also
be served as a lentil. More warm water may be added if a thinner consistency is desired.*

*Soup is not commonly served in India. However, due to contacts with the international community and,
of course, our legacy from the British, many of us have adopted Western soups to suit our tastes.*

Onion Soup ———————————————— *Pyaz Ka Soup* ————————————

2 medium-size potatoes, washed and scraped clean	4 tablespoons melted butter
1 carrot, washed and scraped clean	4 medium onions, sliced into rings
5½ cups water	2 green spring onions, finely minced
12 peppercorns	⅛ to ¼ teaspoon chili powder
1 whole clove	6 slices whole wheat bread (optional)
1 bay leaf	
¼-inch piece of ginger, scraped and cut	2 to 3 tablespoons butter (optional)
1 stalk celery, with leaves, cut in half	¼ pound grated cheddar (or mozzarella) cheese

Place potatoes and carrot in a 5-quart pot. Add water, peppercorns, clove, bay leaf, ginger, and celery. Bring to a boil, then reduce heat, and simmer, covered, 1 hour.

Remove potatoes and mash them thoroughly. Discard other vegetables and spices. Return mashed potatoes to pot.

Heat the melted butter in a skillet and fry the onion rings until they are golden brown (about 15 to 20 minutes). Add them to the pot and simmer, covered, 25 minutes. Then stir in the spring onions and chili powder, and simmer, covered, an additional 5 minutes.

Meanwhile, toast the bread (if used) and then cut into cubes. In a large skillet, melt the 2 to 3 tablespoons butter. Stir in the bread cubes and fry over medium heat until they are golden brown (about 3 to 5 minutes).

To serve, place 4 tablespoons grated cheese in each bowl. Ladle hot soup over cheese and sprinkle with a handful of fried bread cubes.

Serves 6

Remarks

This soup is not "typically" Indian, but has been Indianized to suit our tastes.

You may choose to ladle only the soup into each bowl and serve the cheese and toasted cubes as accompaniments. Desired amounts of cheese and bread may then be added accordingly.

———————————————————————————————

Paras Joshi was a shy Nepali boy who earned the nickname "Tweety" of bird fame! These three were the "regulars." Other friends included Siba Das, a very talented young man who had a flair for the dramatic. He and my mother were the directors of many a drama or play that we staged for a captive audience consisting of M. B., Baba, Asho, Madhu, Babuji, and as many friends as we could find. Mama imbibed this love for drama during her childhood at Abdullah Lodge. Her sister, Khurshid (Appi), is a very well known actress. We had a ready-made entertainment item in the shape of our three tribal friends, Gallant, Sanbah, and Biban, who were members of a local singing group.

They sang songs ranging from typical folk songs to popular Elvis Presley hits of the time. A favorite song was the Khasi Lament, which tells of the heartbreak of a mother deer lamenting the death of her son. The adventurous young buck was curious to find out what life was like in the city. The mother pleaded with him not to leave the jungle. The buck disregarded her pleas and bounded over hill and vale until he reached civilization. He was shot the moment he was seen. The unhappy mother lamented, "Why did you not listen to my warnings? Now I am left all alone in the world and there is no peace or happiness for me." Though the song is tragic, the rhythm is hypnotic and when little Lama, Asho's son, would hear the familiar strains he would come running and clap and sway with the beat, along with the rest of us.

A Flair for Parties

Mama had a flair for throwing successful parties. With Babuji to provide the food and our local band to provide the music, we had the important ingredients already.

My mother always took great pains with aesthetics, the actual presentation of food. She would make sure that there were a number of colorful fruit and vegetable dishes. The table arrangements, in fact the arrangement of the whole room was a major part of her party-planning. She is qualified to teach *ikebana* (Japanese floral arrangement) but has developed her own unique style in floral decoration. It was always a pleasure to enter the dining room when Mama threw a party. The air was fragrant with the combined aromas of Babuji's culinary wizardry and with Mama's precious flowers. When we had a party out-of-doors, we would all pool in to help Mama with her elaborate flower decorations, her seating arrangements on the lower lawn, and with the focal point of many of our parties, the huge pine bonfire in the garden.

Pine trees are everywhere in Shillong. To this day, whenever I see those tall, proud trees anywhere, I feel very much at home. I remember Baba's joy when he was old enough to be allowed to start a fire of his own. We used strips of pine wood saturated with resin to begin the fire. The pine wood lights up like a torch and throws off a wonderful fragrant aroma as well. We carried armloads of dry pine leaves and heaps of pine cones, to build the huge edifice of our bonfire. Most people have wood or coal fires at home that require strenuous beginnings, so the pine torch is a much appreciated friend by the hearth.

The guests at our parties might include the Governor of the State, his wife, and our *chaprasi's* daughter, Kali (named after the goddess, Kali), my constant companion. A *chaprasi* is a clerk, low on the official and social scale. This was part of the charm of Shillong which, of course, we then took for granted. Persons high or low on the social scale could mingle together happily and without embarrassment.

vegetables

Adrak Phulgobi

Gingered Cauliflower

1 large cauliflower (about 2¾ pounds)

2-inch piece of ginger (about 2¾ to 3 tablespoons)

4 to 6 tablespoons mustard oil or vegetable oil

½ to 1 teaspoon turmeric powder

1 small green chili, minced (optional)

2 to 4 small green chilies

1 tablespoon water (optional)

Wash the cauliflower under cold running water. Cut into quarters and trim off only the very tip of the stem. Then cut into 1½-inch pieces, including the stem portion. Leave any tender green leaves to use with the cauliflower.

Scrape the ginger and cut lengthwise. Then cut into very thin slivers, about ¼ to ½ inch in length.

In a *karhai* or wok, heat the oil over moderately high heat. Fry the ginger slivers, turmeric powder, and minced chili (if used) until the ginger is golden brown (about 1 minute).

Immediately add the cauliflower and whole chilies, stir well, cover, and cook over low heat until the cauliflower is tender (about 20 minutes). Stir occasionally during cooking. Sprinkle with water, only if needed.

Serves 6

Babuji Kay Alu Kay Katlay

Babuji's Curried Potato Slices

2 pounds potatoes

3½ tablespoons mustard oil or vegetable oil

1⅓ tablespoons scraped and finely sliced ginger

1⅓ teaspoons cumin seeds

8 *kardi patta*, curry leaves

⅔ teaspoon turmeric powder

¼ to ½ teaspoon chili powder

½ cup warm water

1 to 2 tablespoons chopped coriander leaves

Wash the potatoes and cut into ½-inch slices. Wash the slices and set aside.

In a *karhai* or skillet, heat the oil until it is almost smoking. Reduce heat to moderate and fry the ginger 1 minute. Add the cumin seeds and curry leaves. Fry and stir until the ginger becomes a golden brown. Stir in the turmeric powder and chili powder and fry a few seconds. Add the potatoes and fry 5 minutes while gently stirring.

Pour in the water and when it becomes hot, cover, and cook over moderate heat 30 to 40 minutes. During this time, do not stir. Occasionally lift the *karhai* by the handles and shake gently but thoroughly. Cook until the potatoes are soft but not disintegrated.

Tilt the *karhai* to slide the potatoes into a warm serving dish. Garnish with coriander leaves.

Serves 6

Remarks

Babuji's **Alu Kay Katlay** *were out of this world! He used only potatoes, vegetable oil, a hint of turmeric, and salt. I find I need the help of a few extra spices to achieve good results!*

Alu Chaat

A Tangy Potato Dish

6 medium-size potatoes (about 2 pounds)	¼ teaspoon freshly ground black pepper
3 tablespoons tamarind pulp	1¼ teaspoons cumin powder
1 cup hot water	⅛ to ¼ teaspoon chili powder
1 teaspoon vegetable oil	1 tablespoon lemon juice (optional)
¼ teaspoon *heeng,* asafetida	2 to 3 tablespoons chopped coriander leaves
1¼ teaspoons grated jaggery, or ½ teaspoon honey and 1 teaspoon molasses	6 small green chilies
¼ teaspoon ginger powder	

Boil the potatoes in enough water to cover them.

Soak the tamarind pulp in the hot water while the potatoes are boiling.

Drain the potatoes and cut into ½-inch cubes.

Squeeze the tamarind pulp thoroughly to extract as much juice as possible. Strain and discard the pulp.

In a small skillet, heat the oil and drop in the asafetida. Immediately add the tamarind juice, jaggery, ginger powder, black pepper, cumin powder, and chili powder. Cook over moderate heat about 10 minutes. Lower heat and simmer until the juice thickens (about 10 minutes). You should have 4 to 4½ tablespoons of thickened tamarind juice left after cooking. Remove from heat.

Add the lemon juice to the tamarind juice if a tangy flavor is desired.

In a bowl, combine the potatoes and tamarind sauce and mix thoroughly. Transfer to a serving bowl and garnish with coriander leaves and chilies.

Serves 6

Remarks

This zesty dish is usually served as a teatime snack, but can be presented as a potato salad or a vegetable dish to accompany a meal.

The green chilies can be used in several ways—cut slits down the length of the chilies, deseeding them to remove the "hottest" part; chop a few and sprinkle them over the potatoes; or leave them whole, as we have done.

Alu, Dosay Kay Liyay

Curried Potato with Fresh Coconut, to Accompany Dosa

6 small potatoes	1½ teaspoons husked *urad daal,* a lentil
3 tablespoons grated coconut	3 tablespoons plus 1 teaspoon *chana daal,* a lentil
4 green chilies, chopped	
1 tablespoon scraped and finely chopped ginger	3 *kardi patta,* curry leaves
	pinch of *heeng,* asafetida
1 teaspoon cumin seeds	¾ teaspoon turmeric powder
2 to 4 tablespoons water	¼ to ½ teaspoon chili powder
5½ tablespoons coconut oil or vegetable oil	1 cup chopped onions
1½ teaspoons black mustard seeds	¼ to ½ cup warm water

Boil the potatoes. Drain, dice, and set aside.

Grind the coconut, 2 chilies, ginger, and cumin seeds into a paste. Add a few tablespoons of water as needed.

Heat the oil. Add the mustard seeds and when they sputter, stir in the *urad daal, chana daal,* curry leaves, and asafetida, and fry until the *urad daal* is light brown. Add turmeric powder, chili powder, 2 chilies, and onions. Fry over medium heat until onions are a light golden color. Add the potatoes and coconut paste. Stir well, cover, and simmer 3 minutes. Add ¼ cup warm water, stir well, and simmer 5 to 10 minutes.

Serves 6

Remarks

This savory potato dish is traditionally served with dosas. *A large scoop is placed in the middle of a* dosa, *the* dosa *folded over it, and both served as a stuffed* dosa.

It is also served with Chapatis, *Whole Wheat, Flat Round Bread,* Bhaturas, *Leavened, Deep-Fried Bread, or other* rotis. *See Index for these breads.*

Alu Saag

Curried Potatoes and Spinach, Dry

1½ pounds potatoes	⅛ to ¼ teaspoon chili powder
1½ pounds spinach, fresh or frozen	½ teaspoon turmeric powder
2 tablespoons mustard oil and 5 tablespoons vegetable oil, or 7 tablespoons vegetable oil	1 teaspoon cumin powder
	1 teaspoon *amchoor,* powdered mango (optional)
2 cups finely sliced onion	2 tablespoons water
1 tablespoon scraped and grated ginger	
1 tablespoon minced garlic	

Wash the potatoes well and boil 10 minutes. Drain, allow to cool slightly, and cut into ¾-inch cubes. Wash and finely chop the spinach. If using frozen spinach, allow to defrost.

In a large skillet, heat the mustard oil over moderately high heat and after 1 minute, add 4 tablespoons of the vegetable oil. Fry the potatoes until they become a golden brown. Stir often. Remove the potatoes and strain the oil. Set the potatoes aside.

Return the strained oil to the skillet. Fry the onion over moderate heat until a pale golden brown. Add the remaining 1 tablespoon oil if needed. Stir in the ginger and garlic and fry until the garlic becomes brown as well (about 3 to 4 minutes).

Add the chili powder, turmeric powder, and cumin powder to the pan and fry, while stirring, 2 minutes over moderate heat. Stir in the spinach, cover, and cook over low heat 10 to 15 minutes. Uncover and stir thoroughly to blend the spinach with the spices.

Add the potatoes and powdered mango, stir gently, sprinkle water on top, cover, and simmer until the potatoes are soft when lightly poked with a fork (about 15 minutes). Serve hot.

Serves 6

Remarks

Alu Saag *is very popular throughout north India. This particular recipe is Asho's way of making it—a simple method that always yields good results. Generally, in India, we remove the potato skins, but Asho's method is equally delicious and retains important nutrients.*

Serve with any kind of roti.

Appi Kay Aloo

Appi's Potato Curry with Raw Mangoes

2 pounds potatoes	2 teaspoons *amchoor,* powdered mango
1 unripened mango	1½ to 2 tablespoons lemon juice
5 cups water	2½ teaspoons vegetable oil
2 teaspoons coriander powder	⅛ teaspoon *heeng,* asafetida
1¼ teaspoons turmeric powder	1 teaspoon cumin seeds
¼ teaspoon chili powder	2 or 3 small green chilies, minced (optional)
½ teaspoon cumin powder	

Boil the potatoes until soft. Drain and cool slightly.

Wash the mango. Peel the skin using a small sharp knife. Cut the flesh away from the seed in large chunks. Cut the flesh into slivers 2 inches long and ½ inch wide. Set aside, covered.

With your fingers, break the boiled potatoes into large, uneven pieces into a large saucepan. Add the water, coriander powder, turmeric powder, chili powder, cumin powder, and powdered mango and bring to a boil. Reduce heat to low and simmer, covered, 40 minutes.

Add the mango slivers and lemon juice and continue to simmer another 20 to 25 minutes, covered.

Heat the oil in a small skillet, drop in the asafetida and then the cumin seeds, and fry just 10 to 15 seconds. Add to the cooking potatoes along with the chilies (if used). Simmer, uncovered, another 15 minutes.

Serves 6

Remarks

Serve in small individual katoris *(bowls) to accompany* puris.

This dish without the mango slivers (Appi's own specialty) is most popular in all small hotels and roadside eating places. It is as common to go out for aloo puri *(a fried bread served with curried potatoes) in India as it is to go out for hamburgers in the United States!*

Asparagus Bhaji

Curried Asparagus

1½ pounds tender asparagus

3½ tablespoons vegetable oil

¼ teaspoon fenugreek seeds (optional)

¼ teaspoon cumin seeds

¼ teaspoon fennel seeds

¼ teaspoon black mustard seeds

¼ teaspoon *kelonji,* onion seeds

⅛ teaspoon chili powder

2 tablespoons lemon juice

½ teaspoon paprika

Wash the asparagus. Chop off the woody ends and discard. Divide the asparagus stalks into 3 bundles. Tie each around the middle with string. Stand the bundles upright in a very tall pot with about 1 inch boiling water. Cover securely and steam 5 minutes. Cut asparagus into 1-inch pieces and drain.

Heat the oil in a large, heavy skillet with a tight-fitting lid. Add the fenugreek seeds (if used) and fry over moderate heat until very lightly browned (about 2 minutes). Then stir in the cumin seeds, fennel seeds, mustard seeds, onion seeds, and chili powder. Fry 30 seconds.

Add asparagus pieces and stir 1 minute. Stir in the lemon juice, sprinkle with paprika, and remove from heat.

Serves 6

Remarks

We cut our asparagus into 1-inch pieces because we use our fingers to gather up these tender, bite-size morsels along with our rice or roti. *You may prefer to serve your asparagus in 2- to 3-inch pieces.*

The combination of fenugreek seeds, cumin seeds, fennel seeds, mustard seeds, and onion seeds is what we call panch phuran *(Panch means 5). This spicy mixture creates an exotic and unique flavor which is quite popular in India and is often made in large quantities and stored in airtight containers.*

Serve with Tehri, *Lightly Spiced Rice with Hard-Cooked Eggs (see Index) or another rice dish.* Asparagus Bhaji *also goes well with a Western entree.*

Baingun Bhaja

Savory Shallow-Fried Eggplant Slices

1 medium-size eggplant (about ¾ pound)	½ teaspoon *amchoor,* powdered mango
3 teaspoons turmeric powder	¼ teaspoon ginger powder
¼ to ½ teaspoon chili powder	10 to 15 tablespoons mustard oil or vegetable oil
1 teaspoon *kashmiri mirch,* a chili, or paprika	

Wash the eggplant. Pat dry and cut into ½-inch slices. You will get about 10 to 15 slices in a medium-size eggplant.

Mix together the turmeric powder, chili powder, *kashmiri mirch,* powdered mango, and ginger powder. Sprinkle this mixture over a flat plate.

Coat each eggplant slice on both sides with this mixture by quickly pressing the slice into the mixture and lifting immediately.

Heat 3 tablespoons oil in a large, heavy skillet until it is almost smoking. (I use 2 skillets simultaneously, each with 3 tablespoons of oil.) Then reduce heat to moderate. Place the eggplant slices, side by side, in the skillet and fry over moderately high heat until the eggplant is lightly browned (about 3 to 5 minutes). Lift the skillet off the heat and shake gently once or twice during cooking. Turn over and fry the other side. Add oil as needed, 1 tablespoon at a time.

Serves 6

Remarks

You can serve eggplant slices crisp or quite soft. To make them crisp, fry an extra minute or two, carefully watching to prevent burning.

If you wish, place the slices on a double layer of paper toweling for a few seconds before serving to absorb the excess oil. (We do not.)

Serve with rice and a fish curry. This Bengali dish is traditionally cooked in mustard oil with just turmeric and salt to flavor the eggplant slices.

Baingun Bharta

Eggplant Crush

2 medium-size eggplants (about 2 pounds)	⅓ cup minced spring onions
3 tablespoons mustard oil or vegetable oil	⅓ teaspoon black pepper
½ cup minced onions	1 tablespoon lemon juice
¾ teaspoon turmeric powder	½ teaspoon *garam masalla,* a spice mixture (see page 42)
1½ cups chopped tomatoes	
2 or 3 small green chilies, minced	1 tablespoon chopped coriander leaves

Wash the eggplants and wipe dry. Wrap very securely with aluminum foil and bake 1 hour and 40 minutes at 350°F. Turn the oven off and leave the eggplant inside for 10 to 15 additional minutes.

In a *karhai* or wok, heat the oil until it is almost at the smoking point. Turn the heat to moderately high and fry the onions and turmeric powder 3 to 4 minutes.

Add the tomatoes, green chilies, spring onions, and black pepper and cook until the tomatoes become pulpy (about 5 minutes). Keep the *karhai* on warm.

Peel the eggplant. Reserve the liquid that may collect in the foil. Mash the eggplant and add it to the onions and tomatoes. Cook over low heat 5 minutes. Add lemon juice, *garam masalla,* and coriander leaves. Stir well and simmer 1 to 2 minutes before serving.

Serves 6

Remarks

This typical Punjabi delicacy is loved all over India. In the East, it is served with rice. In northern India, it is generally served with Chapatis, Whole Wheat, Flat Round Bread *(see Index).*

In India we prepare the eggplant by roasting it on a charcoal grill until the skin is burnt on all sides, instead of baking it.

Bhara Kerela

Stuffed Bitter Gourd

6 large or 12 small bitter gourds (about 1 pound)

2 teaspoons turmeric powder

1 tablespoon salt (to be discarded)

6 tablespoons mustard oil or vegetable oil

1¾ cups coarsely grated onions

2 tablespoons coriander powder

3 cups minced tomatoes

1 teaspoon chili powder

1½ teaspoons jaggery or honey

Wash the gourds and pat dry. Make a long slit, lengthwise, in the side of each vegetable. Rub liberally with the turmeric powder, including the inside of the slit, and set aside for 30 minutes. Squeeze out surplus liquid. Rub the gourds with the salt. Rinse thoroughly to wash off the salt and squeeze again to remove all the excess liquid.

Heat 4 tablespoons oil in a skillet and fry the onions until golden brown. Stir frequently. Add the coriander powder, tomatoes, chili powder, and jaggery and continue to fry until the tomatoes are well mashed and oil appears at the sides of the skillet. Remove from heat and allow to cool slightly.

Stuff the mixture into the bitter gourds. Lightly brush a baking sheet with 1 to 2 teaspoons of mustard oil. Arrange the gourds side by side on the baking sheet with the slit side facing upwards. Pour the remaining oil evenly over the top of the gourds. Bake at 350°F until the gourds become golden brown (about 45 minutes).

Serves 6

Remarks

The bitter gourds should be crisp on the outside but soft inside. They are considered a great delicacy, but most people must acquire a taste for them! It will be well worth it; they are delicious!

Rubbing the gourds with salt, then rinsing them, removes the bitterness. It is not possible to use this wonderful vegetable without employing this method.

Babuji was well known for his kerela *preparations. He used different stuffings to create a special dish each time.*

Serve the stuffed kerela *with thin* Chapatis, Whole Wheat, Flat Round Bread *(see Index), kabobs, and lentils.*

Bhara Simla Mirch

Stuffed Green Peppers

1½ pounds potatoes (6 small), diced	2 spring onions, minced
6 small green peppers	1 tablespoon water (optional)
5 tablespoons poppy seed oil or vegetable oil	1½ teaspoons *amchoor,* powdered mango, or 3 tablespoons lemon juice
1 tablespoon coarsely crushed cumin seeds or cumin powder	¼ cup chopped green coriander leaves or a mixture of 2 tablespoons dried parsley flakes and a few sprigs parsley
¼ teaspoon turmeric powder	
1 teaspoon chili powder	

Wash, peel, and boil the potatoes until soft. Drain and coarsely mash.

Wash and dry the peppers. Slice off the tops and reserve. Remove most of the white membrane and seeds. Chop the softer parts of the membrane and set aside with the seeds.

In a large skillet, heat 4 tablespoons of the oil and fry the cumin seeds, turmeric powder, chili powder, and spring onions 1 minute. Add the potatoes and fry 2 to 3 minutes, while stirring. Sprinkle with water, if needed. Add the powdered mango and coriander leaves, remove from heat, and mix well.

Stuff the potatoes into the peppers and replace the tops. Grease a baking dish and lightly brush the remaining oil over the peppers. Bake at 350°F until done (about 40 to 60 minutes).

Serves 6

Remarks

In India, we usually cook the green peppers in a pan with a little oil, on top of the range, sprinkling a little water over them when needed.

This dish goes well with Western meals.

For variety, stuff the peppers with cooked minced meat instead of potatoes.

Bharay Band Gobi Kay Pattay

Stuffed Cabbage Rolls

5 cups water	1 tablespoon minced spring onions
2½ tablespoons white vinegar	1 to 3 teaspoons minced small green chilies
1½ tablespoons honey	½ teaspoon freshly ground black pepper
12 large cabbage leaves or 24 small cabbage leaves	1 teaspoon *garam masalla,* a spice mixture (see page 42)
1¼ cups deseeded and chopped dates	1 tablespoon lemon juice
2½ cups cored and grated tart apples (about 3 or 4 apples)	4 tablespoons butter
¾ cup finely chopped walnuts	

Bring the water to a boil in a 4-quart pot. Mix the vinegar and honey and stir into the pot. When the water is fully boiling, immerse the leaves for 4 minutes. Pour the water out immediately and drain the leaves in a colander while you prepare the filling.

In a bowl, mix and stir thoroughly together the dates, apples, 6 tablespoons of the walnuts, spring onions, green chilies, and black pepper.

Heat a *tava* or griddle and roast the *garam masalla* for 6 to 7 seconds, while stirring. Immediately remove from the heat and place the *garam masalla* in a small bowl. Add the lemon juice and stir.

Trim only the thick, tough end of the center rib of each cabbage leaf. Spread the leaves out on a large flat surface. If smaller leaves are used, overlap two leaves in order to form a larger one.

Dip your fingers into the *garam masalla* mixture and spread it evenly over the surface of the leaves. Spoon about 2 tablespoons of the date mixture into the middle of each leaf. Roll the sides over to form a roll. Tuck the edges of the rolls in to make a neat appearance and to seal the stuffing inside.

Grease a large or 2 medium-size baking dishes and place the rolls side by side in the baking dishes. Dot with 3 tablespoons of the butter. Bake at 350°F until the rolls are lightly browned and have a translucent look (about 15 to 20 minutes).

Meanwhile, fry the remaining walnuts in 1 tablespoon butter. Sprinkle over the rolls during the last minute of cooking.

Serves 6

Remarks

Whenever I serve this dish, it is always greeted with great delight.

The stuffing is not typically Indian. It is a mixture my mother invented one day when we were in a hurry! You'll enjoy making this quick and easy recipe packed with goodies!

Dum Alu

Small Potatoes with Mustard Oil and Spices

1¾ pounds walnut-size potatoes or medium-size potatoes

1 cup mustard oil or 4 tablespoons mustard oil plus enough vegetable oil to equal 1 cup

2 teaspoons coriander seeds

1 teaspoon black cumin seeds or cumin seeds

3 whole cloves

5 peppercorns

seeds of 1 large dark brown cardamom pod

2 tablespoons vegetable oil

¼ to ½ teaspoon chili powder

1 cup water

½ teaspoon *kelonji,* onion seeds

3 tablespoons chopped coriander leaves or 2 tablespoons minced parsley

1 small green chili, minced (optional)

pinch of nutmeg powder

pinch of mace powder

⅛ teaspoon cinnamon powder

Boil potatoes until soft. Drain, cool slightly, and peel. Prick lightly with a fork in several places. If larger potatoes are used, cut them into walnut-size pieces.

Heat the mustard oil in a *karhai* until almost smoking. Add the potatoes and fry until they are golden. Turn occasionally. Remove with a slotted spoon and set aside.

Grind the coriander seeds and cumin seeds and set aside. Then grind the cloves, peppercorns, and cardamom seeds and set aside.

In a large skillet, heat the vegetable oil and fry the freshly ground coriander and cumin seeds along with the chili powder for 30 seconds. Carefully pour in the water and bring to a boil. Cook over moderate heat 2 to 3 minutes, then add the potatoes and cook, covered, over low heat until the potatoes are tender and about ¼ cup water is left.

Stir in the ground cloves, peppercorns, and cardamom seeds, onion seeds, coriander leaves, green chili (if used), nutmeg powder, mace powder, and cinnamon powder. Stir gently and cover tightly.

Heat a *tava* or griddle. Transfer the covered skillet to the *tava.* Keep the *tava* over moderate heat for 20 to 30 minutes before serving, or keep the potatoes tightly covered in a warm oven for 20 to 30 minutes.

Serves 6

Remarks

The last process is known as the "dum" process. The food is kept over low heat to enhance the flavors before serving. Dum Alu is very popular and is made in many different ways. Serve with puris *or another* roti, *or serve as a snack with toothpicks.*

Gajar Bean Bhaji

Lightly Curried Carrots and Beans with Coconut

½	pound carrots (about 3)	¼	teaspoon turmeric powder
½	pound green beans	1	teaspoon minced green chili
2½	tablespoons vegetable oil	1 to 2	tablespoons desiccated coconut
½	teaspoon black or red mustard seeds	2	tablespoons warm water
1	tablespoon chopped peanuts		

Wash the carrots and cut into ¼-inch slices. Cut the larger slices into four pieces and the smaller ones into two pieces.

Wash the beans and trim just the ends. Cut diagonally into ½-inch diamond-shaped pieces.

Heat the oil in a *karhai* or large skillet and fry the mustard seeds. When they begin to sputter, add the peanuts and fry over moderate heat 1 minute.

Add the turmeric powder, chili, and coconut and stir ½ minute. Add the vegetables and fry 3 minutes over moderate heat, while stirring. Stir in warm water, reduce heat to low, and simmer, covered, 14 to 18 minutes. Uncover and cook 1 minute.

Serves 6

Remarks

You will love this simple dish. It is so easy to make and adds a lovely touch of color to the table.

In the south Indian recipe, taught to me by our friend, Jaya Parmasivan, safed urad daal, *a lentil, is used instead of* peanuts.

Haaq

Whole Spinach Greens

1	pound spinach (after trimming)	⅓	teaspoon *heeng,* asafetida
1½	teaspoons crushed fennel seeds	2 or 3	dried red chilies
¾	teaspoon ginger powder	2 or 3	small green chilies
3	tablespoons mustard oil or vegetable oil		

Thoroughly wash the spinach. Trim off only the edges of the stems. Do not chop the leaves. Drain.

On a *tava* or griddle, stir the crushed fennel seeds and ginger powder over moderate heat until the powders become slightly brown (about 2 minutes). Remove from heat and set aside.

In a large skillet, heat the mustard oil to smoking point. Reduce heat to medium. Sprinkle the asafetida on the oil and immediately add the red and green chilies, then the greens. Stir in the fennel seeds and ginger and fry 1 minute. Cover for 3 to 4 minutes, then uncover, and stir until the spinach is ready.

Serves 6

Remarks

It is important not to overcook the spinach since the beauty of this preparation lies in the fresh flavor of the greens seasoned with choice spices.

Haag is the name of a green, leafy vegetable, similar to spinach and is very popular in Kashmir.

Serve with rice and **Kashmiri Kofta,** *Small, Sausagelike Minced Meat Rolls (see Index), or another meat dish.*

Gobi Gajar

Lightly Curried Cauliflower with Carrot Slivers

2 pounds cauliflower (1¾ pounds after trimming)

3 large carrots (about ¾ pound)

5 tablespoons vegetable oil

½ tablespoon cumin seeds

1 teaspoon turmeric powder

¼ to ½ teaspoon chili powder

2 to 3 tablespoons chopped coriander leaves

Cut the cauliflower into 1-inch cubes. Discard the hard part of the stem. Cut the softer part of the stem and any green leaves into ½-inch cubes. Immerse in enough water to completely cover the cauliflower.

Wash the carrots. Cut into 2-inch pieces. Then cut each piece into ¼- to ½-inch slivers. Immerse in enough water to cover.

Heat the oil in a 5-quart pot over moderately high heat. Add the cumin seeds and fry 6 to 7 seconds. Remove the pot from the heat. Scoop half the cauliflower from the water, add to the pot, and return to the heat. Scoop the rest of the cauliflower from the water and add to the pot.

Drain the carrots and add them to the cauliflower along with the turmeric and chili powders.

Stir the vegetables for 1 minute, reduce the heat to low, and simmer, tightly covered, 20 minutes. Stir once. Add the coriander leaves, stir, and continue to simmer, covered, until the vegetables are cooked to desired tenderness.

Serves 6 to 8

Remarks

This delightful Punjabi dish was taught to my mother by Zainab Bi, who cooks for family friends. Zainab Bi has magic in her hands and is such a good teacher that we can duplicate her results very well.

Serve with a rice dish.

Kaila Bhaji

Curried Unripened Banana with Coconut, Dry

6 unripened bananas (each about 6 inches long)

3½ cups cold water

1 cup watercress

1 teaspoon tamari soy sauce

3 small green chilies (2½ to 3½ inches long)

3 tablespoons vegetable oil

6 tablespoons minced onion

1 tablespoon minced garlic

2¼ teaspoons scraped and minced ginger

¼ teaspoon turmeric powder

½ teaspoon freshly ground cumin seeds or cumin powder

¼ teaspoon chili powder

5 tablespoons finely grated coconut

5 tablespoons lemon juice

3 tablespoons warm water

Peel the bananas, cut into 1-inch pieces and marinate, covered, in cold water with the watercress and tamari for 1 hour.

Cut the chilies in half, lengthwise. Remove the seeds (if desired) and wash hands carefully afterwards.

In a large skillet, heat the oil and fry the onion, garlic, and ginger over moderate heat 5 minutes. Add the chilies, turmeric powder, cumin seeds, and chili powder and cook over low heat 6 minutes. Stir occasionally.

Drain the bananas. Discard the water. Reserve 1½ tablespoons watercress leaves. Stir the bananas into the skillet, cover, and simmer until they are soft but not pulpy (about 5 minutes).

Add the coconut, lemon juice, and warm water. Stir very carefully, cover, and simmer over very low heat about 5 minutes. Garnish with the 1½ tablespoons watercress leaves and serve at once.

Serves 6

Remarks

This fragrant and delicate dish is at its best when served immediately after cooking. You may keep it at room temperature and warm it again before serving. However, if refrigerated and then reheated, it loses some of its flavor.

Kanday Chi Pati Chi Bhaji I

Curried Spring Onions and Lentil, Dry

¾ cup yellow and split *moong daal,* a lentil

1½ cups water

¾ pound spring onions (about 3 bundles)

3¾ tablespoons vegetable oil

1 teaspoon black or red mustard seeds

¾ teaspoon cumin seeds

1 cup minced onions

¾ tablespoon scraped and grated ginger

¾ tablespoon minced garlic

2 tablespoons chopped coriander leaves or parsley

⅓ teaspoon turmeric powder

1 or 2 small green chilies, minced

1 small buff or pale green cardamom pod

8 whole cloves

Remove small stones from the *daal.* Wash the *daal* 2 or 3 times and soak in the water for at least 30 minutes.

Wash the spring onions, trim off the roots, and mince both the green and white parts. Drain in a colander.

Heat the oil in a large skillet with a heavy base and a tight-fitting lid. Drop in the mustard seeds and cumin seeds. When the mustard seeds begin to sputter, add the minced onions. Fry the onions, while stirring, until pale brown. Then add the ginger and garlic. Fry 2 minutes, while stirring, over moderately high heat. Stir in the coriander, turmeric powder, and chilies and then add the spring onions. Reduce the heat to moderate and cook, covered, 2 minutes.

Drain the *moong daal* and stir into the pan. Cook, covered, over moderate heat 4 minutes.

Meanwhile, peel the skin from the cardamom pod and wrap the cardamom seeds and cloves in thick paper toweling. Pound until you have a coarse powder. Sprinkle this powder into the pan, stir once, reduce the heat to low, cover tightly, and use the *dum* process of cooking (in its own juices) 20 to 25 minutes. During this time, stir once and quickly replace the lid.

Serves 6

Remarks

A superb Maharastrian cook, Ganga Bai, taught me this delightful dish. It is both delicious and nutritious.

Serve with Khamiri Roti, *Whole Wheat, Leavened, Quick-Baked Bread,* Chapati, *Whole Wheat, Flat Round Bread (see Index), or any other* roti.

Kanday Chi Pati Chi Bhaji II

Curried Spring Onions with Tomatoes

1 pound spring onions (about 4 bundles)

5 tablespoons vegetable oil

1 cup minced onions

1 tablespoon scraped and grated ginger

1 tablespoon minced garlic

2½ cups minced tomatoes

½ teaspoon turmeric powder

1 or 2 small green chilies, chopped

2 teaspoons *garam masalla,* a spice mixture (see page 42)

¼ teaspoon cumin powder

Wash the spring onions, trim off the roots, and mince both the white and green parts. Drain in a colander.

Heat the oil in a large skillet with a heavy base and a tight-fitting lid. Fry the 1 cup minced onions over moderately high heat 3 minutes. Add the ginger and garlic and fry, while stirring, 1 minute. Then add the tomatoes and fry 3 minutes. Stir in the turmeric powder and chilies, then add the spring onions and cook, covered, 1 minute.

Stir in the *garam masalla* and cumin powder, reduce heat to low, and cook, covered, 25 to 30 minutes. Stir twice.

Serves 6

Remarks

This Maharastrian dish is also cooked by the process of "dum." No water is used. The vegetables cook in their own juices over low heat.

Serve with rotis.

Matar Bhaji

Spicy Green Peas

20 ounces green peas (after shelling), fresh or frozen

3½ tablespoons corn oil or vegetable oil

⅛ teaspoon *heeng,* asafetida

½ teaspoon *ajwain,* oregano seeds

½ teaspoon cumin seeds

½ tablespoon scraped and grated ginger

¼ teaspoon turmeric powder

6 dried red chilies

Shell the peas. If frozen peas are used, partially defrost.

In a small skillet, heat the oil. Drop in the asafetida, then the oregano seeds, and then immediately add the cumin seeds. Stir and fry over medium heat 1 minute. Then add the ginger and turmeric powder and fry 1 minute. Add the peas and chilies. Stir for 1 minute, turn heat to low, and cook, covered, 5 to 8 minutes. Uncover and fry 1 to 2 minutes, while stirring.

Serves 6

Remarks

Serve warm with puris *or* Parathas, *Shallow-Fried Bread (see Index), and a meat or lentil dish.*

Khat Mithi Gobi

Sweet and Sour Cabbage with Almonds

1 large cabbage (about 1½ pounds)	½ teaspoon turmeric powder
3 tablespoons vegetable oil	1 tablespoon water
¼ to ½ teaspoon chili powder	2 tablespoons jaggery or 1½ tablespoons honey
2 teaspoons scraped and grated ginger	
pinch of *heeng,* asafetida	2½ tablespoons white vinegar
1 teaspoon coarsely crushed black or red mustard seeds	2 tablespoons unsalted almonds
	¼ teaspoon paprika

Wash and dry the cabbage. Shred finely and set aside, covered.

Heat the oil in a 5-quart pot. Add chili powder, ginger, asafetida, mustard seeds, and turmeric powder and fry 1 minute over moderately high heat, while stirring. Add the shredded cabbage. Reduce heat to moderate. Stir in the water, cover, and cook 10 to 12 minutes. Stir in jaggery and vinegar and cook, uncovered, 10 to 15 minutes. Stir occasionally.

Slice the almonds. Heat a *tava* or griddle. Roast the almonds on the *tava* for about 1½ minutes. Remove from heat and set aside.

To remove any excess liquid in the cabbage, increase heat to moderately high and stir until the liquid evaporates. Reduce heat to moderate, add the almonds and paprika, stir 1 to 2 minutes, and serve.

Serves 6

Remarks

This delicious vegetable can be served with rice or roti. *It is also an ideal dish to serve with a Western meal.*

Khat Mithi Kaddu

Sweet and Sour Pumpkin or Acorn Squash

1 medium-size pumpkin or acorn squash (about 3 pounds)

4 tablespoons mustard oil

1¾ cups minced onions

1½ teaspoons finely minced garlic

1½ teaspoons scraped and minced ginger

½ teaspoon cumin powder

½ teaspoon turmeric powder

2½ cups chopped tomatoes

1 to 3 small green chilies

6 to 8 teaspoons honey

2 tablespoons lemon juice or white vinegar

3 spring onions, minced

½ cup chopped coriander leaves or parsley

1 teaspoon paprika

½ to 1 teaspoon chili powder (optional)

1 teaspoon *garam masalla,* a spice mixture (see page 42)

Cut the pumpkin into 4 or more pieces, then peel. Cut into 1-inch cubes and set aside, covered.

Heat the oil in a *karhai* or wok until it is almost smoking. Reduce heat to moderate and fry the onions until they turn pink (about 5 minutes). Add the garlic and ginger and fry until they become a light brown. Stir in the cumin powder and turmeric powder and fry 1 minute. Add the tomatoes and fry over moderately high heat, while stirring and pressing, until the tomatoes are soft and a paste is formed.

Add the pumpkin and chilies, stir thoroughly, cover, and cook 30 minutes. Stir in the honey and lemon juice, and cook, covered, another 15 minutes. Add the spring onions, coriander leaves, paprika, chili powder (if used), and *garam masalla.* Stir well and cook until the pumpkin is very soft and pulpy.

Serves 6

Remarks

Serve hot with puris. *In eastern India the pumpkin is often served with rice.*

Muli Bhaji

Curried Radishes with Radish Leaves

8	large radishes (about ½ pound)
½	pound radish leaves
¼	pound spinach leaves
3	tablespoons mustard oil
1½	teaspoons scraped and grated ginger

2	teaspoons black or red mustard seeds
1	teaspoon *amchoor*, powdered mango or 1 tablespoon lemon juice
1	teaspoon jaggery or ¾ teaspoon honey
⅛ to ¼	teaspoon chili powder

Wash the radishes thoroughly under cold running water. Cut into ¼-inch pieces. Wash and finely chop the leaves and tender stems. Wash and chop the spinach leaves and stems.

Heat the oil in a large skillet. Stir in the ginger. After 10 seconds, add the radishes, radish leaves, and spinach.

Wrap the mustard seeds in thick paper toweling and pound until they are crushed but not ground. Add them to the skillet along with the powdered mango, jaggery, and chili powder. Stir well and cook, covered, over moderate heat 10 to 18 minutes.

Serves 6

Remarks

This delicately flavored dish can be served with either rice or rotis. *I prefer to serve it with rice.*
The radish leaves and mustard oil give the Muli Bhaji *a unique flavor.*

Muli Ki Phalli Ki Sabzi

Radish Pods with Cumin Seeds

1¼	pounds tender radish pods (about 1½ inches long)
4 to 5	tablespoons mustard oil or vegetable oil
⅛	teaspoon *heeng*, asafetida

1¼ to 1½	tablespoons minced garlic
1½	teaspoons crushed cumin seeds
⅛ to ¼	teaspoon chili powder

Wash the radish pods thoroughly. Cut off the ends that are attached to the stems.

In a large skillet, heat the oil over moderately high heat. Stir in the asafetida, and then immediately add the garlic. Fry 1 minute over moderate heat. Add the cumin seeds, stir, and then add the radish pods and chili powder. Increase the heat to moderately high again and stir 3 to 6 minutes.

Serves 6

Remarks

This fresh, unusual vegetable is always greeted with delight whenever I serve it.

In India, we often allow our radishes to remain unplucked, "go to seed." When small tender pods appear and reach about 1 to 1½ inches in length, we use these pods as a vegetable.

I was delighted when our friends Marilyn and Marvin Williams, both very keen gardeners, rang us up one day to say, "We have uprooted our radishes; do you want the pods?" It was the first time I had been able to get the pods since coming to the States.

Do try and grow a few extra radishes this year so you can enjoy this really wonderful treat!

Khumma/Palak Bhaji

Curried Mushroom/Spinach

1 pound white mushrooms	1 pound spinach
½ cup white vinegar	6 whole cloves
3 to 4 tablespoons honey	¼ to ½ teaspoon chili powder (optional)
1-inch piece ginger root	½ teaspoon garlic powder
3 tablespoons vegetable oil	½ teaspoon paprika

Wash the mushrooms thoroughly. Trim the very tips of the stems, slice each mushroom in half, and place in a bowl.

Mix the vinegar and honey thoroughly, pour over the mushrooms, and marinate for 1 hour. Then drain the mushrooms. Wrap them in 2 layers of paper toweling and squeeze thoroughly to remove as much of the absorbed liquid as possible.

Scrape the ginger and cut into slivers ½-inch long and as thin as possible.

Heat 2 tablespoons oil in a large skillet over moderate heat. Stir in the ginger and fry ½ minute. Add the mushrooms and fry 3 to 5 minutes over moderately high heat, while stirring. Remove from heat and set aside.

Wash, drain, and chop the spinach. Set aside.

Pound the cloves with a mallet, or grind for only a few seconds in a grinder, so that they are crushed but not ground to a powder.

Heat 1 tablespoon oil in another skillet. Add the spinach, cloves, chili powder (if used), and garlic powder and cover. Cook over moderate heat 3 to 4 minutes. Transfer to the mushroom pan. Stir together over moderately high heat ½ minute. Sprinkle with paprika. Serve hot or warm.

Serves 6

Remarks

Serve this tasty dish with either rice or rotis. *I usually serve it with rice.*

Khat Mithi Simla Mirch

Sweet and Sour Green Peppers

6 medium-size green peppers (about 2 pounds)	¼ teaspoon turmeric powder
4½ tablespoons vegetable oil	¼ teaspoon chili powder (optional)
1½ cups minced onions	2 cups chopped tomatoes
1½ tablespoons scraped and minced ginger	1½ tablespoons jaggery or 1 tablespoon honey
1½ tablespoons minced garlic	1 tablespoon plus ¾ teaspoon white vinegar
¾ tablespoon coriander powder	

Wash the peppers and pat dry. Slice into ½-inch rings and then cut each ring into 4 pieces. Discard the white membrane but retain as many seeds as possible.

In a 5-quart pot, heat the oil over moderate heat. Fry the onions 5 to 6 minutes over moderately high heat. Add the ginger and garlic and fry until the mixture is a golden brown.

Stir in the coriander powder, turmeric powder, and chili powder (if used) and fry 1 minute, while stirring. Add the tomatoes and fry until they are well mashed and soft.

Mix together the jaggery and vinegar and stir into the pot. Then add the peppers. Stir thoroughly. Cover and cook over moderate heat 6 to 10 minutes. Uncover and stir 1 minute before serving.

Serves 6 to 8

Remarks

If you like your green peppers crisp, cook them for only 4 to 5 minutes.

I like to include the seeds because they seem to contain the essence of the green pepper flavor! You may remove the seeds if you prefer.

Puri Bean Ki Sabzi

Whole Green Beans, Delicately Flavored

1½ pounds green beans

3½ cups water

pinch of baking soda (optional)

3½ tablespoons mustard oil or vegetable oil

2 or 3 small green chilies, slit into halves lengthwise

⅛ teaspoon *heeng*, asafetida

½-inch piece ginger, grated and finely minced

3 large garlic cloves, minced

1½ tablespoons lemon juice

1 teaspoon paprika

Wash the beans under cold running water. Trim off the stem ends with a small sharp knife. Bring the water to a boil. Drop in baking soda (if used). Then add the beans, stir, and cook for 4 to 5 minutes. Do not overcook. Drain immediately and set aside.

In a large, heavy skillet, heat the oil to almost smoking point. Remove from heat, add chilies, and return to moderate heat. Drop in the asafetida and then immediately add the finely minced ginger and garlic. Fry until a light brown (about 2 to 3 minutes). Stir in the beans and fry 3 to 4 minutes. Stir carefully.

Pour the lemon juice over the beans, stir, and turn off heat. Sprinkle with paprika and serve hot on a large flat serving dish.

Serves 6

Remarks

This dish is a good accompaniment to various Western meals. My friend, Joan, likes to serve Puri Bean Ki Sabzi *with her favorite meat loaf.*

Tok

Sweet and Sour Tomatoes

4 large tomatoes (5½ cups when chopped)

2 tablespoons mustard oil

¾ teaspoon scraped and grated ginger

1 teaspoon minced garlic

pinch of chili powder

½ teaspoon turmeric powder

4 teaspoons jaggery

1 tablespoon black currants or raisins

¼ teaspoon fenugreek seeds

¼ teaspoon mustard seeds

¼ teaspoon anise seeds

¼ teaspoon *kelonji*, onion seeds

1 to 3 red chilies

Dice tomatoes and set aside.

In a large, heavy skillet, heat 1 tablespoon oil and fry ginger and garlic until they turn light brown (about 2 minutes). Add the tomatoes, chili powder, turmeric powder, jaggery, and currants. Cook, uncovered, over moderate heat 20 minutes.

In another skillet, heat 1 tablespoon oil and fry fenugreek seeds about 1½ minutes. Add the mustard seeds, anise seeds, onion seeds, and chilies and fry another minute. Then add these spices to the tomato mixture and cook another 10 to 15 minutes.

Serves 6

Puri Phulgobi

Whole Cauliflower with Carrots and Potatoes

1 large cauliflower, whole	4 tomatoes, diced
2 whole cloves	2 to 3 potatoes, peeled and cut into 2½ × 1-inch wedges
½ to 1 teaspoon chili powder	
5 tablespoons vegetable oil	3 carrots, cut into 2 × ½-inch wedges
1 cup minced onions	
2 teaspoons crushed garlic	1 teaspoon paprika
1½ tablespoons scraped and crushed ginger or 2 teaspoons ginger powder	¼ teaspoon cumin powder
	¼ teaspoon powdered cloves
2 tablespoons freshly ground coriander seeds	¼ teaspoon cinnamon powder
	¼ teaspoon cardamom powder
1 teaspoon crushed cumin seeds	3 tablespoons chopped coriander leaves or watercress
¼ teaspoon turmeric powder	

Parboil the cauliflower with the whole cloves and chili powder. Drain.

In a *karhai* or deep pan, heat 3 tablespoons oil and fry the onions until brown. Stir in the garlic and ginger and fry 3 to 5 minutes. Add the ground coriander seeds, cumin seeds, and turmeric powder and fry 1 minute. Then add the tomatoes and fry, while stirring, until mashed. Place cauliflower gently in pan and spoon the cooked spices over it. Sprinkle a few teaspoons of warm water on top, cover, and cook over medium heat for 10 minutes.

Meanwhile, parboil potato and carrot wedges. Drain. In another pan, heat the remaining oil and fry the potatoes and carrots until crisp and brown. Remove any surplus oil and keep warm.

Add the paprika, cumin powder, powdered cloves, cinnamon powder, and cardamom powder to the cauliflower. Stir gently. Turn the cauliflower over and fry, uncovered, over moderate heat until cauliflower is light brown.

Place cauliflower in the center of a large flat dish and arrange the carrot and potato wedges around it. Garnish with coriander leaves.

Serves 6 to 9

Remarks

A number of my Indian friends have mentioned to me that they like to serve Puri Phulgobi *for a party because it looks so festive.*

Sabzi Ki Tikki

Spicy Mixed Vegetable Cutlets

1¼ pounds potatoes	⅛ teaspoon chili powder
3 cups water	1¼ teaspoons crushed mustard seeds
1 onion, coarsely chopped	½ to ¾ teaspoon ginger powder
3 large garlic cloves	½ teaspoon black pepper
1-inch piece ginger	1 to 2 small green chilies, chopped
¼ pound carrots (2 medium-size carrots)	¼ to ½ teaspoon garlic powder
¼ pound green beans	1½ tablespoons lemon juice
¼ pound cauliflower florets	2 eggs, beaten
5 to 6 tablespoons vegetable oil	½ to ¾ cup whole grain bread crumbs

Boil the potatoes in enough water to cover. Peel, mash coarsely, and set aside.

Boil 3 cups water with the onion and garlic. Scrape the ginger lightly, pound once with a mallet, and drop it into the pot.

Scrub the carrots and cut each in half. Cut each half into 4 to 8 slivers. Place the slivers in the boiling water. Trim the stem end of the beans. Drop the beans and the cauliflower into the pot after the carrots have been in the boiling water for 3 minutes. Continue boiling all the vegetables for 5 to 6 minutes. Drain.

Discard the onion, garlic, and ginger. Mash the carrots. Cut the beans and cauliflower finely.

In a large, heavy skillet, heat 1½ tablespoons oil. Stir in the mashed potatoes, carrots, chopped beans, cauliflower, chili powder, mustard seeds, ginger powder, black pepper, chilies, and garlic powder. Fry over moderately high heat 1 to 2 minutes while stirring. Add lemon juice and remove from heat. Cool slightly and place in a large bowl.

Add the eggs to the mixed vegetables in the bowl. Divide into 24 portions and shape each portion into a round patty about 2 to 2½ inches in diameter.

Heat 3 tablespoons oil in a large, clean skillet. Coat each cutlet lightly with bread crumbs and fry, side by side, over moderate heat about 6 to 7 minutes. Turn over and fry until brown (about 5 minutes). Add 1 to 2 teaspoons oil around the edges of the skillet and between the cutlets as needed.

Yields: 24 cutlets

Remarks

These cutlets have a lovely gingery flavor. They are absolutely delicious served with a dab of butter. Serve with Pudina Chutney, *Mint Chutney, or* Dhania Chutney, *Fresh Coriander Chutney (see Index).*

Same Bhaji I

Fava or Green Beans with Coconut, Peanuts, and Mustard Seeds

1½ pounds fava or green beans (5½ cups when cut)

3 tablespoons raw whole unsalted peanuts with skins

6 tablespoons *ghee* (see page 40) or vegetable oil

1½ teaspoons black mustard seeds

1½ teaspoons scraped and finely cut ginger

¾ cup finely chopped onions

⅛ teaspoon freshly ground black pepper

¼ to ½ teaspoon chili powder

½ cup finely grated coconut

8 tablespoons well-mixed Homemade Yogurt (see page 41)

2 tablespoons chopped green coriander leaves or parsley

Remove the string from the beans and slice into ¼-inch pieces.

Heat a *tava* or griddle and roast the peanuts, while stirring, for 35–45 seconds. Cool, remove the skins, coarsely chop, and set aside.

In a *karhai* or large, heavy skillet, heat the *ghee*. Drop in the mustard seeds and when they sputter, add the peanuts and stir 1 minute. Stir in the ginger, onions, pepper, and chili powder. Then add the beans and cook 5 minutes over medium heat. Stir frequently.

Add the coconut and yogurt, stir thoroughly, reduce heat to low, cover, and cook 15 minutes. Stir once.

Stir in the coriander leaves, cover, and cook another 5 to 10 minutes. Serve immediately or at room temperature.

Serves 6

Remarks

This dish keeps well. It can be refrigerated for 3 to 4 days, reheated, and served.

Same Bhaji II

Diamond-Cut Fava or Green Beans with Mustard Seeds

1½ pounds fava or green beans	¾ teaspoon turmeric powder
3 teaspoons black or red mustard seeds	½ to 1 teaspoon *kashmiri mirch,* a chili
5½ tablespoons mustard oil	½ to 1 tablespoon lemon juice (optional)
⅜ teaspoon *heeng,* asafetida	

Wash the beans and cut them into long thin, diamond-shaped pieces and set aside.

Wrap the mustard seeds in two layers of thick paper toweling and pound with a small mallet until the seeds are split and crushed but not ground.

In a large skillet, heat the mustard oil. Sprinkle the asafetida into the oil and immediately add the beans. Stir quickly and add the crushed mustard seeds, turmeric powder, and *kashmiri mirch.* Cook over moderate heat about 5 minutes. Stir occasionally.

Reduce heat to low, cover, and cook another 5 minutes. Uncover, and cook until the liquid evaporates and the beans are tender. Stir occasionally.

Stir in the lemon juice (if used) and serve.

Serves 6

Remarks

Same Bhaji *goes well with many dishes. It can be served with rice and a meat, fish, or chicken preparation.*

Saral Bean Bhaji

Quick and Easy Lightly Curried Beans

1½ pounds green beans	1 tablespoon plus ¾ teaspoon finely minced garlic
8 to 10 cups water	1 tablespoon plus ¾ teaspoon cumin seeds
3½ tablespoons vegetable oil	
⅛ teaspoon *heeng,* asafetida	1 to 1½ teaspoons *kashmiri mirch,* a chili
¾ teaspoon turmeric powder	

Wash the beans and trim the stem ends.

Bring the water to a boil. Add the beans and boil for 4 minutes. Immediately drain and cool the beans slightly. Cut into 1-inch pieces.

In a large skillet, heat the oil. Drop in the asafetida and then immediately add the turmeric powder and garlic. Fry until the garlic becomes a light brown (about 2 to 3 minutes). Add the cumin seeds, stir, then add the beans and *kashmiri mirch.* Stir for 2 to 3 minutes over moderately high heat. Serve hot.

Serves 6

Remarks

I like to serve this vegetable with rice and a lentil or a meat dish with lots of gravy. It takes only about 15 minutes to prepare, and I often make it just before guests are due to arrive.

—————————————————————— *Soya Alu* ——————————————————————

Curried Potatoes with Fresh Dill Leaves

1½ pounds potatoes, scrubbed	1 teaspoon lemon juice
3 tablespoons mustard oil or vegetable oil	2 tablespoons water
1 teaspoon scraped and finely chopped ginger	1 teaspoon freshly ground black pepper
¾ teaspoon ground fennel seeds	½ to ¾ cup chopped dill leaves
1 to 3 small green chillies, chopped	

Boil the potatoes. Cool slightly and cut into ½-inch cubes.

In a large skillet, heat the oil until it is almost smoking. Reduce heat to moderate. Drop in the ginger and after a minute add the potatoes, fennel seeds, and chilies. Stir 1 minute, sprinkle with lemon and water, reduce heat to low, and cook, covered, for about 5 minutes. Sprinkle with pepper and dill leaves, simmer 3 to 4 minutes, and serve.

Serves 6

Remarks

Serve with **Chapati**, *Whole Wheat, Flat Round Bread*, or *Paratha*, Shallow-Fried Bread (see Index).
In India we peel the potatoes after boiling, but I like to use this nutritional part of the potato in as many recipes as possible.

—————————————————————— *Turai Bhaji* ——————————————————————

Curried Zucchini

3 zucchini, 7 to 8 inches long (1 pound, 10 ounces)	1½ teaspoons coriander powder
4 tablespoons vegetable oil	½ teaspoon turmeric powder
pinch of *heeng,* asafetida	¼ teaspoon chili powder (optional)
½ tablespoon cumin seeds	½ cup water
1¼ cup minced tomatoes	¼ teaspoon *garam masalla,* a spice mixture (see page 42)

Wash the zucchini, pat dry, and cut into ¼-inch slices.

In a *karhai* or wok, heat the oil over moderately high heat. Drop in the asafetida, then the cumin seeds, and quickly stir in the tomatoes. Add the coriander powder, turmeric powder, and chili powder (if used) and cook 2 to 3 minutes over moderately high heat. Add the zucchini and water and cook, covered, for 15 minutes over moderate heat. Stir once during this time. Uncover and sprinkle with the *garam masalla.* Stir gently and cook another few minutes, uncovered.

Serves 6

Remarks

You may serve the zucchini after five minutes of cooking it uncovered, or after 20 minutes, depending on the degree of tenderness you prefer.

Serve hot with rice or roti. *We prefer to serve this typical dish from Ulter Pradesh in north India with rice because the "gravy" is very thin.*

Tandoori Sabzi

Mixed Baked Vegetables

½ pound eggplant	1¾ cups milk
2 teaspoons turmeric powder	5 tablespoons minced spring onions
2 teaspoons paprika	2 tablespoons chopped green coriander leaves or parsley
8 to 10 tablespoons vegetable oil	
2½ cups green beans (about ½ pound)	2½ to 3 cups grated cheese
3 cups water	2 teaspoons cumin powder
3 cups cauliflower florets (about ½ pound)	1 teaspoon black pepper
3½ tablespoons *ghee* (see page 40) or butter	25 to 30 whole cashew nuts, roasted
1 tablespoon arrowroot	1 to 3 small green chilies, minced (optional)

Wash the eggplant and pat dry. Cut into ½-inch slices. Mix the turmeric powder and paprika together on a flat platter. Coat the eggplant slices lightly with the mixture.

Heat 3 tablespoons oil in a large, heavy skillet. Fry the eggplant slices until light brown (about 4 to 5 minutes). Add oil as needed. Turn over and fry the other side until light brown. Set aside.

Trim the stem ends of the green beans. Bring the water to a boil. Add the beans and cook for 3 minutes. Drain and chop into ½-inch pieces. Set aside.

Cut the cauliflower into ½-inch cubes.

In a large skillet, melt the *ghee*. Stir in the arrowroot and cook over moderate heat about 1 minute. Stir continuously. Add ¾ cup milk and stir well. Stir in 3 tablespoons minced spring onions, coriander leaves, 1 cup grated cheese, cumin powder, and black pepper. Add the cauliflower and the rest of the milk and cook over moderate heat until the sauce thickens (about 5 minutes).

Cut the eggplant into small pieces and place in a large bowl. Add the beans, sauce, and remaining spring onions.

Pour the vegetables with sauce into one large or 2 small casseroles. Decorate with cashew nuts by placing each nut partially into the vegetables so that more than half of each nut is visible on top. Sprinkle with the remaining cheese and green chilies (if used). Bake at 400°F for 10 minutes. Reduce oven temperature to 250°F and bake another 10 to 15 minutes.

Serves 6 to 8

Remarks

Serve hot with a meat or fish dish and rotis.

lentíls

Arhar Daal Aur Lauki

Lentil with Garden Marrow

4½ cups *arhar daal,* a lentil

4 cups water

3 cups coarsely chopped garden marrow or zucchini squash

⅛ teaspoon *heeng,* asafetida

1 teaspoon minced garlic

¼ teaspoon chili powder

½ teaspoon *amchoor,* powdered mango

1 teaspoon coriander powder

¾ teaspoon turmeric powder

¼ teaspoon *garam masalla,* a spice mixture (see page 42)

4 tablespoons vegetable oil

1 tablespoon plus ¾ teaspoon slivered garlic

4 dried red chilies

Remove stones and discolored lentils from the *daal.* Wash the *daal* thoroughly and soak in water while preparing other ingredients.

Transfer *daal* and soaking water to a heavy-bottomed 4-quart pot. Add the marrow, asafetida, minced garlic, chili powder, powdered mango, coriander powder, and turmeric powder. Stir well and bring to a boil. Reduce heat to moderate, partially cover, and cook 30 minutes.

Add *garam masalla,* stir well, reduce heat to low, and simmer, tightly covered, another 30 minutes.

In a skillet, heat the oil and fry the slivered garlic until lightly browned. Add the chilies and fry until the chilies become very dark and the garlic becomes a dark brown (about 1 minute).

Transfer the contents of the skillet to the pot, stir once, and simmer, uncovered, 4 to 5 minutes before serving, topped with a dab of *ghee* and paired with rice or rotis.

Serves 6

Kali Daal Chilkay Vali

A Lentil Dish of Small Split Black Beans

1⅓ cups *kali chilkay ki daal,* a lentil

4 to 5 cups water

½ teaspoon turmeric powder

1 tablespoon minced garlic

1 tablespoon scraped and grated ginger

1 to 3 small green chilies

pinch of *heeng,* asafetida

½ teaspoon cumin powder

2 tablespoons *ghee* (see page 40) or vegetable oil

1½ teaspoons chopped garlic

6 dried red chilies

Remove stones from the *daal.* Wash *daal* thoroughly several times.

Place the *daal* in a heavy 4-quart pot with 4 cups water, turmeric powder, minced garlic, ginger, green chilies, asafetida, and cumin powder and bring to a boil. Stir well, reduce heat to low, and simmer, covered, until the lentil is soft (about 1 hour). Add ½ to 1 cup boiling water if the liquid in the pot has been absorbed.

In a skillet, heat the *ghee* and fry the chopped garlic until it becomes a golden brown. Add the red chilies and fry about 1 minute. Pour the *ghee,* garlic, and chilies into the pot with the *daal.* Stir well, simmer 1 minute, and serve hot or warm. Top each serving with a dab of *ghee.* Serve with rice or roti.

Serves 6 to 8

Arhar Daal Aur Saag

Lentil with Spinach

1 cup *arhar daal,* a lentil

½ teaspoon turmeric powder

½ teaspoon chopped garlic

⅛ teaspoon *heeng,* asafetida

4 cups cold water

   tamarind pulp, the size of a walnut

½ cup hot water

½ pound spinach

½ to 1 teaspoon *garam masalla,* a spice mixture (see page 42)

½ tablespoon lemon juice

2 tablespoons *ghee* (see page 40) or vegetable oil

2 teaspoons minced garlic

1 to 3 green chilies, halved

1 teaspoon cumin seeds

Remove stones from the *daal.* Wash *arhar daal* thoroughly and place in a 2-quart pot with turmeric powder, chopped garlic, asafetida, and cold water. Bring to a boil, lower heat to moderate, and cook, covered, 30 to 40 minutes.

Meanwhile, soak the tamarind in hot water for 15 to 20 minutes.

Chop the spinach leaves and stems and add them to the lentils.

Squeeze the tamarind pulp to extract as much juice as possible. Strain through a sieve, then through a thin muslin cloth. Add the tamarind juice to the lentils.

Stir in the *garam masalla* and lemon juice and cook, partially covered, for 10 to 15 minutes. If necessary, add ¼ to ½ cup boiling water.

Heat the *ghee* in a large skillet and brown the minced garlic for 2 minutes. Add chilies and fry another 1 to 2 minutes. Stir in the cumin seeds and after ½ minute pour the contents of the skillet into the lentil pot. Stir and simmer 1 minute, then serve.

Serves 6

Remarks

The process of frying certain spices in oil and then adding them to the lentils is called tarka *or* baghar.
Serve the daal *with rice.*

Daal Aur Soya Saag

Lentil with Fresh Dill Leaves

½ cup *sabut moong daal,* a lentil

5¾ cups water

1½ cups *arhar (tuar) daal,* a lentil

2 medium-size tomatoes

3 cups boiling water

1 tablespoon coriander powder

½ teaspoon turmeric powder

1 tablespoon plus 1 teaspoon minced garlic

pinch of *heeng,* asafetida

½ teaspoon *garam masalla,* a spice mixture (see page 42)

2 tablespoons *ghee* (see page 40) or butter

1 teaspoon black or red mustard seeds

3 or 4 dried red chilies

½ to ¾ cup minced dill leaves

Remove stones from *moong daal.* Wash the *daal* thoroughly and soak overnight in 2 cups water.

Remove stones, sticks, and discolored lentils from the *arhar daal.* Wash lentils thoroughly and place in a 3-quart pot with 3¾ cups water.

Drain the *moong daal* and add to the pot with the *arhar daal.*

Immerse the tomatoes in the boiling water for ½ minute. Drain and peel. Chop the tomatoes and add to the pot. Stir in the coriander powder, turmeric powder, 1 teaspoon garlic, asafetida, and *garam masalla.*

Bring the *daal* to a boil and remove the scum. Stir well, reduce heat to moderate, and cook, partially covered, for 15 minutes. Stir again, reduce heat to low, and simmer, tightly covered, until the *daal* is very soft and cooked (about 20 to 30 minutes). With a *ghotni* or potato masher, or just the back of a large spoon, mash some of the *daal* to thicken the liquid. Keep *daal* warm.

In a skillet, heat the *ghee* and fry the mustard seeds until they begin to sputter. Add the 1 tablespoon garlic and the chilies and fry until the garlic is browned. Pour the contents of the skillet and the dill leaves into the *daal,* stir well, and simmer a few minutes before serving.

Serves 6

Remarks

If you prefer your daal *with more liquid, add ½ cup boiling water when you add the dill leaves.*

I usually make this nutritious daal *when my family is in a vegetarian mood! We have rice,* daal, *a vegetable or two, and a* chutney. *The* daal *is spooned over a heap of rice on individual* thalis *or plates.*

Dhansak

Richly Pureed Lentils and Vegetables with Chicken

3½ pounds chicken pieces

1 tablespoon plus ¾ teaspoon scraped and grated ginger

1 tablespoon grated garlic

½ cup *chilka masur daal,* a lentil

¼ cup *(pili) moong daal,* a lentil

¾ cup *arhar (tuar) daal,* a lentil

¼ cup *chana daal,* a lentil

7 cups water

7 tablespoons *ghee* (see page 40)

2 tablespoons coriander seeds

1 tablespoon cumin seeds

2 dried red chilies

10 peppercorns

5 whole cloves

½-inch cinnamon stick

1 teaspoon minced garlic

1 teaspoon minced ginger

5 tablespoons water

1¾ teaspoons turmeric powder

2 cups chopped pumpkin or acorn squash

2 cups chopped eggplant

1 cup tightly packed chopped spinach

1 cup minced tomato

¾ cup minced onions

1⅓ cup finely sliced onions

2 or 3 small green chilies, minced

2 tablespoons chopped mint

4 tablespoons chopped coriander leaves

Remove the skin and fat from the chicken pieces. Wash and drain in a colander. Then rub the grated ginger and garlic into the chicken pieces and set aside.

Remove stones from the lentils. Wash all the *daals* thoroughly and soak them in enough water to cover for 15 minutes.

Drain the *daals* and bring them to a boil with the 7 cups of water in a 5 to 6-quart heavy-based pot. Remove the scum, reduce heat to low, and simmer, covered, 30 minutes.

Meanwhile, heat 4 tablespoons *ghee* in a pan and fry the chicken pieces until browned.

While the *daals* and chicken are cooking, grind the coriander seeds, cumin seeds, red chilies, peppercorns, cloves, and cinnamon to a powder. Add the minced garlic and ginger, the 5 tablespoons of water, and grind until you have a fine paste. Mix the turmeric powder into the paste.

Add the pumpkin, eggplant, spinach, tomato, and minced onions to the *daal* and bring to a boil while stirring. Reduce heat to low again and simmer, covered, until the vegetables are very tender (about 40 minutes).

Meanwhile, heat 3 tablespoons *ghee* in a large skillet and fry the sliced onions until brown. Stir occasionally. Add the ground paste and fry. Stir frequently. Add 1 to 2 tablespoons water as the paste dries. Repeat this process until the paste is well fried (about 10 minutes).

When the vegetables are tender, place 1 cup of the *daal* and vegetables in a blender and blend to a puree. Repeat this process until all the *daal* is pureed. Return this thick puree to the pot and add the fried paste, green chilies, mint, and 1 tablespoon coriander leaves. Bring the *daal* to a boil again, while stirring, and simmer, covered, 5 minutes.

Add the chicken and continue to simmer, covered, 20 to 25 minutes.

Stir in the rest of the coriander and simmer 10 minutes. Serve hot, with rice.

Serves 8 to 12

Kali Sabut Urad Daal

Small Whole Black Lentils

1½ cups *urad daal,* a lentil

6 cups water

¾ tablespoon minced garlic

1 teaspoon minced ginger

¾ teaspoon turmeric powder

2 or 3 small green chilies

2¾ tablespoons vegetable oil

¾ cup minced onions

½ teaspoon grated garlic

¼ teaspoon scraped and grated ginger

2 teaspoons water

½ teaspoon cumin powder

1 teaspoon coriander powder

1 cup chopped tomatoes

3 tablespoons well-mixed Homemade Yogurt (see page 41)

Remove stones from the *daal.* Wash the *urad daal* thoroughly, then soak in the water for 8 hours.

Transfer the lentils and soaking water to a heavy-bottomed 5-quart pot. Add the minced garlic, ginger, turmeric powder, and chilies and bring to a boil. Reduce heat to low, partially cover, and simmer 15 minutes. Cover and continue to simmer until the lentils are soft and can be easily mashed (about 1½ hours).

In a large skillet, heat the oil and fry the onions over moderately high heat until golden brown (about 5 minutes). Stir occasionally. Add the grated garlic and ginger and fry 1 minute. Add 1 teaspoon water and fry 1 minute, then add another teaspoon of water and fry another minute. Stir in the cumin powder and coriander powder and fry 2 to 3 minutes.

Add the tomatoes and fry until they are well mashed (about 3 minutes). Reduce heat to low, add yogurt, and stir constantly 1 minute. Pour the contents of the skillet into the lentil pot, stir well, and simmer for 5 minutes.

Serves 6 to 8

Remarks

This highly nutritious lentil dish is a favorite in most Punjabi households. Generally, it is served with roti.

Khatta Chana (Cholay)

Curried Dark Chick-Peas with a Sour Tang

2 cups *kala chana,* small, dark chick-peas

6 cups cold water

6 or 7 small green chilies

1 tablespoon minced garlic

1 tablespoon scraped and minced ginger

1 cup finely chopped onions

½ teaspoon turmeric powder

1¼-inch cinnamon stick

4 whole cloves

2 large dark brown cardamom pods

1 teaspoon black pepper

1 teaspoon cumin powder

1 tablespoon freshly ground coriander powder

1 cup finely chopped tomatoes

tamarind pulp, the size of a medium-size egg

⅓ cup boiling water

2 teaspoons *anar dana,* pomegranate seeds

4 to 5 tablespoons *ghee* (see page 40) or vegetable oil

¼ teaspoon *heeng,* asafetida

4 to 6 dried red chilies

3 tablespoons green coriander leaves or any green herb

Wash the *chana* several times and then soak in cold water for 24 hours.

Place the *chana* and its soaking water in a 4-quart pot. Add 2 green chilies, garlic, ginger, onions, turmeric powder, cinnamon, cloves, cardamom pods, black pepper, cumin powder, coriander powder, and tomatoes. Bring to a boil, reduce heat to low, and simmer, covered, 2 hours.

Soak the tamarind pulp in the boiling water for at least 15 minutes. Then squeeze the pulp to extract all the juices. Strain the tamarind juice and discard the pulp. You will have about 2 tablespoons of thick tamarind juice.

Wrap the pomegranate seeds in kitchen cloth and pound a few times with a mallet to lightly crush the seeds.

Add the tamarind juice and crushed pomegranate seeds to the pot, stir well, and continue to cook until the *chana* is very tender. If necessary, add up to 1½ cups boiling water and continue to simmer. I like to cook my *chana* for about 3 to 4 hours, until it is very tender and there is about 1 cup of liquid in the pot.

Heat the *ghee* in a small skillet and fry the asafetida for 2 seconds. Add the red chilies and fry for about 2 minutes over moderate heat. Pour *ghee* and chilies into the *chana* and stir. Sprinkle coriander leaves on top and simmer, uncovered, 1 to 2 minutes before serving.

Garnish with the remaining green chilies, whole or slit in halves.

Serves 6

Remarks

This popular north Indian dish may be served with puris *or* Bhatura, *A Leavened, Deep-Fried Bread (see Index), as we often do, or with rice.*

Rajma

Red Kidney Beans Cooked as a Lentil

1¾ cups red kidney beans

1 to 3 small green chilies

1 tablespoon scraped and minced ginger

½ tablespoon minced garlic

¾ teaspoon tumeric powder

4½ tablespoons ground nut oil or vegetable oil

2 cups finely sliced onions

1 teaspoon grated garlic

¾ teaspoon scraped and grated ginger

1 tablespoon coriander powder

1 teaspoon cumin powder

1½ cups chopped tomatoes

¾ teaspoon *garam masalla,* a spice mixture (see page 42)

2 tablespoons chopped coriander leaves or parsley

Wash the kidney beans thoroughly. Soak them overnight (the water level should be about 2 inches above the beans). Drain the beans and reserve the soaking water. Transfer beans and 4½ cups of water including soaking water to a 5-quart heavy-based pot. Add chilies, the minced ginger and garlic, and tumeric powder. Bring to a boil, reduce heat to low, and simmer until the beans are very tender (about 2 to 3 hours). Mash some of the beans to thicken the liquid.

In a large skillet, heat the oil and fry the onions until they are browned (about 10 to 12 minutes). Stir occasionally. Add the grated garlic and ginger and fry over moderate heat until the garlic is lightly browned. Stir in the coriander powder and cumin powder and fry another 2 minutes. Add the tomatoes and cook until the tomatoes are well mashed and pulpy and oil appears at the sides of the pan (about 4 to 5 minutes). Transfer the tomato mixture to the bean pot and add the *garam masalla.* Simmer 5 to 10 minutes, sprinkle with coriander leaves, and serve.

Serves 6 to 8

Remarks

Rajma *is a great favorite with Punjabis. It is generally served with a* roti, *yet it is also nice as an accompaniment to rice.*

In hot weather, a white foam may collect on top of the water when the beans are soaked. If this happens, drain the beans, discard the water, and add 4½ cups of fresh water.

Sabut Masur Aur Tamatar

A Spiced Lentil Dish with Tomatoes

1¼ cups *sabut masur daal,* a lentil

3 tomatoes

4½ cups water

¾ teaspoon tumeric powder

1 tablespoon ground coriander

1 or 2 green chilies or ¼ to ½ teaspoon chili powder

2 teaspoons minced garlic

1½ teaspoons scraped and chopped ginger

½ cup finely chopped onions

6 *kardi patta,* curry leaves

2 tablespoons *ghee* (see page 40) or vegetable oil

¼ teaspoon *heeng,* asafetida

¾ teaspoon cumin seeds

½ teaspoon *garam masalla,* a spice mixture (see page 42)

2 tablespoons chopped coriander leaves or parsley

Remove stones from the *daal.* Wash the *daal* under cold running water and set aside.

Boil some water, and drop the tomatoes in for about 1 minute. Drain, peel, and chop.

Put the daal in a heavy 4-quart pot with the chopped tomatoes, 4 cups water, tumeric powder, coriander powder, chilies, garlic, ginger, onions, and curry leaves. Bring to a boil, reduce heat to low, cover partially, and simmer about 1 hour. Add ¼ to ½ cup boiling water if the liquid is absorbed.

Heat the *ghee* in a skillet over moderately high heat. Drop in the asafetida and then immediately add the cumin seeds. Fry a few seconds and then carefully transfer the contents of the skillet to the *daal.* Stir in *garam masalla* and simmer, uncovered, a few minutes.

Pour into a warmed serving bowl and garnish with coriander leaves before serving.

Serves 6 to 8

Remarks

Babuji often made this simple lentil with variations. Frequently I was the despair of this fine cook. Every time he would ask me, "Baby, kya khaogi?" *(What do you want to eat?), I would reply, "Daal chaval" (Lentil and rice).*

Most Indians love lentils and rice. After eating different or exotic foods for a while, one finds one develops a craving for simple daal chaval *or* daal roti.

Sambar

Lentils with Vegetables

tamarind pulp, the size of a lemon

2¼ cups boiling water

1¼ cups *arhar daal,* a lentil

6 cups water

1 teaspoon tumeric powder

1 cup finely sliced spring onions

1½ cups diced eggplant

1½ cups coarsely chopped okra

1 tomato

3 tablespoons *ghee* (see page 40) or vegetable oil

¼ teaspoon *heeng,* asafetida

½ teaspoon fenugreek seeds

1½ tablespoons coriander seeds

2¼ teaspoons cumin seeds

2 tablespoons grated coconut or desiccated coconut

1 teaspoon black or red mustard seeds

3 *kardi patta,* curry leaves, or bay leaves

1 to 2 small green chilies, chopped

1 to 2 dried red chilies

Soak the tamarind pulp in ¼ cup boiling water for 15 minutes. Squeeze the pulp and strain. Collect the juice and discard the pulp.

Meanwhile, remove any sticks or stones from the *daal.* Wash thoroughly and soak in 5 cups water for 20 minutes.

In a heavy 5-quart pot, bring the *daal,* its soaking water, and turmeric powder to a boil. Reduce heat to moderate and cook, partially covered, about 40 minutes.

Add the spring onions, eggplant, and okra to the cooked *daal.* Cook 2 minutes. Then add the tamarind juice. Stir well and cook, covered, over low heat 10 minutes.

Meanwhile, immerse the tomato in 2 cups boiling water for less than 1 minute. Drain, quickly peel, and chop the tomato. Then add it to the lentils.

In a skillet, heat the *ghee.* Drop in the asafetida, then the fenugreek seeds, coriander seeds, and cumin seeds. Fry a few seconds, then add the coconut and fry, while stirring, until the coconut becomes a light brown. With a slotted spoon, remove all the fried spices from the *ghee* and grind them to a fine paste. Add this paste to the lentils and simmer another 5 minutes.

In the same skillet and using the same oil, fry the mustard seeds until they sputter. Add the curry leaves and green and red chilies. Fry 1 minute and then add the contents of the skillet to the lentils. If the liquid in the pot is too thick, add a cup of boiling water, stir, bring to a boil again, and then serve.

Serves 6

Remarks

It is difficult to go wrong with this lovely south Indian favorite! I learned it years ago from my friend, Jaya Parmasivan. Serve with plain rice, idli, *or* dosa.

the extended family of our household

Baba and I were never alone. If my parents went out, we had Asho, Babuji, Hansraj Hussain, Lalsingh and often the other household help with us. They were a mixed bunch, but we all got along very well together, as everyone knew each others' foibles and made allowances for these. Ever since I could remember, there was Babuji. He was a strong, self-willed man, and much of the family life revolved around him. He was always in "his" kitchen, from which the most elusive and tempting aromas wafted. The sound of ginger or coriander seeds being ground would blend with the sudden sizzle of *baghar* (see Glossary) being added to his incomparable lentils. Sometimes he could be heard scolding his kitchen helpers, or calling out for Asho.

Babuji was the old, faithful family retainer who had learned his art in my father's household in Lucknow. He was trained by superb chefs in my great-grandfather's house. This was a large feudal household and Babuji began his career (as his father did before him) as a gentleman butler.

Sharafat Bibi, my father's mother was a kindly lady who managed a large retinue of servants with flair, sympathy, and efficiency. Babuji was one of her favorites and she took special care to see that he achieved his ambition of becoming a "major domo" in his own right. When he was younger, he had to act as a general helper to the senior servants. He was meticulous in every respect, beginning with a thorough cleaning of the kitchen before he was even allowed near the *chula* (earthen cooking range).

How Babuji's Kitchen Was Run

The kitchen was run very efficiently. It had to be, to cater to the dozens of extended family members that sat down for each meal. Before the actual cooking began, the herbs and spices were prepared, some freshly plucked, some roasted and ground, in various combinations, for the day's use. As a child, I remember being fascinated with the colorful assortment of spices—some ground, some whole, arranged attractively on a large *thali* or the flat lid of one of Babuji's enormous *degchis* (pans). It was all a big mystery to me. I would ask, *"Babuji, yeh kya hai?*—Babuji, what is this?" He would say, "Can't you smell it? It is cardamom."

An added fascination was Babuji's *hookah* (water pipe). After he had finished his cooking, and done all his ablutions, he would change into a loose *lungi* (a cloth wrapped around his waist), elaborately clear his throat, and light up his *hookah.* It was an old, silver *hookah,* presented to him by my father's family. He would sit smoking contently, while the water which acted as a filter for the tobacco gurgled with each satisfying puff. I would sit at his feet, and he would tell me marvelous fairy tales. My favorite story was about the handsome prince who rode a flying white horse and saved the beautiful princess from all kinds of calamities. I'm sure he must have related this story to me a hundred times, as his father had before him, to my father. The fascination lay in that each time he told the story, it was as if he was telling it anew. He never showed his boredom, and always punctuated his narrative with generous gestures.

When he was in a very good mood, Babuji would even let me have a puff from his *hookah.* I used to wait for these precious moments! I was his great favorite. I suspect this was because I would greet him so respectfully every time I even caught

"He would sit smoking contentedly while the water which acted as a filter for the tobacco gurgled with each satisfying puff."

a glimpse of him. The Muslim form of greeting is to bend low and raise your right hand to your forehead. You are expected to do this when you greet anyone older than yourself. (The response to this greeting is that the person being so greeted replies *"Jiti raho"* meaning literally, "Keep on living," or really, "May you have a long life.") However, it is not expected that one repeat this greeting constantly to the same person, yet I would do this—sometimes up to twenty times a day! It was another family joke, but it suited both Babuji and me fine! It was our own special little ritual.

The Art of Cooking with Flair and Gusto

I absorbed not so much the actual art of cooking from Babuji as the attitude of approaching the preparation of even simple meals with great flair and gusto. And of course, the most important thing Babuji gave to us all was an appreciation of the culinary art, and the experience of having tasted the best Moghul foods. Later, when I began to cook, I found this experience invaluable. Even if I didn't have a recipe, I knew what a dish should taste like, and it was not too difficult to achieve some degree of success, with this unwritten guide always in my mind.

I remember an occasion which I always refer to as Babuji's finest hour! There was great excitement, bustle, and nervousness in the house. The Aga Khan was coming to dinner. He was visiting Assam as the leader of the International Refugee Committee.

At last Babuji felt vindicated—he had triumphed. Old, loyal, zealous Babuji, the family retainer for decades, had been asked by the State Government to supervise the banquet in honor of the Khan. He knew he was a superb cook, but did the ungrateful family he had served so long? Now they'd know!

Babuji looked smug that day, and he shouted a little louder at his kitchen helpers. He had a half dozen kitchen helpers bustling around; one grinding onions and garlic, another crushing tumeric root, yet another pounding cloves and cardamom pods.

The Great Banquet for the Khan

Finally, his great moment came. He hovered around my mother as she supervised setting the table, unwilling to delegate any of his power. At dinner time, there was a feast laid out on the table. Imagine: *kababs* of all kinds, delicate, melting in the mouth, the piéce de resistance, *Mussalam Raan, Korma,* stuffed *kerelas,* and peppers, many different *daals, pillaus, chapatis*—paper-thin, soft pliable *parathas,* curried pea and potato, *Murgh Mussallam,* aromatic mutton curry, fish in tamarind sauce, his delectable *Shahi Tukray.* All were cooked just right! There was no end to the culinary delights produced that night by the magic wave of Babuji's hand.

―――――――――― *Dhuli Maash Ki Daal* ―――――――――― Split White
Lentils with Onion Crisps

1½ cups *dhuli maash daal,* a lentil

2¼ cups water

1 tablespoon scraped and thinly sliced ginger

½ teaspoon turmeric powder (optional)

2 tablespoons plus ¾ teaspoon vegetable oil

1¾ cups finely sliced onions

2 or 3 tablespoons *ghee* (see page 40) or butter

2 or 3 small green chilies, halved or minced (optional)

Remove the stones and other foreign matter from the *daal.* Wash the *daal* thoroughly and soak for 30 minutes in just enough water to cover the *daal.*

Drain the *daal* and place in a 4-quart pot. Add water, ginger, and turmeric powder (if used) and bring to a boil. Reduce heat to low, remove the scum, cover tightly, and simmer until the lentils are soft and break easily when pressed with your fingers (about 30 minutes).

Simmer, uncovered, until all the liquid is absorbed.

Meanwhile, heat the oil in a skillet and fry the onions until they are crisp and a dark, reddish brown color. Stir occasionally.

Melt the *ghee* and combine with the fried onions in a small serving bowl to accompany the lentils. Spoon the lentils into a serving dish and garnish with chilies. Place the fried onions and *ghee* next to the lentils as added garnish.

Serves 6

Remarks

This lentil preparation was one of Babuji's specialties. The lentils should be soft but not mushy. Each lentil should remain whole. For this reason, you should not stir the lentils during the cooking period. The appearance should be somewhat like that of plain, cooked rice.

The onion crisps in melted **ghee** *are an important part of this dish. Each lentil serving is topped with the desired amount of onions.*

This daal *goes best with* Chapati, Whole Wheat, Flat Round Bread *(see Index).*

Succulent ———————————— *Korma II* ————————————
Lamb or Beef Curry

4 tablespoons Homemade Yogurt (see page 41)

1½ pounds lean round of lamb or beef

4 tablespoons vegetable oil

2 cups finely sliced onions

2 to 4 dried red chilies

1¼ tablespoons coriander seeds

8 tablespoons warm water

4 whole cloves

4 small pale green cardamom pods

1½ tablespoons scraped and finely grated ginger

1½ tablespoons minced garlic

3 to 4½ cups water

pinch ground nutmeg

pinch ground mace

¼ teaspoon *kewra* water or rose water

Beat the yogurt lightly and keep it at room temperature until it is slightly sour (preferably a few hours).

Wash the meat and trim off excess fat. Cut into 1-inch cubes.

Heat the oil in a 5-quart pot and fry the onions until lightly browned. Remove the onions from the pan and grind them along with the chilies, coriander seeds, warm water, cloves, and cardamom pods to a fine paste. Return the ground spices to the pot. Add the meat, ginger, and garlic and fry until brown (about 7 to 10 minutes).

Add 2¼ cups water and bring to a boil. Reduce the heat to low and cook, covered, until the meat is tender (about 1 to 1½ hours). Stir in yogurt. If there is too little liquid, add 1 cup hot water to yield a rich, slightly thick gravy. Add the nutmeg, mace, and *kewra* and stir thoroughly. Simmer a few minutes before serving.

Serves 6

Pea and ———————————— *Matar Alu* ————————————
Potato Curry with Cumin Seeds, Dry

1¼ pounds potatoes (about 3 medium-size)

10 ounces green peas, fresh or frozen

3 tablespoons vegetable oil

2 teaspoons cumin seeds

½ teaspoon cumin powder

¼ teaspoon turmeric powder

1 or 2 small green chilies, minced

Boil the potatoes until tender. Drain and cut into ½-inch cubes.

Shell the peas. If frozen peas are used, defrost partially.

In a large skillet, heat the oil. Add the potatoes, cumin seeds, cumin powder, and turmeric powder and stir 2 minutes. Stir in the peas, cover, and cook over moderate heat 5 to 10 minutes. Stir in the chilies and serve hot.

Serves 6

—————————— *Raan* —————————— Spicy Leg of
Lamb

5 to 5½	pounds leg of lamb, fat trimmed	2½	tablespoons minced garlic
7	tablespoons grated coconut	¾	cup thick Homemade Yogurt (see page 41)
½	cup raw, unsalted peanuts		
3	tablespoons *khas khas,* white poppy seeds	⅛	teaspoon nutmeg powder
		⅛	teaspoon mace powder
1½	tablespoons cumin seeds	8	tablespoons *ghee* (see page 40) or vegetable oil
3	tablespoons coriander seeds		
7	small cardamom pods	3½ to 4	cups minced onions
3	large cardamom pods	1	teaspoon *kashmiri mirch,* a chili, or 1 teaspoon paprika
	1½-inch cinnamon stick		
10	whole cloves	¼	cup whole cashew nuts (optional)
20	peppercorns	12	fresh pink rose petals (optional)
2½	tablespoons scraped and grated ginger	2	tablespoons chopped coriander leaves or mint

Heat a *tava* or griddle and roast the peanuts until golden brown. Grind to a coarse powder in a coffee grinder or blender and set aside. In the same *tava,* roast the white poppy seeds, cumin seeds, and coriander seeds, while stirring, until lightly browned. Grind to a fine powder and set aside.

Remove the cardamom seeds from the pods. Break the cinnamon into pieces. Grind the cardamom, cinnamon, cloves, and peppercorns to a powder and set aside.

Place the leg of lamb in a large bowl and thoroughly rub the coconut, ground peanuts, white poppy seeds, cumin, coriander, cardamom, cinnamon, cloves, and peppercorns into it. Add the ginger, garlic, yogurt, nutmeg powder, and mace powder and work all the spices into the meat. Cover the bowl and marinate in the refrigerator for 24 hours or at room temperature for at least 8 hours.

When ready to cook, heat 6 tablespoons *ghee* in an 8-quart pot with a heavy bottom and fry the onions until golden brown over moderately high heat. Carefully add the leg of lamb with all the spices. Stir once, then reduce heat to moderate, and cook, covered, for 12 to 15 minutes. Quickly stir again, reduce heat to low, and continue to cook, covered, for 30 minutes.

Add the chili, stir, cover, and cook for 1 hour. Turn the leg of lamb over, stir, and continue cooking, covered, until the lamb is soft and the thick gravy looks red (about 1 hour). Turn the heat off and keep the lamb covered.

Heat 2 tablespoons *ghee* in a skillet and fry the cashew nuts until golden brown. Drain on paper toweling.

Place the *raan* on a large, flat, warmed serving dish. Garnish with fried cashew nuts. To add a delightful touch to the *raan,* arrange the rose petals (if used) in clusters of 3 or 4 petals each to form small flower shapes. Sprinkle coriander leaves on top and serve hot.

Serves 8

Princely ————————————— *Shahi Tukray* —————————————

Delicacy of Fried Toast Cooked in Milk

6 slices of thick, whole wheat bread	10 tablespoons powdered milk
9 to 10 tablespoons *ghee* (see page 40) or butter	3½ to 4 tablespoons water
½ cup milk	4 tablespoons heavy cream
¼ teaspoon *zafraan,* saffron threads	¾ tablespoon *kewra* water
4 tablespoons grated jaggery	12 whole almonds
	1 tablespoon pistachio nuts

Trim the crusts from the bread slices.

In a large skillet, heat 2 tablespoons *ghee* and fry 3 slices of bread until golden brown on one side. Remove the bread. Add 2 tablespoons *ghee* to the skillet and fry the other side of the bread until golden brown. Repeat this process with the 3 remaining slices.

In a small pan, warm the milk with the saffron threads and jaggery, stirring until the jaggery dissolves completely.

Lightly grease a thick baking sheet with a little *ghee* and arrange the slices close to each other. Pour the warm milk mixture over the slices and allow to soak for 15 to 20 minutes.

In the small pan, stir together 1 tablespoon *ghee,* the powdered milk, and water and cook over low heat until you have a smooth paste. Remove from heat and stir in the cream and *kewra* water.

Reserve 2 to 3 tablespoons of the milk/cream mixture and pour the rest evenly over the bread. Place the baking sheet on the burner and simmer for 6 to 10 minutes.

Lift 1 slice with a spatula and lightly brush the baking sheet with *ghee*. Replace the slice on the greased baking sheet so that the side with milk on top now faces downwards. Repeat this process with all the slices, turning one at a time. Pour the reserved paste over the slices and simmer another 5 to 8 minutes.

Slice the almonds into very thin slivers. Wrap the pistachio nuts in thick paper toweling and pound with a mallet until the nuts resemble large crumbs.

In a skillet, roast the nuts over moderate heat until lightly browned (about 3 to 4 minutes). Add a little *ghee* if necessary. Sprinkle the roasted nuts evenly over the *Shahi Tukray.*

When ready to serve, warm the slices. Then, lift one slice off the baking sheet for each serving.

Serves 6

Remarks

This popular soft, moist dessert is at its best when served immediately. If crisper Shahi Tukray *are preferred, warm them in a moderate oven before serving.*

———————————————————————————————————

The Aga Khan, as is the tradition in old families, asked for the chef, after the meal. Babuji came forward, frail but triumphant. He was handsomely rewarded for his labors. This public approbation served to keep him happy for months basking in remembered glory!

Differences in the Household

Babuji, of course, was a very strict Muslim observing all the required rituals and prayers. Ashna, or Asho as we called her, is a high caste Hindu. Initially, this was a barrier to any understanding between them. Babuji's insistence on cleanliness, his determination not to allow any "unclean meat" (like the Jews, Muslims believe that an animal has to be killed in a certain way, before it can be considered "clean" meat) into the house, was another irritant to Asho's already busy life. Babuji, on the other hand, was horrified at Asho's easygoing ways, and her enjoyment of the forbidden meat (pork) was the last straw for him.

But there was a powerful bond that Babuji and Asho shared. They were both devoted to us, as we were to both of them. Gradually through this shared bond they overcame their differences, and developed an understanding of each other. Babuji continued to fuss about Asho's tardiness or her neglect of him, but increasingly, as he got older, he began to depend more and more on her.

Asho would grumble about having to do all Babuji's work for him, but they made a great team, and Asho slowly climbed to second place in the domestic hierarchy. Babuji's position was so strong in the household that my mother's friends would tease her about it, referring to him as her mother-in-law!

Asho came to our household before my brother was born. She is a Nepali, who had left her home and country for the love of an Indian man, Indar, who happened to be a chef at a hotel in Shillong. She was young, attractive, and very vivacious. When Rashid (Baba) was born, he became her special charge. He was a happy, contented baby. Asho would tie him onto her back with the ends of her *sari*, piggyback style, and take him for walks around the Shillong Ward Lakes, with Baba snug as a butterfly in a cocoon.

Asho's Knowledge of Nature Was Put to Use

Asho knew all kinds of grasses and mushrooms, having spent her childhood in rural Nepal, and could concoct a delicious dish seemingly out of nothing. So my brother tasted all kinds of grasses and berries from his vantage point on Asho's safe back! To this day, his favorite dishes are Asho's tomato chutney, her potato pickle, and her mutton curry garnished with some wild leaves such as wood sorrel, and her *Tandoori Tukray*.

Asho was a carefree person, but deeply superstitious. She would not allow us to pluck flowers after the sun had set, for fear of offending the garden spirits, who, she said, liked to rest in peace in the evening.

The day a man finally landed on the moon was not a very happy one for Asho. I remember Baba was divided between a mischievous urge to break this sacrilegious piece of news to her, and his concern for her feelings. To Asho the moon was sacred and of course, man could never desecrate it by setting foot on it. So, at first she refused to believe that the moon landing had actually happened. Finally, when everyone repeated the astounding news, she was heard muttering under her breath. "No good will come to the man who has committed this foolhardy act," she declared. According to her, the world was in peril, as the forces of Bhagvan (God) would surely punish man for this act. No wonder we love Asho so much! We consider ourselves

Asho's *Tandoori* Chicken Breast Pieces — *Asho Kay Tandoori Tukray*

3 to 3¼ pounds chicken breasts	1½ teaspoons cumin seeds
2⅓ tablespoons scraped and grated ginger	2 tablespoons melted *ghee* (see page 40) or vegetable oil
2 tablespoons minced garlic	⅔ to 1 teaspoon chili powder
3 tablespoons thick Homemade Yogurt (see page 41)	

Trim any excess fat from chicken. Cut each breast piece into 2 or 3 pieces, bone and all. Wash and let drain in a colander for 15 minutes.

Rub the ginger, garlic, and yogurt into the chicken pieces and refrigerate, covered, for about 48 hours.

Heat a *tava* or griddle and roast the cumin seeds 12 seconds, while stirring. Remove the *tava* from the heat. Place the cumin seeds in a double layer of thick paper towels and pound with a small mallet until the seeds are crushed to a coarse powder.

Mix the powdered cumin, *ghee,* and chili powder thoroughly with the chicken. Then place the chicken pieces side by side on a large baking tray and broil 6 to 8 minutes. Turn the pieces over and broil until browned (about 6 to 8 minutes). Serve hot or warm.

Serves 6 to 8

Remarks:

Adapted from my grandmother's Moghul recipe, this is one of my favorites. Asho made it often for us, barbecuing it over pine logs instead of broiling it.

Serve with Khamiri Roti, Whole Wheat, Leavened, Quick-Baked Bread, Naan, Leavened, Baked, Whole Wheat Bread *(see Index), or any other* roti.

---

very fortunate, that even in these changed times (in India) we still have Asho with us, with her children, Madhu and Lama, who are like aunt and uncle to my children.

Hansraj, the Blood Brother

All of us are very fond of Hansraj, a special family favorite. Once when my mother had been very ill, Hansraj donated his blood for her. She always called him her blood brother after that. Hansraj is fairly typical of a certain class of Indian. He is from a high-caste, but poor, *Brahmin* family in Bihar, where they own a few acres of land.

As they were not able to make ends meet on cultivation alone, Hansraj came to seek a job in Shillong. My father had him employed as a government peon (a low grade clerk), and later he spent more and more time at our house. He was very conscientious, saving all his money to send home to his family in Bihar. He really had two occupations, one as a clerk and the other as a shopkeeper during evenings. He made and sold the most delicious *pakoras* and *alu tikkis* (potato cutlets) washed down with that popular Punjabi drink, *Lassi,* and was a familiar sight to all our friends, who specially patronized his shop.

──────────── *Alu Ki Tikki* ──────────── Thin Potato
Cutlets

1½ pounds potatoes

2 tablespoons lemon juice

3 tablespoons chopped coriander
   leaves or parsley

1 teaspoon *garam masalla,* a spice
   mixture (see page 42)

2 or 3 small green chilies, minced

1 teaspoon cumin powder

3 tablespoons soya flour or *besan,*
   chick-pea flour

¼ teaspoon garlic powder (optional)

5 to 6 tablespoons vegetable oil

Boil the potatoes. Cool slightly, then peel and mash the potatoes thoroughly.

In a large bowl, mix the potatoes with lemon juice, coriander leaves, *garam masalla,*
and chilies.

Heat a *tava* or griddle and roast the cumin powder over moderately high heat 10
seconds. Remove and add to the potatoes.

Knead the potatoes until soft and pliable. Form into 12 cutlets, less than ½ inch thick
and 2 to 3 inches in diameter.

Sift the flour and garlic powder (if used) together and spread thinly over a platter.
Lightly coat the potato cutlets with the flour mixture on both sides.

Heat 2 tablespoons oil in a large skillet and place 6 cutlets in it, side by side. Fry until
golden brown (about 5 to 6 minutes). Turn the cutlets over carefully, add 1 or 2 tablespoons oil, and fry over moderate heat until golden brown.

Serves 6

──────────── *Lassi* ──────────── A Yogurt-
Based Cool Drink

3 cups Homemade Yogurt (see
   page 41)

2¼ cups cold water

2¼ to 5 teaspoons honey

Put 1½ cups yogurt, 1½ cups water, and 2¼ teaspoons honey in a blender and blend
at high speed for a few seconds. Pour out the liquid and set aside.

Put the remaining yogurt and water in the blender and blend at high speed for a few
seconds.

Return the first batch of blended yogurt to the blender and blend everything together at high speed for 3 to 4 seconds. If you prefer a sweeter drink, add more honey.

Serve over ice cubes in individual glasses.

Yields about 6 cups

Remarks:

Lassi *is a typical Punjabi drink, meant for refreshing the spirit on hot summer days.*

*If refrigerated, remember to stir thoroughly before serving; the yogurt tends to settle at the bottom of
the container if not served immediately.*

Deep-Fried Onions in Batter
Pyaz Pakora

2 large onions (about 2½ cups when sliced)	¼ cup chopped coriander leaves or dried parsley flakes
1 cup *besan,* chick-pea flour	1 teaspoon *garam masalla,* a spice mixture (see page 42) or cumin powder
2½ tablespoons lemon juice	
¼ teaspoon chili powder	½ cup water
2 teaspoons minced small green chilies	oil for deep frying
¼ teaspoon turmeric powder	

Slice the onions and cut each slice in half.

In a bowl, mix the chick-pea flour, lemon juice, chili powder, chilies, turmeric powder, coriander leaves, and *garam masalla.* Add the water slowly and continue stirring so that the batter is smooth and free of lumps.

Add the onion slivers to the batter and mix thoroughly.

Heat the oil in a *karhai,* or wok, or deep-frying pan. Test the oil by dropping in just one onion sliver. If it rises immediately to the surface, the oil is ready. Drop the batter by the rounded teaspoonful into the oil and fry until the *pakoras* are golden brown. Remove with a slotted spoon and place in an oven-proof dish lined with paper towels. Keep in a warm oven until all the *pakoras* are made. Serve immediately with mint or coriander chutney.

Yields 24 to 26 *pakoras*

Remarks

Serve with Pudina Chutney, *Mint Chutney, or* Dhania Chutney, *Fresh Coriander Chutney (see Index).* Pakoras *are very easy to make and are invariably loved by everyone. I use less chick-pea flour than is commonly used in India so that the* pakoras *are light and airy.*

Hansraj was unique. He was the kindest soul in the world, incapable of harshness, even under provocation. His voice was so soft and gentle that we often had to strain to catch what he was saying. He was deeply religious, yet very tolerant of others beliefs. He loved to read whenever he had a spare moment, and I remember seeing him with his steel-rimmed glasses, catching up on his latest reading, which included the *Bhagavad Gita* (see Glossary). His respect for learning spilled over to veneration for the books themselves. He taught us to revere books and never be careless with them. If we accidentally brushed a book with our feet, we would immediately pick it up and touch it to our foreheads, as we had always seen him do. On the days that Babuji made *Chewra (Poha),* Pounded Rice Flakes (see Index), Hansraj could always be seen tucked away in a corner of the kitchen, on his *mura.* This *mura,* a sort of stool, beautifully worked in cane, is still in our kitchen in Shillong, as is Babuji's favorite *mura.*

rice

———————————————— *Asaan Pullau* ————————————————

Easy Rice/Lamb Pilaf with Saffron

1½ pounds lean round of lamb or beef	8 to 10 *kardi patta,* curry leaves
1 tablespoon scraped and grated ginger	2 cups long grain brown rice
¾ tablespoon minced garlic	¼ to ½ teaspoon *zafraan,* saffron powder, or ¼ teaspoon *zafraan,* saffron threads
½ teaspoon freshly ground black pepper	
4 cups water	1 tablespoon hot milk
5 tablespoons vegetable oil	3 tablespoons chopped coriander leaves or dill leaves
1¼ cups finely sliced onions	
2 teaspoons freshly ground cumin powder	
2 teaspoons crushed *khas khas,* white poppy seeds	

Trim any fat from the meat. Cut the meat into 1-inch cubes and rub with the ginger, garlic, and black pepper. Set aside for about 30 minutes.

Bring water to a boil in a 4-quart pot and cook the spiced meat 35 to 45 minutes over moderate heat. Drain and reserve the stock.

In a large skillet, heat 3 tablespoons oil and fry the onions until brown (about 8 to 10 minutes). Add the cumin powder, poppy seeds, 6 curry leaves, and the meat and fry until the meat is lightly browned. Stir occasionally.

Wash the rice under cold running water and drain. In a heavy 5-quart pot, heat 2 tablespoons oil. Fry the rice 5 to 10 minutes over moderate heat. Stir gently.

Meanwhile, soak the saffron in the milk.

Add the saffron, remaining curry leaves, meat, and stock to the rice. If the stock is less than 4 cups, add fresh water to equal 4 cups of liquid. Bring to a boil, reduce heat to low, and simmer, tightly covered, until the rice is cooked.

Transfer to a large warm serving platter and fluff up the rice with a fork. Garnish with coriander leaves.

Serves 6

Remarks

   This fragrant dish has the exquisite flavors and aromas of both zafraan *and* kardi patta. *We like to serve it with* Dhania Chutney, *Fresh Coriander Chutney,* Pudina Chutney, *Mint Chutney, or* Tazay Tamatar Ki Chutney, *Fresh Tomato Chutney (see Index) and a* raita.

Biryani E Mahi

Rice Pilaf with Fish

1¼ pounds firm white fish

1½ teaspoons ground fennel seeds

1½ teaspoons cumin powder

4 tablespoons *besan,* chick-pea flour

9 tablespoons thick Homemade Yogurt (see page 41)

6½ tablespoons melted *ghee* (see page 40) or butter

1 tablespoon plus ¾ teaspoon coriander powder

¼ teaspoon powdered cloves

½ teaspoon cardamom powder

¼ cup finely grated onions

1 tablespoon finely grated ginger

½ teaspoon chili powder

¼ teaspoon *zafraan*, saffron powder

3¼ cups milk

2 cups long grain brown rice

¼ teaspoon rose water

2 to 3 tablespoons chopped coriander leaves

Cut the fish into 2-inch squares. Remove the skin and bones.

Mix together the fennel seeds, cumin powder, and chick-pea flour. Coat the fish pieces with this mixture, leave for 5 minutes, then rinse lightly, and let the fish dry on paper towels.

Beat yogurt lightly. In a large bowl, mix together the yogurt, *ghee,* coriander powder, cloves, cardamom powder, onions, and ½ tablespoon ginger. Squeeze the remaining ginger to extract the juice. Discard the ginger and add the juice to the bowl, with the chili powder.

Carefully mix the fish pieces with the yogurt mixture until the fish is well coated. Marinate the fish for 1 hour.

Soak the saffron powder in 1 tablespoon milk.

Wash the rice thoroughly, drain, and set aside.

When ready to cook, warm a 5-quart, heavy-bottomed pot and slide the fish with its marinade into the pot. Fry the fish 3 to 4 minutes. Shake the pot gently once or twice. Pour the remaining milk over the fish and sprinkle the rice on top. Bring the milk to a boil, then immediately reduce the heat to low and simmer, tightly covered, about 20 minutes.

Uncover and sprinkle the saffron (with milk), rose water, and 1 tablespoon coriander leaves over the rice. Stir very gently; be careful not to break the fish pieces. Cover tightly again and simmer until the rice is cooked (about 20 minutes).

Garnish with remaining coriander leaves and serve hot.

Serves 6

Remarks

This recipe is from a princely home in Rajasthan and was "whispered" to a member of my family.

In India, we would cook Biryani E Mahi *on very low heat with live coals on the lid of the pot. This process is known as* dum *(see Index).*

Serve with Baingun Bharta, *Eggplant Crush (see Index) and one of the green bean recipes.*

Bhuna Chaval

Rice Fried to a Golden Brown

3 cups long grain brown rice

8 tablespoons *ghee* (see page 40) or vegetable oil

2 cups minced onions

3 small pale green cardamom pods

3 to 6 bay leaves

2 teaspoons cumin seeds

¼ teaspoon tumeric powder

6 cups boiling water

3 tablespoons chopped coriander leaves or watercress

Wash the rice under cold running water and soak for 15 minutes in enough water to cover the rice.

In a heavy 5-quart pot, heat the *ghee* over medium-high heat until a light haze forms on top. Fry the onions, while stirring, until they become golden brown. Add the cardamom pods, bay leaves, and cumin seeds and fry 1 minute.

Drain the rice and add to the pot. Fry the rice and turmeric powder, while stirring and gently lifting, until the rice is a light golden brown (about 15 minutes). Pour in the boiling water, stir, bring to a boil, reduce heat, cover tightly, and simmer until the rice is tender but not mushy (about 20 to 40 minutes).

Spoon onto a heated serving dish and lightly fluff up with a fork. Garnish with coriander leaves.

Serves 6

Remarks

This rice dish can accompany most types of foods. It may also be served on its own for a simple family meal with one of our lentils, a chutney, and/or a yogurt dish.

Chana Chaval

Rice with Chick-Peas

¾ cups *kala chana,* small, dark chick-peas, or chick-peas

2½ cups water

1-inch cinnamon stick

2 large dark brown cardamom pods

2 small pale green cardamom pods

8 to 10 garlic cloves

¼ teaspoon chili powder

1 or 2 small green chilies

½ teaspoon tumeric powder

1 teaspoon *amchoor,* powdered mango

2 cups long grain brown rice

4½ tablespoons vegetable oil

½ cup minced spring onions

2 tablespoons scraped and finely sliced ginger

1½ teaspoons cumin seeds

4 bay leaves

1 teaspoon freshly ground black pepper

3 tablespoons chopped green coriander leaves or any green herb

Remove any sticks or stones from the lentils. Wash the *chana* 3 or 4 times and soak for 12 hours in 2½ cups water.

Transfer the *chana* and water to a 3-quart pot and add the cinnamon, large and small cardamom pods, garlic, chili powder, chilies, turmeric powder, and powdered mango. Bring the water to a boil, reduce heat to low, and simmer, covered, until the *chana* is tender (about 1¾ to 2½ hours). Add more water if needed.

Drain the *chana* and reserve the liquid. Remove the cinnamon, cardamom pods, and garlic from the *chana.*

Wash the brown rice and set aside.

Heat the oil in a 5-quart pot and fry the onions in the oil until lightly browned. Stir in the ginger and fry over moderate heat until it becomes a pale brown (about 2 to 3 minutes). Add the cumin seeds, bay leaves, pepper, and prepared *chana.* Stir 3 to 4 minutes, then add the rice, and stir another 2 minutes.

Pour in reserved water from the *chana* plus fresh water to equal 4½ cups. Bring to a boil, reduce heat to low, and simmer, covered, until the water is absorbed by the rice (about 30 to 50 minutes).

Transfer to a heated serving platter by lightly lifting the rice with a fork. Garnish with coriander leaves.

Serves 6

Remarks

This protein-rich dish may be served with just a vegetable, a raita, *and chutney.*

Khitchri I

*A Light Dish Made with Rice and Orange Lentils

2½ cups long grain brown rice

1 cup *chilka masur daal,* a lentil

5 tablespoons *ghee* (see page 40) or vegetable oil

2 cups finely sliced onions

½ teaspoon scraped and finely sliced ginger (optional)

1¼ teaspoons cumin seeds

½ teaspoon tumeric powder

8 cups water

½ to 1 teaspoon *garam masalla,* a spice mixture (see page 42)

Wash the rice and soak in enough water to cover.

Remove any stones from the *daal.* Wash the *daal* and soak in enough water to cover.

Heat 2½ tablespoons of the *ghee* in a 5-quart pot and fry 1 cup onions until brown. Drain the *daal.* Add the *daal,* ginger (if used), cumin seeds, and turmeric powder and fry 4 to 5 minutes.

Add 3 cups water, bring to a boil, lower heat, and simmer, covered, until the water is absorbed.

Drain the rice and add it to the pot with *garam masalla* and 5 cups water. Bring to a boil, reduce heat to low, stir, cover, and cook until the water is absorbed (about 20 to 30 minutes).

Meanwhile heat the remaining *ghee* in a skillet and fry the remaining onions until reddish brown and crisp. Pour *ghee* and onions into a small serving bowl.

Place the *khitchri* in a warmed serving platter and fluff with a fork. Serve the crisped onions and *ghee* separately.

Serves 6

Remarks

This light dish is excellent for young children and invalids because it is very easy to digest. Whenever we had an upset stomach, my mother would make Khitchri *for us without the* garam masalla *and using yellow* moong daal, *which is the lightest* daal.

Khitchri *goes well with* Pudina aur Dhania Chutney *(Mint and Coriander Chutney),* Pudina Chutney *(Mint Chutney),* or Dhania Chutney *(Fresh Coriander Chutney). See index for these chutneys.*

Khitchri II

Split Lentils and Rice

1¼ cups *chilka urad daal,* a split lentil

2 cups long grain brown rice

1 cup finely sliced onions

5 tablespoons *ghee* (see page 40) or butter

1 tablespoon scraped and finely minced ginger

½ tablespoon finely chopped garlic

3 bay leaves

½ teaspoon tumeric powder

2 cups boiling water

¼ teaspoon *garam masalla,* a spice mixture (see page 42)

4½ cups water

Remove stones from the *daal.* Wash the *urad daal* thoroughly and soak in enough cold water to cover for 30 minutes to 1 hour.

Wash the rice and soak in enough cold water to cover.

In a 5-quart pot, fry the onions in 4 tablespoons *ghee* over moderately high heat until they are red and crisp (about 15 minutes). Stir occasionally. Remove from pot with its cooking *ghee* and set aside in a small bowl.

Pour the remaining 1 tablespoon *ghee* into the pot and fry the ginger and garlic 2 minutes. Add bay leaves and fry 1 minute. Drain the *daal* and fry with tumeric powder 5 minutes. Pour in the boiling water and cook, covered, over moderate heat 15 to 20 minutes.

Drain the rice and reserve the soaking water. Add the rice, *garam masalla,* 4½ cups water, and the soaking water and bring to a boil. Reduce heat to low, cover, and simmer until the water is absorbed (about 25 to 45 minutes).

Serves 6 to 8

Remarks

This khitchri *makes a delicious family meal. We serve it with* Tazay Tamatar Ki Chutney *(Fresh Tomato Chutney),* Dhania Chutney *(Fresh Coriander Chutney), plain yogurt or a* raita, *and the crisp onions in* ghee, *which is spooned over each individual serving. See Index for these chutneys.*

Masalla Pullau

A Spicy Rice Dish

3 cups long grain brown rice	2-inch cinnamon stick
6 to 7 tablespoons vegetable oil	6 to 8 whole cloves
2 cups finely sliced onions	1 tablespoon scraped and grated ginger
1 tablespoon minced garlic	2 tablespoons plus ¾ teaspoon *garam masalla,* a spice mixture (see page 42)
20 to 30 peppercorns	1 tablespoon cumin seeds
6 small green cardamom pods	6 cups water
4 bay leaves	

Wash the rice and soak it in enough water to cover.

In a 5-quart pot, heat the oil and fry 1 cup onions until they are reddish brown and crisp. Remove with a slotted spoon and set aside.

In the same pot, fry the remaining 1 cup onions and garlic over medium heat until they are golden brown. Add peppercorns, cardamom pods, bay leaves, cinnamon, and cloves, and after 1 minute add the ginger. Fry until the ginger becomes a light brown (about 2 minutes). Add the *garam masalla* and fry ½ minute.

Drain the rice and reserve the soaking water. Fry the rice and cumin seeds with the other spices for 4 to 5 minutes. Stir carefully. Add 6 cups water including the soaking water and bring to a boil. Reduce heat to low, cover, and cook until the water is absorbed (about 20 to 40 minutes).

Transfer rice to a large flat serving dish and sprinkle the fried onions over the top.

Serves 6

Remarks

You may prefer to remove the cardamom pods, bay leaves, and other whole spices before serving. Though we don't eat them, we like to leave them in.

Matar Pullau

Rice Pilaf with Peas

2 cups finely sliced onions	4 to 6 whole cloves
5 tablespoons *ghee* (see page 40) or vegetable oil	12 peppercorns
2½ cups brown rice	6 bay leaves
2 large dark brown cardamom pods	½ teaspoon tumeric powder
2 small green or buff-colored cardamom pods	2½ cups peas, fresh or frozen
	5 cups cold water

In a 5-quart heavy-bottomed pot, fry the onions in 3 tablespoons *ghee* over moderate heat until they are a deep reddish brown and just begin to turn crisp (about 20 to 25 minutes). Stir frequently. Remove the onions with a slotted spoon and set aside.

Wash the rice and leave it in just enough water to cover it.

Add 2 tablespoons *ghee* to the pot. Lightly press the cardamom pods between your fingers to partially break the skin of the pods. Just a slit is enough to allow the flavors to escape fully. Drop the cardamom pods, cloves, and peppercorns into the pot and fry 1 minute over moderate heat. Add the bay leaves and remove pot from heat.

Drain the rice thoroughly. Reserve any liquid. Fry rice and tumeric powder with the spices in the pot 3 to 4 minutes. Add the peas and continue frying another 2 to 3 minutes. Add water drained from rice and enough fresh water to equal 5 cups. Stir gently and bring to a boil. Reduce heat to low and simmer, tightly covered, until the rice is cooked and the water is absorbed (about 25 to 35 minutes).

Spoon onto a large flat serving dish and lightly fluff up the rice with a fork. Garnish with crisped onions.

Serves 6

Remarks

Matar Pullau *is a great favorite with everyone and can be served with any meat or vegetable dish. Often, a family meal consists of just* matar pullau *with a* raita *and* chutney.

Matar, Soya Pullau

A Delicate Rice Dish with Green Peas and Fresh Dill Leaves

3 cups long grain brown rice	1 teaspoon crushed cumin seeds
3 tablespoons vegetable oil	4 cups peas
1 cup finely sliced onions	6¼ cups water
1½ tablespoons scraped and grated ginger	½ cup coarsely chopped dill leaves
¾ tablespoon *garam masalla,* a spice mixture (see page 42)	

Wash the rice and soak it in enough water to cover.

Heat the oil in a heavy 5-quart pot and fry the onions to a golden brown (about 10 to 12 minutes). Add the ginger and fry until the ginger is a light brown (about 2 minutes). Stir in the *garam masalla* and cumin seeds and fry ½ minute. Remove the pot from the heat.

Drain the rice and reserve the soaking water.

Return the pot to the heat and fry the rice for 4 to 5 minutes. Add the peas and fry another 2 to 3 minutes. Stir in the 6¼ cups water and the soaking water. Bring to a boil, reduce heat to low, cover tightly, and simmer 20 to 40 minutes until the water is completely absorbed.

Transfer to a large flat serving dish and gently stir in some dill leaves. Reserve a few to sprinkle on top as garnish.

Serves 6

Remarks

This fragrant rice dish is a popular family meal. Serve with just a chutney and a raita.

Sada Chaval

Plain Boiled Rice

3 cups long grain brown rice	1 teaspoon *kewra* water, or rose water (optional)
6 cups water	

Wash the rice and place in a 5-quart pot with a tight-fitting lid. Add water and bring to a rapid boil. Reduce heat to low, add *kewra* water (if used), cover tightly, and cook until the water is absorbed (about 25 to 40 minutes).

Transfer the rice to a large, flat serving dish and fluff with a fork.

Serves 6 to 8

Remarks

Serve with any curried dish with gravy or with a lentil and vegetable dish.

Murgh Pullau

Rice and Chicken Pilaf

4 pounds chicken pieces	3 tablespoons well-mixed Homemade Yogurt (see page 41)
1½ tablespoons coriander powder	
1½ teaspoons cumin powder	2½ cups long grain brown rice
1 tablespoon plus ¾ teaspoon scraped and grated ginger	4 to 6 bay leaves
1 tablespoon plus ¾ teaspoon minced garlic	6 small pale green cardamom pods
	½-inch cinnamon stick
¾ teaspoon chili powder	5 cups cold water
6 tablespoons vegetable oil	¼ teaspoon turmeric powder

Remove the skin and fat from the chicken. Cut the chicken into 2- to 3-inch pieces (including bones), wash well, and drain in a colander.

Mix together the coriander powder, cumin powder, ginger, garlic, and ½ teaspoon chili powder and rub into the chicken pieces.

Heat 3 tablespoons oil and fry the chicken pieces over moderately high heat 15 minutes. Stir frequently. Add the ¼ teaspoon chili powder and yogurt, stir well, and reduce heat to moderate. Cover and cook 30 to 35 minutes. Stir occasionally.

Wash the rice and set aside.

Heat 3 tablespoons oil in a 5-quart pot. Fry the bay leaves, cardamom pods, and cinnamon 1 minute. Fry the washed rice 2 to 3 minutes. Add the water and turmeric powder and bring to a boil. Reduce heat to low, cover, and simmer 20 to 25 minutes.

Uncover and spoon two-thirds of the rice into a bowl. Place half the cooked chicken evenly over the rice remaining in the pot. Sprinkle one-third of the rice on the chicken. Layer with the remaining half of the chicken and then with the remaining rice. Tightly cover, place pot on a warm *tava* or griddle, and keep on warm heat 10 to 15 minutes so that the rice can absorb all the flavors.

Serves 6

Remarks

Serve hot with a yogurt preparation and a vegetable or chutney. Murgh Pullau *is very popular in Utter Pradesh, in north India.*

Nariyal Chaval

Rice Cooked in Coconut Milk

3 cups long grain brown rice	1¼ cups finely sliced onions
1 coconut	10 to 15 peppercorns
6 cups boiling water	¾ teaspoon turmeric powder
5 tablespoons *ghee* (see page 40) or vegetable oil	10 *kardi patta,* curry leaves

Wash the rice and soak it at least 30 minutes in enough water to cover the rice.

Break the coconut. (For procedure, see page 40.) Grate 2½ cups of the coconut. Cut 2 tablespoons coconut into thin slices, ½ inch × ¼ inch. Soak the grated coconut in the boiling water 8 to 10 minutes. Cool. Blend one-third of the coconut and water in an electric blender. Pour out the coconut milk and blend the other two thirds the same way. Strain all the milk through a fine sieve. Collect the coconut milk and discard the pulp after squeezing thoroughly to extract all the juice.

In a 5-quart pot, heat 3 tablespoons *ghee* and fry the onions until they are dark brown. Remove with a slotted spoon and set aside.

In the same *ghee,* fry the sliced coconut until golden brown. Remove with a slotted spoon and set aside. Drain the rice.

Add 1 tablespoon *ghee* to the pot and fry the drained rice, peppercorns, turmeric powder, and curry leaves 5 to 6 minutes over moderately high heat.

Add the 6 cups coconut milk. If you do not have 6 cups, add enough plain water to equal 6 cups. Bring to a boil, reduce heat to low, and cook, covered, until the rice is tender and the liquid has evaporated. This takes 20 to 35 minutes.

Spoon into a large flat serving platter. Fluff up the rice gently with a fork. Sprinkle the fried onions and fried coconut slices on top as garnish.

Serves 6

Remarks

This delightful dish is light and appetizing. The rice takes on a lovely lemon color.

The original recipe from Bengal does not have the fried coconut slices. I find it adds a very nice touch.

Rajma Chaval

Delicately Flavored Rice with Kidney Beans

1 cup red kidney beans	4 bay leaves
3 cups water	4 whole cloves
2 cups long grain brown rice	½ teaspoon turmeric powder
6 tablespoons vegetable oil	1½ tablespoons cumin seeds
¾ cup chopped onions	3 small green chilies
½ tablespoon scraped and grated ginger	6 or 7 sprigs mint or ¼ cup minced chives

Wash and then soak the kidney beans in the water overnight. Drain the beans and reserve the soaking water.

Rinse the rice under clear running water and set aside.

In a heavy 5-quart pot with a tight-fitting lid, heat the oil. Fry the onions over high heat 1½ minutes while stirring and another 1 minute over moderately high heat. Add the ginger and fry 30 seconds. Stir constantly. Add the bay leaves, cloves, turmeric powder, and 1 tablespoon cumin seeds and fry 1 minute. Stir in the drained kidney beans and fry 3 to 4 minutes.

Add ½ cup plus 3 tablespoons of the reserved soaking water, reduce heat to moderate, cover, and cook until the beans are tender and the water is absorbed (about 40 minutes to 1 hour, 15 minutes). Add a little water if needed.

Uncover, add rice, and cook 3 to 4 minutes. Stir frequently. Add the rest of the soaking water and enough cold water to equal 4½ cups. Bring to a boil, reduce heat to low, cover, and cook about 40 to 50 minutes. If necessary, uncover and continue cooking until all the water evaporates.

Heat a *tava* or griddle and roast the remaining cumin seeds a few seconds. Wrap the seeds in thick paper towels and pound until lightly crushed.

Slit the chilies into quarters and rinse out the seeds under cold running water.

Fluff up the rice in a warm serving dish and garnish with roasted cumin, chilies, and mint.

Serves 6

Remarks

Serve hot with a chutney and raita.

Shahi Biryani

A Royal Rice and Lamb Dish

2	pounds lean round of lamb or beef	
8½	tablespoons *ghee* (see page 40)	
1¾	cups finely sliced onions	
¾	cup grated onions	
1	tablespoon plus ¾ teaspoon scraped and minced ginger	
½	tablespoon minced garlic	
1¼	teaspoons cumin seeds	
¼ to ½	teaspoon chili powder	
	2½-inch cinnamon stick	
6	whole cloves	
12 to 15	peppercorns	

5	small pale green cardamom pods
⅛	teaspoon ground nutmeg
⅛	teaspoon ground mace
¾	cup thick Homemade Yogurt (see page 41)
1¼	cups light cream
1¼	cups water
2	cups long grain brown rice
¼	teaspoon *zafraan,* saffron threads
1	tablespoon boiling water
2 to 2½	tablespoons slivered almonds
2	tablespoons raisins

Trim any fat from the meat. Cut the meat into 1-inch cubes.

Heat 4 tablespoons *ghee* in a 5-quart pot and fry ¾ cup of the sliced onions and the grated onions until brown. Add the ginger, garlic, cumin seeds, and chili powder and fry to brown garlic lightly.

Add the meat, cinnamon, cloves, peppercorns, cardamom pods, nutmeg, and mace and fry until the meat mixture is a reddish brown. Stir frequently. If needed, sprinkle with a few drops of water.

Beat yogurt lightly. Mix the yogurt, cream, and water together and stir into the meat mixture. Bring slowly to a boil, lower heat, and simmer, covered, about 35 to 40 minutes. Remove from heat and leave the pot covered.

Wash the rice and soak it in enough water to cover.

Remove the meat from the stock and set both aside separately.

Wash and dry the pot, or in another 5-quart pot, heat 2½ tablespoons *ghee.* Fry the meat until it looks reddish. Remove and set aside.

Drain the rice and fry it in the same pot for 3 to 4 minutes. Add the stock with enough water to equal 4 cups liquid and bring to a boil. Lower heat and simmer, covered, 10 to 12 minutes.

Meanwhile, soak the saffron threads in the hot water.

Heat 2 tablespoons *ghee* in a skillet and fry the remaining 1 cup sliced onions until reddish brown and crisp. Remove with a slotted spoon and place in a small bowl. Fry the almonds and raisins until they are lightly browned. Add a little *ghee* if needed. Remove and set aside with the onions.

Uncover the rice and spoon out more than half of it. Sprinkle a few drops of the dissolved saffron threads on the rice remaining in the pot. Add a layer of meat. Top this with a layer of rice and saffron threads. Again add a layer of meat, then a final layer of rice and sprinkle saffron threads on top. Sprinkle the fried onions, almonds, and raisins over the rice. Cover the pot tightly and place over very low heat until the rice is cooked (about 20 to 25 minutes).

Serves 6

Remarks

This festive dish was often prepared for us by Babuji on our birthdays or other special occasions. For a family meal we savored its rich flavor with just a raita *and chutney to accompany it.*

Tehri

Lightly Spiced Rice with Hard-Cooked Eggs

2½ cups long grain brown rice	1¾ cups finely sliced onions
3¾ cups water	½ teaspoon turmeric powder
8 eggs	⅛ to ¼ teaspoon chili powder
4½ tablespoons vegetable oil	6 to 8 *kardi patta*, curry leaves

Wash the rice and place it in a 4-quart pot with the water. Bring the water to a boil, reduce heat to low, and simmer, covered, until the water evaporates. Remove from heat and keep rice warm.

Meanwhile, boil the eggs for about 7 to 8 minutes in enough water to cover them. Then remove shells and set aside.

In a 5-quart pot with a heavy base and tight-fitting lid, heat the oil. Fry the onions until they become golden brown. Add the turmeric powder, chili powder, and curry leaves and stir 2 to 3 minutes.

Carefully add the cooked eggs and fry 2 to 3 minutes over moderately high heat. Stir gently. The eggs should become a yellow brown.

Scoop the rice out of its pan and spoon it into the egg mixture. Stir gently so as not to break the eggs. Sprinkle a tablespoon of water on top of the rice and cover very tightly.

Place a *tava* or griddle over moderately high heat and place the tightly covered pan of rice on top of the *tava* until the rice is cooked (about 5 minutes). Serve immediately.

Serves 6

Remarks

In Shillong, Asho used to make Tehri *for us using* kathal *(jack fruit) seeds instead of the eggs.*

When making Tehri, *it is important that you do not completely cook the rice in the first stage of preparation. It will cook by the process of "dum" (in its own natural juices over very low heat). This happens when we add the rice to the egg mixture and remove the pan from direct heat.*

We serve Tehri *with a raita, or Dahi Bara, Deep-Fried Rissoles Made from Lentils, in Yogurt (see Index). It is a wonderful dish to make when you are in a hurry, since it takes only 30 minutes to prepare.*

dairy-based dishes and raitas

Chenna Aur Tinday Ki Halki Sabzi

Lightly Curried Homemade Cheese and Frizzle Squash

8 cups milk

¾ cup well-mixed Homemade Yogurt (see page 41)

3 tablespoons lemon juice

1 pound white frizzle squash (about 3)

4½ tablespoons vegetable oil

½ cup minced onions

¼ cup grated onions

1 tablespoon plus 1½ teaspoons coriander powder

2½ teaspoons cumin powder

¼ teaspoon turmeric powder

¼ teaspoon chili powder

1¼ cups chopped tomatoes

4 tablespoons minced onion shoots

1 or 2 small green chilies

3 tablespoons chopped coriander leaves or parsley

Bring the milk to a boil in a heavy 5-quart pot. Lower heat and quickly stir in the yogurt and lemon juice. Continue stirring until the milk curdles and forms small lumps of white cheese. The rest of the milk will turn into a watery, light-colored liquid. Remove from heat.

Place a clean cloth over a 3-quart pot. Strain the curdled milk through the cloth so that the cheese *(chenna)* collects in the cloth and the liquid collects in the pot below. Loosely tie the cloth and allow the cheese to drain.

Dice the frizzle squash, including seeds, and set aside. If the squash is tough, use only the soft parts. You should have about 2¾ cups of squash.

In a 5-quart pot, heat the oil and fry the onions until golden brown. Stir occasionally. Add the coriander powder, cumin powder, turmeric powder, and chili powder and fry over medium heat 3 to 4 minutes. Stir in the tomatoes and cook until they are soft and pulpy.

Add the squash, 1 cup of the reserved liquid, and onion shoots. Stir over moderately high heat until the liquid is bubbling. Cover and cook until the squash is tender (about 12 to 15 minutes).

Break up the larger lumps of the *chenna* with your fingers as you add it to the pot. Add another cup of the reserved liquid, chilies, and coriander leaves and bring to a boil. Reduce heat to low and simmer 2 minutes before serving.

Serves 6

Remarks

Serve with rice and a "hot" chutney.

Kailay Ka Raita

Yogurt with Banana and Nuts

2½ cups thick, Homemade Yogurt (see page 41)

1¾ tablespoons melted *ghee* (see page 40) or butter

⅔ teaspoon black or red mustard seeds

1 tablespoon plus ¾ teaspoon minced unsalted, skinned peanuts

2 to 3 teaspoons minced small green chilies

½ teaspoon cumin seeds

3 medium-size firm bananas (about 7 or 8 inches long)

1 tablespoon chopped coriander leaves

1½ teaspoons vegetable oil

2 tablespoons almond slivers

½ teaspoon *garam masalla,* a spice mixture (see page 42)

Beat the yogurt lightly with a fork and set aside.

In a small skillet, heat the *ghee* and fry the mustard seeds. When they begin to sputter, add the peanuts. Fry 1 minute, while stirring, over moderate heat. Add the green chilies and cumin seeds, stir, and reduce heat to low.

Peel and cut 2½ bananas into ¼-inch slices. Gently stir them into the skillet and then remove from heat.

In a serving bowl, lightly mix together the yogurt, the contents of the skillet, and the coriander leaves.

In another small skillet, heat the vegetable oil and stirring frequently, fry the almond slivers until they become golden brown. Drain off any surplus oil and stir the almonds into the *raita* (the yogurt mixture).

Heat a *tava* or griddle and, stirring often, fry the *garam masalla* until lightly browned. (This will take just a few seconds.) Immediately remove from heat and sprinkle over the *raita* as a garnish.

Remarks:

When you want to add a quick Indian touch to a non-Indian meal, try this raita.

Kheeray Ka Raita

Spicy Yogurt with Cucumber

1 large cucumber (about ¾ pound)	1 teaspoon cumin seeds
2¾ cups thick Homemade Yogurt (see 41)	½ teaspoon *garam masalla,* a spice mixture (see 42)
¼ to ½ teaspoon freshly ground black pepper	
2 small green chilies, chopped	
3 tablespoons chopped coriander leaves or parsley	

Wash and peel the cucumber. Grate coarsely. Squeeze a handful at a time and discard the surplus liquid.

In a large bowl, beat the yogurt thoroughly.

Mix together the cucumber, yogurt, and black pepper.

Transfer the mixture to a serving bowl and sprinkle with chilies and coriander leaves.

Heat a *tava* or griddle and roast the cumin seeds over moderate heat until lightly browned (about 30 seconds). Then grind the seeds coarsely.

On a hot *tava* or griddle, roast the *garam masalla* a few seconds and sprinkle it with the cumin over the yogurt as a garnish.

Serves 6

Remarks

Raita *is served as an accompaniment to any kind of meal. Only a small quantity is needed for each serving.*

Lauki Ka Raita

Yogurt with Curried Garden Marrow

2¾ cups garden marrow or yellow squash	¼ cup water
2 tablespoons vegetable oil	¼ teaspoon *garam masalla,* a spice mixture (see page 42)
1 teaspoon scraped and grated ginger	2½ cups Homemade Yogurt (see page 41)
¾ teaspoon minced garlic	2 tablespoons chopped coriander leaves or watercress
1 teaspoon cumin seeds	
1 to 2 small green chilies, chopped (optional)	

Wash the garden marrow and cut it into very small pieces.

In a skillet heat the oil. Fry the ginger and garlic over moderate heat until light brown (about 2 to 3 minutes). Stir in the cumin seeds and chilies (if used) and fry 1 minute.

Add the garden marrow and fry about 3 minutes. Stir occasionally. Add the water, stir well, and cook, covered, 8 to 10 minutes.

Uncover and add the *garam masalla.* Stir occasionally until the water evaporates.

Combine the cooked garden marrow and yogurt. Stir thoroughly. Transfer the mixture to a serving bowl, garnish with coriander leaves, and chill before serving.

Serves 6

Tamatar Raita

Yogurt with Tomatoes

1 tablespoon vegetable oil

⅛ teaspoon *heeng,* asafetida

1 teaspoon *chana daal,* a lentil, or peanuts, each split into 4 pieces

½ tablespoon scraped and finely sliced ginger

½ to ¾ cup finely chopped spring onions

1 cup finely chopped tomatoes

3 cups thick Homemade Yogurt (see page 41)

½ teaspoon *garam masalla,* a spice mixture (see page 42)

2 tablespoons chopped green coriander leaves

1 to 3 small green chilies, chopped (optional)

Heat the oil, drop in the asafetida, and then immediately add the *daal.* Fry 2 minutes. Add the ginger and fry 2 to 3 minutes. Stir in the onions and fry 1 minute. Stir in the tomatoes and remove from the heat.

Beat the yogurt well and stir into the fried tomato mixture. Transfer to a serving bowl.

Heat a *tava* or griddle and roast the *garam masalla* until an aroma becomes apparent (about 3 to 5 seconds). Stir into the mixture.

Garnish with coriander leaves and chilies (if used). Chill before serving.

Serves 6

Remarks

Generally, a raita *does not taste as well if it is kept for longer than a day. It is meant to be served fresh, only slightly chilled before serving.*

A raita *is a delightful addition to most meals.*

Matar Panir I

Lightly Curried Homemade Cheese and Peas

8 cups water

3 cups low-fat powdered milk

1 cup well-mixed Homemade Yogurt (see page 41)

3 tablespoons lemon juice

2 medium-size tomatoes

½ pound shelled peas, fresh or frozen

5 tablespoons vegetable oil

½ cup grated onions

¼ cup minced onions

1 tablespoon scraped and grated ginger

¾ tablespoon minced garlic

1 teaspoon turmeric powder

¼ to ½ teaspoon chili powder

2 tablespoons chopped coriander leaves

Bring the water to a boil in a heavy-bottomed 5-quart pot. Stir in the powdered milk with a wire whisk. Return to a boil. Quickly stir in the yogurt and lemon juice, and continue stirring until the milk becomes a watery liquid with little lumps of cheese forming. Remove from heat.

Place a clean cloth over another container and strain the curdled milk into the cloth, so that the cheese will collect in the cloth and the liquid will collect in the container. Set the liquid aside.

Tie the cheese and hang it up for 15 minutes to allow it to drain. Squeeze gently with your fingers to remove any remaining liquid and place the cheese, still inside the cloth, on a wooden board. Flatten the cheese as much as possible by pressing down and spreading it, without allowing it to break. Fold a layer of cloth over the cheese and place a pan over both the cloth and the cheese. Put a heavy weight in the pan and allow the cheese to further flatten and form for about 45 minutes to 1 hour. You will have about ½ pound cheese.

Meanwhile, in a saucepan, bring the tomatoes, peas, and 1 cup of the reserved liquid to a boil. Reduce heat to low and simmer, covered, 15 minutes. Remove from heat. Remove the tomatoes from the pan, peel, and pass through a sieve by pressing down with a flat utensil: Collect the pureed tomato.

In a large skillet, heat the oil and fry the onions until they are a light brown. Add the ginger, garlic, turmeric powder, chili powder and 2 tablespoons of the reserved liquid and fry until the mixture is evenly browned (about 4 or 5 minutes). Stir in the tomato puree and cook over moderate heat until the tomatoes and spices are well blended and a thick paste is formed (about 10 minutes).

Add the peas and their cooking liquid to the tomatoes. Add another 1½ cups of the reserved liquid and coriander leaves and cook 1 minute.

Cut the block of cheese into ¾-inch cubes and then add to the skillet. Bring the *Matar Panir* to a boil, stir, remove from the heat, and serve hot.

Serves 6

Remarks

Matar Panir I, *Lightly Curried Homemade Cheese and Peas (see Index), is a typical north Indian favorite. Zainab Bi taught my mother this recipe. We prefer it to the better-known* Matar Panir II, *Curried Homemade Cheese and Peas (see Index). Serve with either rice or* rotis, *or both.*

Matar Panir II

Curried Homemade Cheese and Peas

8 cups water	¾ tablespoon minced garlic
3 cups powdered non-fat milk	1 tablespoon coriander powder
1 cup well-mixed Homemade Yogurt (see page 41)	1 teaspoon cumin powder
3 tablespoons lemon juice	1 teaspoon turmeric powder
7 tablespoons vegetable oil	½ to 1 teaspoon chili powder
½ cups grated onions	2 cups minced tomatoes
¼ cups minced onions	½ pound shelled peas, fresh or frozen
¾ tablespoon scraped and peeled ginger	2 to 3 tablespoons chopped coriander leaves

Bring the water to a boil in a heavy 5-quart pot. Stir in the powdered milk with a wire whisk. Return to a boil. Quickly stir in the yogurt and lemon juice and continue stirring until the milk becomes a watery liquid with little lumps of cheese forming. Remove from heat.

Place a clean cloth over another container and strain the curdled milk into the cloth, so that the cheese will collect in the cloth and the liquid will collect in the container. Set the liquid aside.

Tie the cheese and hang it up for 15 minutes to allow it to drain. Squeeze gently with your fingers to remove any remaining liquid and place the cheese, still inside the cloth, on a wooden board. Flatten the cheese as much as possible by pressing down and spreading it, without allowing it to break. Fold a layer of cloth over the cheese and then place a pan over both the cloth and the cheese. Put a heavy weight into the pan and allow the cheese to further flatten and form for about 3 hours. You will have about ½ pound of cheese.

When the cheese is well flattened, cut it into 1-inch cubes. Heat 2 tablespoons oil in a large skillet and fry the cubes of cheese until they are a golden brown. Remove from skillet and set aside.

Add the remaining oil to the skillet and fry the onions until they are a light brown. Add the ginger and garlic and fry until the mixture is a golden brown. Add the coriander powder, cumin powder, turmeric powder, and chili powder and fry 2 minutes over moderately high heat.

Stir in the tomatoes and fry until they are well mashed and oil appears at the sides of the pan.

Add 2½ cups of the reserved liquid, and the peas and simmer until the peas are tender. Carefully add the fried cheese cubes and coriander leaves and simmer about 5 to 10 minutes before serving.

Serves 6

Remarks

Matar panir *is such a well-loved, nutritious dish, that I have included 2 versions. It is a special favorite with vegetarians. Serve with either rice or* rotis, *or both.*

Saadi Kardi, Haray Pyaz Kay Saath

A Yogurt and Chick-Pea Flour Based Curry with Spring Onions

½ cup *besan,* chick-pea flour

5½ cups water

1¼ cups Homemade Yogurt (see page 41)

4 *kardi patta,* curry leaves

1 tablespoon scraped and finely grated ginger

½ tablespoon finely grated garlic

½ teaspoon turmeric powder

2 small green chilies

¼ teaspoon chili powder

⅛ teaspoon *heeng,* asafetida

1½ tablespoons vegetable oil

pinch of *heeng,* asafetida

½ teaspoon black or red mustard seeds

¾ teaspoon cumin seeds

4 to 6 dried red chilies (optional)

½ cup finely chopped spring onions

Thoroughly mix the chick-pea flour with ½ cup of water. Begin with 2 tablespoons of water and gradually add the rest of the ½ cup. Stir continuously. Beat the yogurt and stir it into the chick-pea flour. Pour the mixture into a heavy 5-quart pot. Gradually add the remaining 5 cups of water. Stir vigorously.

Add the curry leaves, ginger, garlic, turmeric powder, green chilies, chili powder, and the ⅛ teaspoon asafetida. Stir well, and bring to a boil. Immediately remove from the heat, stir the *kardi* thoroughly, return to low heat, and cook, covered, for about 1 hour, 15 minutes. Stir occasionally. Turn heat to moderate and cook, uncovered, until the *kardi* thickens (about 15 to 25 minutes). Stir occasionally.

Heat the oil in a small skillet and drop in a pinch of asafetida. Add the mustard seeds and when they begin to sputter, stir in the cumin seeds and red chilies (if used) and cook ½ minute. Add the spring onions, stir for a few seconds, and pour the entire contents of the skillet into the *kardi* pot. Stir again, simmer 2 minutes, and serve.

Serves 6 to 8

Remarks

Serve kardi *hot as an accompaniment to a rice preparation—preferably plain boiled rice.*

breads

Adai

Pancakes Made from Mixed Lentils and Rice

½ cup *arhar daal,* a lentil

½ cup *safed urad daal,* a lentil

2 cups long grain brown rice

5 cups water

¼ cup chick-peas

1-inch piece ginger, scraped and chopped

1 cup minced onions

¼ teaspoon *heeng,* asafetida

4 tablespoons chopped coriander leaves or parsley

½ cup grated coconut

½ cup water

1 tablespoon lemon juice

1 to 3 small green chilies, minced (optional)

½ teaspoon coarsely crushed dry red chilies or ¾ teaspoon freshly ground black pepper

4 to 6 tablespoons coconut oil or vegetable oil

Remove stones from the *daals.* Wash the *arhar* and *urad daals* together in a pan two or three times. (Discard the water and use clean water each time.) Rub the *daals* between your fingers lightly as you wash. Do the same with the rice. Soak the *daals* and rice together with about 4 cups cold water for 3 hours. If you find the *daals* have swollen to above the water level, add more water to cover them.

Wash the chick-peas well and soak them in about 1 cup of water.

After 3 hours of soaking, spoon a quarter of the *daals* and rice into a blender with some of the chick-peas and part of the ginger. Blend until the mixture is reduced to a puree. Scoop the mixture into a large bowl. Repeat this process until the *daals,* rice, chick-peas, and ginger are all pureed. If blending is difficult, add a teaspoon of water at a time, stir gently, and blend.

Cover the bowl and let the mixture ferment for 4 to 5 hours for best results. If you are pressed for time, allow to ferment for at least an hour.

Add the onions, asafetida, coriander leaves, coconut, ½ cup water, lemon juice, green chilies (if used), and red chilies and mix thoroughly to form a thick batter. Stir in 1 tablespoon water if the batter won't slip off the spoon easily.

In a large skillet, heat 1 tablespoon of oil. Tilt the skillet to allow the oil to evenly coat the surface. (I use 2 skillets simultaneously so that I can cook about 3 or 4 *adais* in each skillet at the same time.) Using a ⅓ cup measure, drop batter into the skillet and spread it until it is a circular shape, about 4 to 5 inches in diameter, or an oval shape. Fry over moderate heat until browned (about 5 minutes). Turn over and spoon another 1 to 2 teaspoons of oil around the edge. After 1 minute, lift the skillet and gently shake it so that oil spreads under the *adai.* Cook until the second side is also golden brown.

Yields 14 to 16 *adais*

Remarks

Serve hot with Nariyal Chutney I *(Coconut Chutney with Yogurt),* Pudina Chutney *(Mint Chutney), or* Dhania Chutney *(Fresh Coriander Chutney). See Index for these recipes.*

This nutritious "bread" can make a full meal served with a yogurt dish and a vegetable; or you may wish to serve it as a snack, in which case smaller adais *may be more convenient.*

Bhatura

A Leavened, Deep-Fried Bread

4 cups whole wheat flour

2 teaspoons baking soda

1 cup plus 2 tablespoons thick Homemade
Yogurt (see page 41)

1 or 2 eggs

3 tablespoons melted *ghee* (see page 40) or
vegetable oil

1 teaspoon honey

3 to 4 cups vegetable oil for deep frying

Warm the flour slightly in an oven on very low heat. In a large mixing bowl, sift the flour and baking soda together.

Warm the yogurt slightly and beat it until it is smooth. Set 4 tablespoons aside and pour the rest into the middle of the flour.   .

Add 1 egg, 1 tablespoon melted ghee, and honey to the flour. Mix together and gather into one mass. If the particles won't adhere, add the reserved yogurt gradually until one solid mass is formed. If more liquid is required, add the remaining egg.

Dip your fingers into the melted *ghee* and knead the dough on a lightly floured surface. Knead until the dough becomes soft and pliable (about 5 to 10 minutes). Gather the dough into a large ball and place it in a large bowl. Smear the remaining *ghee* on the top of the dough and cover with a dampened cloth. Allow the dough to rise in a warm place for at least 3 hours.

Heat the oil in a *karhai* or wok. Separate the dough into 24 portions. Shape each portion into a ball, then flatten. Roll out each flattened ball until 4½ to 5½ inches in diameter. While you work, keep the rolled out *bhaturas* covered with a slightly dampened cloth to prevent them from drying.

When the oil is almost at smoking point, reduce the heat to moderate. Slide the first *bhatura* into the oil. When the lower side becomes a deep golden brown (about 1 minute), turn over with a slotted spatula. Cook the second side until golden brown (about 1 minute). It will puff up by itself during the cooking. Remove from oil and place in a dish lined with thick paper toweling. Continue until all the *bhaturas* are fried, alternating the heat between high and moderately high as you cook.

Yields 24 *bhaturas*

Remarks

Bhaturas *are at their best if served immediately. However, they are very good even if cooked ahead and reheated in a moderate oven before serving.*

They are traditionally served with a potato or dark chick-pea curry (see Index for Appi Kay Aloo, *Appi's Potato Curry with Raw Mangoes, and* Sukha Kala Chana, *Dry Curried Dark Chick-Peas) and are often served as a teatime snack or at a leisurely family breakfast.*

If you serve a rice dish as well, each person will require 2 Bhaturas, *at the most, for a serving. You can freeze the rest in plastic wrap and warm them in a moderate oven before serving.*

We make Bhaturas *with white flour in India. Since whole wheat flour is heavier, you will need to press down firmly with the rolling pin when rolling them out. You will find them well worth the effort!*

Dosa

Thin Ground Rice and Lentil Bread

1½ cups long grain brown rice

4¾ cups cold water

½ cup *safed urad daal,* a lentil

2 tablespoons scraped and finely chopped ginger

3 tablespoons chopped coriander leaves

1 small green chili, minced (optional)

4 to 5 tablespoons *ghee* (see page 40) or vegetable oil

Wash the rice and soak in 2½ cups cold water for at least 3 hours.

Remove any stones or sticks from the *daal* and wash 2 or 3 times. Soak in 2 cups clean cold water for at least 3 hours.

Drain the rice. Reserve the soaking water. Place the rice in a blender, add ½ cup of the reserved water, and blend until the rice is ground to a puree. Set aside in a bowl.

Drain the *daal.* Reserve the soaking water. Place the *daal* in the blender, add ½ cup of its soaking water, and blend until the *daal* becomes a thick batter. Add it to the rice, cover the bowl securely with a thick damp cloth, and allow the mixture to ferment for at least 12 hours.

When ready to cook, add the ginger, coriander leaves, chili (if used), and ¼ cup cold water to the mixture and stir well. You will now have a thin batter.

Heat ½ teaspoon *ghee* in a medium-size heavy skillet over moderate heat. Put in about ⅓ cup of the batter and tilt the skillet from side to side to spread it evenly into a thin, flat bread, about 6 to 6½ inches in diameter. Let it cook until you see bubbles forming on top (about 2 to 3 minutes). Dribble ½ teaspoon *ghee* over the top and sides and turn the *dosa* over. Cook 1½ minutes until the *dosa* is lightly browned (about another 1½ minutes).

Lift the *dosa* onto a heated serving dish and keep covered until all the *dosas* are made and you are ready to serve. They are at their best when served immediately.

Yields 10 to 12 *dosas*

Remarks

This great south Indian favorite has become popular all over India. It is traditionally served with Nariyal Chutney I, Coconut Chutney with Yogurt, and Sambar, Lentils with Vegetables (see Index).

If you wish to make stuffed dosas, omit the spices from the batter. After the dosas are cooked, place some potato stuffing, Alu, Dosay Kay Liyay (see Index), in the middle of each one and fold the two edges over it as you would a stuffed crepe. Serve with the same accompaniments as for Dosa.

Gobi Paratha

Whole Wheat Bread with Spicy Cauliflower Stuffing

1½	cups *ghee* (see page 40) or butter	
5	cups whole wheat flour	
3	cups water	
1	large cauliflower (about 2 pounds)	
½	cup minced onions	
2	tablespoons minced garlic	

1 tablespoon coarsely crushed cumin seeds

2 tablespoons scraped and minced ginger

1½ tablespoons minced small green chilies

1 teaspoon turmeric powder

⅛ to ¼ teaspoon chili powder (optional)

1 tablespoon lemon juice (optional)

In a medium-size mixing bowl, rub 4 tablespoons *ghee* into the flour with your fingertips until there are no lumps left. Pour 1½ cups of water into the flour and quickly knead. If you cannot gather the mixture into a large ball, add more water gradually, a tablespoon at a time. I usually need about 2 cups plus 2 to 3 tablespoons water.

Sprinkle a little flour on a board and knead the dough until it is pliable and smooth (about 7 to 10 minutes). Gather into a ball and place in a bowl. Sprinkle 2 tablespoons of water on top and cover tightly. Allow the dough to rest for at least 30 minutes.

Wash the cauliflower thoroughly and chop into very tiny pieces, removing only the tougher parts of the stem.

Heat 3½ tablespoons *ghee* in a saucepan and fry the onions and garlic until they are lightly browned. Stir in the cauliflower, cumin seeds, ginger, chilies, turmeric powder, and chili powder (if used). Cover tightly and cook until the cauliflower is tender but not mushy (about 10 to 12 minutes). Stir in lemon juice (if used).

Knead the dough lightly for a few seconds and divide into 12 portions. Divide the cauliflower into 12 portions also.

On a lightly floured surface, roll one portion of dough into a round about 6 to 8 inches in diameter. Place a portion of cauliflower filling in the middle. Gather the edges together in a pleating fashion, pressing the dough lightly to enclose the cauliflower filling. Carefully pat the stuffed ball that is now formed to flatten it as much as possible. Sprinkle ½ teaspoon flour on top and gently roll out the *paratha* until it is betweeen 7 to 8 inches in diameter. Repeat this process until all the *parathas* are made. As you work, keep the dough and the rolled out *parathas* covered with a lightly dampened cloth to retain pliability.

Heat a *tava*, griddle, or cast-iron skillet, then adjust heat to moderate. Place a *paratha* on the tava, dribble 1 teaspoon *ghee* around the edge, and cook 1½ minutes. Turn over, dribble more *ghee* around the edge, and cook for another 1½ minutes. Then dribble ¾ to 1 teaspoon *ghee* on the surface of the *paratha*, turn over, and allow to become golden brown. Dribble ¾ to 1 teaspoon *ghee* on the second surface, turn over again, and cook until the *paratha* is brown. Remove from the *tava* and keep in a warmed dish, covered, until all the *parathas* are ready to serve. Wipe the skillet after each one is cooked.

Yields 12 *parathas*

Remarks

Serve warm with plain yogurt or a raita *and a chutney.*

Khamiri Roti

Whole Wheat, Leavened, Quick-Baked Bread

1 tablespoon whole wheat pastry flour or whole wheat flour

10 tablespoons well-mixed Homemade Yogurt (see page 41)

1 tablespoon honey

3¾ cups whole wheat flour

1½ teaspoons baking powder

½ teaspoon baking soda

2 tablespoons oil

1 cup milk

1 tablespoon lemon juice (optional)

To make the starter, mix thoroughly the pastry flour, 2 tablespoons yogurt, and ½ tablespoon honey and leave covered overnight.

In a large mixing bowl, sift the whole wheat flour, baking powder, and baking soda together. Add the oil and ½ tablespoon honey to the flour.

Warm the remaining 8 tablespoons yogurt, beat slightly, and pour into the center of the flour. Mix in the starter. Warm the milk and pour ¾ cup of the milk into the flour. Mix together and form into a large mass. Add more milk and lemon juice (if used) if needed to form the dough.

On a lightly floured surface, knead the dough until soft and pliable. Gather into a ball, place in a large bowl, and brush 2 tablespoons milk over the surface. Cover with a dampened cloth and let rise for at least 3 hours in a warm place. In winter let rise at least 5 hours.

Lightly knead the dough again and separate into 18 portions. Shape each one into a ball, flatten between your palms, and roll into a round or a teardrop shape. The rounds will be about 4½ inches in diameter. The teardrops will be about 6 inches long—4 inches at the base and tapered at the tip.

Preheat the oven to 350°F and heat 3 baking sheets, each 11 × 17 inches. Place the rolled *rotis* on the warmed baking sheets and bake 6 to 8 minutes. Turn the *rotis* over and bake another 5 to 6 minutes. They should puff up and become a golden brown with some darker spots.

Yields 18 *rotis*

Remarks

We serve this nourishing roti *with* pasanday, korma, *or any meat curry.*

Keema Vali Khamiri Roti

A Bread Stuffed with Minced Meat

1 cup whole wheat flour

1 cup whole wheat pastry flour

4½ tablespoons thick Homemade Yogurt (see page 41)

½ tablespoon granular yeast

1 egg

2 tablespoons melted *ghee* (see page 40) or vegetable oil

2 tablespoons honey

6 tablespoons warm water

½ pound lean round of lamb, minced

¼ teaspoon black pepper

¼ cup plus 2 tablespoons water

2 tablespoons vegetable oil

1 cup finely chopped onions

1 tablespoon scraped and chopped ginger

1 tablespoon chopped garlic

1 green chili, chopped (optional)

¼ teaspoon chili powder

¼ teaspoon turmeric powder

½ teaspoon *garam masalla,* a spice mixture (see page 42)

1 to 2 tablespoons chopped green coriander leaves

½ to 1 tablespoon lemon juice

1 teaspoon *kelonji,* onion seeds, or cumin seeds

Sift together the whole wheat flour and whole wheat pastry flour. Beat yogurt lightly. Mix together the yeast, yogurt, egg, 1 tablespoon *ghee,* and honey. Pour the yeast mixture into the flour with the warm water and mix until a mass of dough is formed. Knead well for 8 to 15 minutes. Cover with a dampened cloth and let rise in a warm place for at least 1 hour.

In a saucepan, bring the minced meat to a boil with pepper and ¼ cup plus 2 tablespoons water. Lower heat and simmer, covered, 20 to 30 minutes.

In a large skillet, heat 2 tablespoons oil and fry onions in oil 2 to 3 minutes. Add ginger, garlic, and chili and continue to fry 3 minutes over moderately high heat. Add the chili powder, turmeric powder, and *garam masalla* and fry another minute. Add the cooked meat, with liquid, and fry until the water evaporates. Add the coriander leaves and lemon juice, stir, and remove from heat. Set aside.

Divide the dough into 12 equal sections. Flatten between the palms of your hands to form rounds about 4 to 5 inches in diameter. Place one section flat on a plate or board and place a heaping tablespoon of meat over the surface and spread evenly to within ½ inch of the entire edge. Then moisten the edge with water. Flatten another section of dough to the same size and place it on top of the meat filling. Press the edges of both sections firmly to seal. Press and pull gently to form a circle 5 to 5½ inches in diameter or to form an oval shape. Repeat this process until you have 6 stuffed *rotis.*

Dip your fingers in 1 tablespoon melted *ghee* and lightly apply to both sides of the *roti.* Dip your fingers in a plate with the onion seeds and apply to the lightly greased *roti.* The seeds will stick to the surface.

Preheat the oven to 375°F. Bake until the rotis are golden brown (about 5 to 9 minutes on each side).

Yields 6 *rotis*

Remarks

The kelonji *give this dish a very distinctive taste.*

Makkay Ki Roti

Cornmeal Bread

4 cups cornmeal	⅓ to ½ cup minced onions
3 to 3½ cups very warm water	1 cup water
1¼ teaspoons *ajwain,* oregano seeds	8 tablespoons *ghee* (see page 40) or butter

Mix together the cornmeal, 3 cups water, oregano seeds, and onions. Add more water gradually, if needed, to form mixture into a loose ball. The mixture need not form a regular dough, but the particles should be able to adhere together.

Warm a *tava* or griddle over moderate heat. Place a small bowl of water at a convenient spot near the *tava.*

Form ⅓ cup of the corn mixture into a round patty in your palm. (You should have 12 portions.) Place the corn patty in the middle of the *tava,* dip your fingers in the water, and quickly spread the *roti* until it is between 5 to 6 inches in diameter and about ¼ inch thick. Cook 4 to 5 minutes. Carefully lift the *roti* and turn it over, using your fingers to help you. Let it cook another 4 to 5 minutes.

Pour 1 teaspoon of melted *ghee* around the edges of the *roti* and spread 1 teaspoon *ghee* evenly over its surface. Turn the heat to moderately high and let the *roti* become a golden brown underneath. Turn and lightly brown the other side. Remove from *tava* and keep warm until you have cooked all the *rotis.*

Yields 12 *rotis*

Remarks

A meal of **Makkay Ki Roti** *and* Saag, *Spicy Mixed Greens, Pureed (see Index) is very popular in the Punjab and United Provinces of India and one for which an Indian feels homesick.*

Roti *is at its best when served immediately with a dab of butter on top.*

If you wish to serve them for a party, plan to make them ahead of time and keep in a warm oven wrapped in foil.

Muli Paratha

Whole Wheat Bread with Spicy Daikon Filling

5 cups whole wheat flour	3 tablespoons lemon juice
1½ cups *ghee* (see page 40) or butter	1 tablespoon minced small green chilies
3 cups water	1 teaspoon *garam masalla,* a spice mixture (see page 42) or allspice
2 pounds white radishes	
1 teaspoon *ajwain,* oregano seeds	

Mix together (using your fingers) the flour and 4 tablespoons *ghee* until there are no lumps left. Pour 1½ cups water into the flour and knead quickly. If the particles of flour do not adhere together and form one solid mass, then gradually add water, 1 tablespoon at a time, until a solid dough is formed. I usually use about 2 cups.

On a lightly floured surface, knead the dough until it is soft and pliable. Gather the dough into a ball and place it in a bowl. Sprinkle 2 tablespoons water over the top, cover tightly, and set aside for at least 30 minutes.

Wash and scrub the white radishes thoroughly. Grate coarsely and drain in a colander. Then squeeze thoroughly to extract surplus liquid and place in a bowl.

Heat 2 teaspoons *ghee* in a small skillet and fry the oregano seeds for a few seconds. Remove from heat and add to the radishes with the lemon juice, chilies, and *garam masalla.* Mix well and set aside.

Knead the dough lightly for a few seconds and divide into 24 portions. Divide the radish filling into 12 portions.

On a large, lightly floured surface, roll out the dough portions, one by one, until each is between 7 to 8 inches in diameter. Keep a lightly dampened cloth over the dough and the rolled *parathas* as you work.

To make a stuffed *paratha,* spread one portion of the filling evenly over one rolled *paratha,* leaving a ½-inch margin along the edge. Moisten the edge with water, place another rolled *paratha* on top, and press the edges of the two together to seal. You will make one stuffed *paratha* using two rolled out portions of dough. Repeat this process until you make twelve.

Heat a *tava,* griddle, or cast-iron skillet, then adjust the heat to moderate. Place a *paratha* on the *tava.* Dribble 1 teaspoon *ghee* along the edge of the *paratha* but on the surface of the skillet. Cook 1½ minutes. Turn over, dribble more *ghee* around the edge, and cook until a golden brown (about another 1½ minutes). Then dribble ¾ to 1 teaspoon *ghee* on the surface of the *paratha,* turn over, and cook until golden brown. Dribble ¾ to 1 teaspoon *ghee* on the second surface, turn over again, and cook until evenly browned. Remove from *tava* and place in a warmed dish, covered, until all the *parathas* are ready to serve. Wipe skillet after each one is cooked to prevent browned particles from sticking to the *parathas.*

Yields 12 large *parathas,* 7 to 8 inches in diameter

Remarks

Muli Paratha *is a typical Punjabi dish but popular in Utter Pradesh as well. Different stuffings, such as cooked potatoes, minced meat, or lentils can be used.*

Parathas *are served warm with plain yogurt or a* raita *and a chutney. If you wish to serve them later, wrap them in foil and warm for a few minutes in the oven before serving.*

I usually cook 2 parathas at the same time on 2 different tavas, *making them as I go along. I make 2, begin to cook them, then roll and make up 2 more while the first 2 are cooking. You can do this, too, with a little practice.*

Since stuffed parathas *take some time to prepare, do not plan to serve them for a large party!*

Naan

Leavened, Baked Whole Wheat Bread

4 cups minus 2 tablespoons whole wheat flour

1 tablespoon baking powder

¼ teaspoon baking soda

2 eggs

1¼ cups plus 2 tablespoons milk

2 tablespoons Homemade Yogurt (see page 41)

2 tablespoons melted *ghee* (see page 40) or vegetable oil

1 teaspoon honey

4 tablespoons granular dry yeast

Sift flour, baking powder, and baking soda into a large mixing bowl. Make a depression in the center of the flour and drop in the eggs.

Warm the 1¼ cups milk and the yogurt in a small pan. Add the *ghee,* honey, and yeast. Pour the warmed mixture in the flour and mix well. Gather into a mass. If necessary, add more milk, 1 tablespoon at a time, until you can form a dough.

On a lightly floured surface, knead the dough until smooth and pliable (about 6 minutes). Gather into a ball and place in a large bowl. Brush the dough with 2 tablespoons milk, cover the bowl with a dampened cloth, and let rise in a warm place for about 3 hours.

When ready to bake, preheat the oven to 450°F and warm 3 baking sheets. Divide the dough into 20 portions and roll each one into a round, about 4½ to 5 inches in diameter and ¼ inch thick, or roll into a teardrop shape, about 5½ to 6 inches long—4 inches at the base and tapered at the top.

Arrange these *naans* side-by-side on the baking sheets and bake 5 minutes. Quickly turn them and bake another 3 minutes. They should be puffed and a golden brown with some darker brown spots. If not, bake another 1 to 2 minutes. Serve hot or at room temperature.

Yields 20 *naans*

Remarks

Naans *are similar to Middle Eastern breads and are typically north Indian. They are very easy to make and are a delightful addition to most meals—especially baked chicken,* Tandoori Murgh *and* Seekh Kababs, *Broiled Kabobs of Minced Meat and Spices (see Index).*

Puri II

Light-Colored, Deep-Fried Whole Wheat Bread

2½ cups whole wheat flour, sifted (1¾ cups after sifting)

1½ cups whole wheat pastry flour, sifted (¾ cup after sifting)

1 tablespoon and ½ teaspoon *ghee* (see page 40) or butter

¾ cup cold water

4 cups vegetable oil for deep frying

Sift the whole wheat flour through a fine sieve. Sift the whole wheat pastry flour in the same way. You will now have 2½ cups of fine sifted flour.

In a mixing bowl, mix the *ghee* with the flour. Use your fingers to rub the flour and *ghee* together lightly until there are no lumps left. Pour in water, a little at a time, while mixing, until you can form a mass of dough. Knead the dough on a flat surface until it is light and pliable (about 5 to 6 minutes). Gather the dough into a ball, place in a bowl, and cover with a metal or plastic bowl. Set aside for 30 minutes.

Separate the dough into 20 portions. Shape each portion into a ball and then flatten it into a patty (*puri*).

Begin to heat the oil in a *karhai* or wok over high heat. Roll out a few *puris* on a flat surface until they are 4½ inches in diameter.

Test the oil by dropping in a tiny piece of dough. If it comes to the surface immediately, the oil is ready for deep-frying the *puris*.

Slide a *puri* into the hot oil. In a few seconds, it will puff up and become round. Cook for about 4 to 6 seconds after it has puffed up, then turn it over, and cook the second side until a golden brown (about 4 to 6 seconds). Immediately lift the *puri* from the oil and drain on paper towels. Continue this procedure until all the *puris* are cooked. Serve warm or hot.

Yields 20 round *puris*

Remarks

Puris *are very easy to make and are quite versatile. They are made for various festivities all over India. Often a midday meal consists of* puri, alu bhaji *(a potato dish),* cholay *(made from chick-peas) or a* halva *(a Cream of Wheat pudding), and a vegetable dish.*

— *Sial Roti* —

A Sweet Bread of Ground Rice and Flour, Shaped Like Doughnuts

¾ cup long grain brown rice

1½ cups water

1 cup whole wheat flour

¾ teaspoon baking powder

⅓ cup Homemade Yogurt (see page 41)

¾ cup lukewarm water

3½ to 4 tablespoons honey

vegetable oil for deep frying

Wash the rice and soak it in 1½ cups water for at least 3 hours.

Drain the rice. Reserve the soaking water. Place the rice in a blender and blend with ⅓ cup of the soaking water until the rice is reduced to a paste. Add 1 to 2 tablespoons water if needed while blending.

In a bowl, mix thoroughly together the rice paste, flour, baking powder, yogurt, lukewarm water, and honey. Cover with a thick dampened cloth and allow to ferment overnight.

Begin to heat the oil in a *karhai* or wok over moderately high heat. Check the batter. If it is too thin, add a little more whole wheat flour to get the desired consistency.

Cut a tiny hole, less than ¼ inch square, in the middle of a thick, clean cloth about 9 inches square. (Or, use an icing tube with a round head, ¼ inch in diameter.) Spoon or pour about ½ cup batter into the cloth. Gather the cloth over the batter. Keeping one hand under the hole, position yourself over the oil. Gently squeeze and press the cloth, forcing the batter out of the whole and forming a circle about 2½ inches in diameter in the oil. Lift your hands and begin another circle. Cook the *rotis* until golden brown (about 8 to 10 minutes). Turn over and cook the other side until golden brown. Remove with a slotted spoon and drain on paper towels.

Yields 20 to 24 *sial rotis*

Remarks

Serve rotis *as an accompaniment to a meal, or as a snack. They are lovely warm or cold. When cool, they can be stored in an airtight container for about a week. Ours never last long; my children and their friends eat them as they are made.*

This recipe is an adaptation of Asho's Nepali Sial Roti.

chutneys

Baingun Ki Chutney

Eggplant Chutney

1 large eggplant (about 1 pound)	4 small pale green cardamom pods
4 tablespoons jaggery	1½-inch cinnamon stick
6 tablespoons white vinegar	6 whole cloves
12 to 14 large garlic cloves	16 to 20 peppercorns
1½-inch piece ginger	8 to 10 tablespoons vegetable oil
4 to 10 dried red chilies	1 teaspoon turmeric powder
1 to 2 tablespoons water	1½ tablespoons black or red mustard seeds

Wash the eggplant and cut into 1-inch cubes.

Mix together the jaggery and vinegar and set aside.

Grind the garlic cloves, ginger, and chilies together, adding water, and set aside.

Pound or grind the cardamom pods, cinnamon, cloves, and peppercorns using a mortar and pestle or coffee grinder and set aside.

Heat the oil in a 2-quart saucepan with a heavy bottom. Fry the garlic paste 3 to 5 minutes until the raw smell disappears and it is lightly browned. Add the turmeric powder and mustard seeds and fry over moderate heat 2 minutes. Add the eggplant, stir well, reduce heat to low, and cook, covered, 8 minutes. Stir again, cover, and cook until eggplant is tender. Stir in the jaggery and vinegar mixture and cook, covered, 5 minutes.

Uncover and simmer until the gravy is thick enough to coat a spoon.

Sprinkle the dry ground spices on top, stir, and remove from heat. Bottle when completely cool.

Yields about 1½ to 2 cups

Remarks

Baingun Ki Chutney *is a welcome addition to any meal. To savor its special flavor, we sometimes eat it with just a* roti *or rice.*

Dhania Chutney

Fresh Coriander Chutney

2 cups green coriander leaves with stems

1 cup coarsely chopped onions

1 tablespoon coarsely chopped garlic

2 to 3 tablespoons lemon juice

1 teaspoon honey

2 to 5 small green chilies, chopped

4 tablespoons grated coconut (optional)

Wash the coriander leaves thoroughly in a colander. Place in a blender and add the onions, garlic, lemon juice, honey, chilies, and coconut (if used). Blend for a few seconds. Scrape down the sides of the container. Blend again for a few seconds until the mixture is reduced to a puree. Add a little water if the puree is too thick.

Pour into a small serving bowl.

Yields 1 cup

Remarks

Serve Dhania Chutney *to accompany a meal, or serve it as a dip for* samosas *and* pakoras *(snacks). We always serve this chutney when we have a family meal of* Khitchri I, *A Light Dish Made with Rice and Orange Lentils (see Index). Since this chutney has a tendency to change color if left standing, it is best when served fresh.*

Pakay Aam Ki Chutney

Quick Sweet and Sour Mango Chutney

2 large semiripe mangoes (2 pounds)

2 tablespoons mustard oil or vegetable oil

⅛ teaspoon *heeng,* asafetida

½ teaspoon ginger powder

2½ teaspoons lemon juice

2 teaspoons honey

2 teaspoons white vinegar

½ teaspoon *garam masalla,* a spice mixture (see page 42)

⅛ to ¼ teaspoon chili powder

Wash the mangoes, wipe dry, and peel the skins off as thinly as possible. Grate the mangoes and set aside. You should have about 3½ cups of mango pulp.

In a *karhai,* wok, or skillet, heat the oil until it is almost smoking. Reduce heat to moderate and drop in the asafetida. Immediately stir in the mango, ginger powder, lemon juice, honey, vinegar, *garam masalla,* and chili powder. Cook, while stirring, about 5 to 10 minutes. Serve hot.

Serves 6

Remarks

This quick, simple chutney makes a delightful addition to almost any meal.

This recipe was invented by Babuji, who would just pluck the semiripe fruit as he needed it from our mango tree.

Nariyal Chutney II

Coconut Chutney with Tamarind

1 coconut	½ tablespoon minced garlic
1½ tablespoons tamarind pulp	3 tablespoons Homemade Yogurt (see page 41)
7 tablespoons hot water	
1½ tablespoons vegetable oil	pinch *heeng,* asafetida
½ teaspoon mustard seeds	½ teaspoon cumin seeds
1 teaspoon *safed urad daal,* a lentil, or ½ teaspoon minced peanuts	6 *kardi patta,* curry leaves
1 dried red chili	2 tablespoons minced coriander leaves or your favorite herb

Break the coconut. (For procedure, see page 40.) Chop half the coconut into small pieces. Place in a blender and blend until finely shredded. You should have 1½ cups.

Soak the tamarind pulp in the hot water for at least 15 minutes. Squeeze the pulp firmly to extract as much juice as possible and strain. Squeeze and press the pulp as you strain. Collect the tamarind juice and discard the pulp.

In a skillet, heat ½ tablespoon oil and fry the mustard seeds until they begin to sputter. Add the *urad daal* and chili and fry until the *daal* is lightly browned. Remove the skillet from the heat and stir in the garlic.

Grind the fried spices. In a clean blender, blend the yogurt with the ground spices for a few seconds. Add the tamarind juice and blend for 2 to 3 seconds.

Combine the coconut and blended mixture thoroughly and transfer to a serving dish.

Heat the remaining oil in the skillet and drop in the asafetida. As the asafetida spreads, add the cumin seeds and curry leaves and fry over moderate heat until the cumin seeds are brown (about 2 minutes).

Stir the fried spices and coriander leaves gently into the coconut. Serve chilled or at room temperature.

Serves 6

Remarks

This lovely chutney has a tangy flavor and can be served with any type of meal.

Papitay Aur Khajur Ki Meethi Chutney

Sweet Chutney with Papaya and Dates

1 pound semiripe papaya	½ teaspoon chili powder
2 tablespoons vegetable oil	2 or 3 *kardi patta*, curry leaves
½ to 1 tablespoon minced ginger or 1½ teaspoons ginger powder	1 tablespoon jaggery
	4 tablespoons white vinegar
1 cup chopped dates	4½ tablespoons lemon juice
½ tablespoon freshly ground coriander powder	1 teaspoon *garam masalla*, a spice mixture (see page 42)
⅛ teaspoon cinnamon powder	

Wash and cut the papaya in half. Peel the skin, remove stringy portion in center, and chop into tiny pieces.

In a large, heavy-based skillet with a cover, heat the oil and fry the ginger until lightly browned. If using ginger powder, do not fry. Add the papaya, dates, coriander powder, cinnamon powder, chili powder, and curry leaves and fry 1 to 2 minutes over moderate heat.

Stir in the jaggery and 2 tablespoons vinegar and cook, while stirring, 5 or 6 minutes. Reduce heat to low and simmer, covered, 7 to 8 minutes.

Add the rest of the vinegar, lemon juice, and *garam masalla*. Stir well and simmer, covered, about 30 minutes. During this time, stir twice, mashing the papaya as you stir. Your chutney is ready when most of the papaya and dates are mashed and pulpy.

Yields about 1½ cups

Remarks

This chutney is a particularly nice addition to a dry type of meat or fowl dish, such as Murgh Ki Tikki, *Deep-Fried Chicken Cutlets (see Index). It also goes well with a Western meal, used as you would cranberry sauce or applesauce.*

Pudina Chutney

Mint Chutney

3 cups mint sprigs	¼ tablespoon jaggery
1 tablespoon *anar dana,* pomegranate seeds	1 tablespoon water
3 tablespoons minced onions	1 tablespoon lemon juice
1 or 2 small green chilies, chopped	

Wash the mint sprigs and remove the leaves from the stems. Discard the stems. You should have about 2 cups of loosely packed mint leaves.

Place the pomegranate seeds in the jar of a blender and blend until well crushed. Add a quarter of the mint leaves and the remaining ingredients and blend. Scrape down the sides of the container and blend again. Add the remaining mint leaves gradually until the mixture becomes a smooth puree.

Serve at room temperature or slightly chilled.

Yields about ½ cup

Remarks

Mint chutney is at its best served the day it is made. However, properly sealed and refrigerated, it can be served up to two days later.

If you do not have pomegranate seeds, use a tablespoon or more of extra lemon juice.

Tazay Tamatar Ki Chutney

Fresh Tomato Chutney

3 tomatoes	1 to 3 small green chilies, chopped
¾ cup finely sliced onions	2 tablespoons chopped coriander leaves or any green herb
2 tablespoons mustard oil	
½ tablespoon grated jaggery or molasses	¼ teaspoon freshly ground black pepper
2 tablespoons lemon juice	

Wash the tomatoes and cut into ¾-inch cubes.

In a large bowl, lightly toss all the ingredients together. Transfer to a serving bowl and serve.

Serves 6

Remarks

Serve chilled or at room temperature as an accompaniment to a khitchri *or a* pullau.

In this simple chutney, it is the mustard oil that gives it a unique flavor.

Sabut Mirch

Whole Anaheim Peppers, Marinated and Fried

½ pound anaheim peppers (about 7 or 8)

1⅓ cups thick Homemade Yogurt (see page 41)

6 tablespoons *besan,* chick-pea flour

½ to 1 teaspoon chili powder

¼ teaspoon turmeric powder

4 to 8 tablespoons water

vegetable oil for deep frying

Wash the anaheim peppers and dry thoroughly. Cut a 3 to 4-inch slit along one side of each pepper without cutting in half.

In a medium-size bowl, beat the yogurt. Add the peppers, mix well with the yogurt, and set aside, covered, for 48 hours.

Drain the excess yogurt. Gently shake the peppers to dislodge the yogurt inside the slits. Let the peppers dry, preferably in the sun, with the slit side facing upwards.

Mix together the chick-pea flour, chili powder, turmeric powder, and enough water to make a thin batter.

Heat the oil in a *karhai,* wok, or deep-frying pan. Lightly coat the peppers with the chick-pea flour mixture and fry until very lightly browned. Serve immediately while crisp.

Serves 6

Remarks

While the whole peppers are not a "chutney," they serve as a substitute for a pickle or chutney.

Use the excess yogurt, seasoned with your favorite fresh herb, as an accompaniment to rice.

salads

———————— *Chana Aur Kachay Tamatar Ka Salaad* ————————

Dark Chick-Pea and Green Tomato Salad

1 cup *kala chana*, small dark chick-peas	1½ teaspoons scraped and grated ginger
2¾ cups cold water	8 to 10 small green tomatoes (2½ cups when cut)
½ teaspoon freshly ground cumin powder	
pinch of *heeng*, asafetida	5 tablespoons white vinegar
½ teaspoon garlic powder	3½ tablespoons honey
¼ to ½ teaspoon chili powder	

Remove stones or sticks from the chick-peas. Wash thoroughly and soak overnight in 2 cups fresh water.

Put the chick-peas, soaking water, ¾ cup fresh water, cumin, asafetida, garlic powder, chili powder, and ginger in a 2-quart saucepan and bring to a boil. Reduce the heat to low and simmer, covered, until the chick-peas are tender and the water is absorbed (about 1½ to 2½ hours).

Meanwhile, wash the tomatoes and cut each one into quarters and each quarter into 3 pieces.

Mix the vinegar and honey in a bowl and fold in the tomatoes. Marinate for at least 30 minutes.

Scoop the chick-peas into a large serving bowl. Drain the tomatoes and fold them gently into the chick-peas. Serve chilled or at room temperature.

Serves 6

Remarks

This unusual, delicious dish can serve as a salad, a lentil, or a vegetable entree.

———————— *Gajar Aur Angur Ka Salaad* ————————

Carrot and Grape Salad

¾ pound carrots (about 3 large carrots)	1 tablespoon honey
½ pound seedless grapes	1 tablespoon white vinegar
2 tablespoons vegetable oil	½ to 1 tablespoon lemon juice
1 to 1½ teaspoons crushed black or red mustard seeds	½ teaspoon freshly ground black pepper
	1 teaspoon paprika

Thoroughly scrub the carrots and cut each in half. Cut each wider half lengthwise into 8 to 12 slivers. Cut each narrower half into 4 to 6 slivers. You should have thin slivers, each ¼ inch thick and 3 to 4 inches long. Rinse and set aside.

Wash the grapes.

Place the carrots and grapes in a large bowl and toss together with the oil, mustard seeds, honey, vinegar, lemon juice, and pepper.

Transfer to serving dish and refrigerate for 15 to 30 minutes before serving. Sprinkle with paprika.

Serves 6

Chana Palak Salaad

Chick-Pea and Spinach Marinade

1½	cups chick-peas		¼	pound spinach leaves
4 to 5	cups water		2	teaspoons vegetable oil
3	large garlic cloves		2	teaspoons black or red mustard seeds
⅛	teaspoon turmeric powder		5	tablespoons lemon juice
½ to ¾	teaspoon chili powder		1	teaspoon honey
1	teaspoon ginger powder		1	teaspoon garlic powder
⅛	teaspoon black pepper			

Remove any stones or sticks from the chick-peas. Wash thoroughly under cold running water and soak overnight in 4 cups water.

Drain the chick-peas. Reserve the soaking water. Place chick-peas in a 4-quart pot, add the soaking water and enough fresh water to equal 4 cups. Add the garlic cloves, turmeric powder, ¼ to ½ teaspoon chili powder, ½ teaspoon ginger powder, and pepper and bring to a boil. Reduce the heat to moderate and simmer, covered, until the chick-peas are tender but not mushy (about 1¾ to 2½ hours). If necessary, remove the lid for the last few minutes of cooking time to allow the excess water to evaporate.

Wash the spinach leaves, tear them by hand, and toss in a large bowl with the oil.

Wrap the mustard seeds in several layers of paper toweling and pound with a mallet until the seeds are crushed but not finely ground.

Add the crushed mustard seeds, ⅛ to ¼ teaspoon chili powder, ½ teaspoon ginger powder, lemon juice, honey, and garlic powder to the spinach. Toss lightly and marinate for at least 30 minutes.

Spoon the chick-peas into a serving bowl. (Remove garlic cloves, if desired.) Fold in the spinach mixture, cover, and chill thoroughly before serving.

Serves 6

Remarks

I prefer to make this delightful salad a day ahead so that it can absorb all the flavors of the marinade.

Dalia Salaad

Salad with Cracked Wheat

1½ cups *dalia*, cracked wheat

1 tablespoon plus ¾ teaspoon white vinegar

1 tablespoon plus ¾ teaspoon lemon juice

½ tablespoon honey

1 medium-size cucumber

12 cherry tomatoes

½ pound spinach leaves

½ pound lettuce

3 tablespoons ground nut oil or vegetable oil

½ teaspoon freshly ground black pepper

2 teaspoons scraped and finely slivered ginger

1 tablespoon white sesame seeds

1 teaspoon paprika (optional)

Soak the cracked wheat in enough water to cover for 1 hour.

In a bowl, mix together the vinegar, lemon juice, and honey.

Wash, dry, and thinly slice the cucumber. Add the cucumber slices and cherry tomatoes to the vinegar marinade and marinate for 15 minutes. Remove the cucumbers and tomatoes and set aside.

Wash and drain the spinach and lettuce. Cut into long thin strips. Toss with 1 tablespoon plus ¾ teaspoon oil, then add to the vinegar marinade, sprinkle with ¼ teaspoon pepper, and lightly toss again. Allow to marinate for a few minutes.

Line a colander with a kitchen cloth and pour the wheat into the cloth. Allow to drain, then hold the cloth tightly and squeeze the excess water from the wheat.

In a skillet, heat the remaining oil and fry the ginger for ½ minute. Add the wheat, ¼ teaspoon pepper, sesame seeds, and paprika (if used). Fry over moderate heat, while stirring gently, 2 to 3 minutes. Remove from heat and cool for a few minutes.

Arrange the greens on a large flat platter. Spoon the wheat over the bed of greens, forming a mound in the center. Arrange the cucumber slices and tomatoes in a ring around the wheat. Garnish with paprika and serve at room temperature or slightly chilled.

Serves 6

Remarks

This salad, which I adapted from my Aunt Apabi's health salad, takes just 15 minutes to prepare. It is wonderful served with either an Indian or Western meal. I sometimes serve it as an appetizer, but often serve it for lunch.

_____ *Phulgobi Ki Kaliyan Ka Salaad* _____

Cauliflower or Broccoli Salad with Mushrooms

1⅛ pounds cauliflower florets or broccoli

5 cups water

4 tablespoons corn oil or salad oil

½-inch piece ginger, scraped and sliced into thin, fine slivers

¼ pound small mushrooms, washed and trimmed

⅛ teaspoon chili powder

2 teaspoons crushed black or red mustard seeds

6 medium-size garlic cloves, minced

2 or 3 tablespoons lemon juice

¼ pound cherry tomatoes

1½ teaspoons honey

Trim the stems off the cauliflower forets. If using broccoli, leave up to 1½ inches of stem on each floret.

Bring the water to a boil and drop in the florets for ½ minute (broccoli for 1 minute). Drain immediately.

Heat the oil in a large skillet. Fry the ginger and mushrooms 3 or 4 minutes. Add the cauliflower, chili powder, and mustard seeds and fry 1 minute over moderately high heat while stirring. Remove from skillet and cool.

In a large serving bowl, mix the garlic, lemon juice, tomatoes, and honey. Add the cauliflower and mushrooms and stir thoroughly. Chill at least 30 minutes before serving.

Serves 6

Remarks

We love this garden fresh salad. It goes beautifully with a Western meal.

_____ *Salaad* _____

Salad to Accompany *Seekh Kababs*

6 large onions

6 to 8 green chilies

¼ cup mint leaves or any herb

2 to 3 tablespoons lemon juice

Seekh Kabab, Broiled Kabobs of Minced Meat and Spices (see Index)

Slice the onions into rings. Slit the chilies, lengthwise, into halves. Mix the mint and lemon juice.

Arrange most of the onion rings on a large flat serving dish and pour three-quarters of the lemon-mint mixture over them. Arrange the *kababs* over the onions. Then sprinkle the remaining onion rings and lemon mixture over the *kababs*. Garnish with green chilies.

Serves 6

Pyaz Ka Salaad

Onion Salad to Accompany *Tandoori Murgh I*

1 teaspoon cumin powder	6 green chilies
2½ cups finely sliced onions	*Tandoori Murgh I,* Whole Tandoori Chickens (see Index)
3 tablespoons lemon juice	
¼ to ½ cup watercress leaves	

Heat a *tava* or griddle. Roast the cumin powder 1 minute over moderate heat. Mix the cumin with onions, lemon juice, and watercress.

Slit the chilies under running water and add them to the salad. You may remove the chili seeds if you prefer.

Spread the onion salad on a large flat serving dish. Arrange the chicken on top of the salad and serve.

Serves 6

Remarks

You can spoon some of the salad over the chicken; or, arrange the salad around the chicken as described in the Tandoori Murgh I, *Whole* Tandoori *Chickens recipe (see Index).*

In India, we use fresh coriander leaves with this salad rather than watercress.

Salaad, Moong Kay Saat

Mixed, Fresh Salad with Sprouted Mung Beans

¾ cup green *moong,* mung beans	¾ teaspoon freshly ground black pepper
1½ cups cold water	1 small green pepper
3 medium-size onions	3 medium-size tomatoes
¼ cup plus 2 tablespoons lemon juice	4 to 6 small green chilies
1 tablespoon finely chopped coriander leaves	18 radishes

Remove any stones or sticks from the mung beans. Wash thoroughly and soak in cold water for 12 hours. Drain. Then soak a paper towel in water and wring it out. Place the wet towel over the beans. Cover the entire bowl with a cloth and set aside for 12 hours, after which time there should be tiny sprouts. Sprinkle a few drops of water over the paper towel, cover the bowl, and set aside for another 24 hours. The mung beans should have swollen to fill over 2 cups.

Cut the onions into rings and set aside.

Mix the 2 cups sprouted mung beans with the lemon juice, coriander leaves, and pepper and set aside.

Cut the green pepper into rings and set aside.

Cut the tomatoes into rings and allow to drain on a paper towel.

Slit the chilies under cold running water and remove the seeds. Trim the radishes and form into rosettes.

Line a large, flat serving dish with the onion rings. Sprinkle half the mung bean-lemon juice mixture over them. Then arrange the pepper and tomato slices alternately on top of the mung beans. Sprinkle with the rest of the mung bean mixture and then decorate the top with radishes and chilies.

Serves 6

our favorite festivals

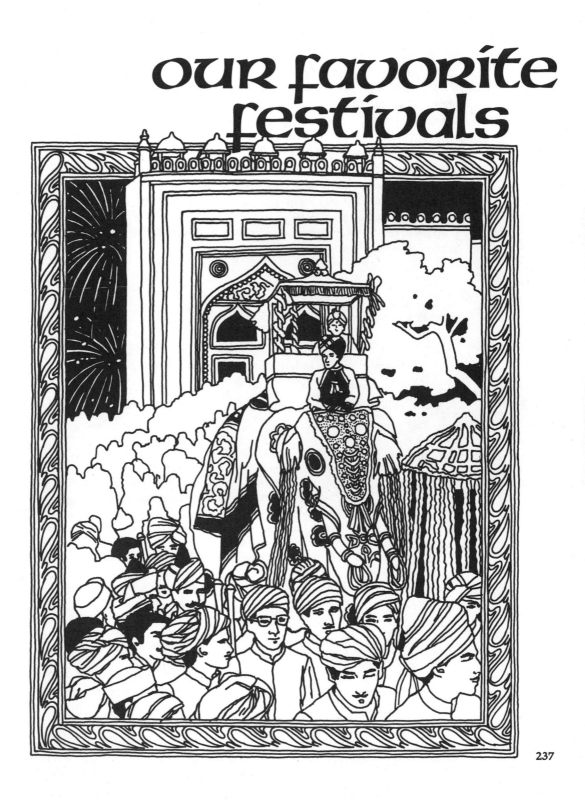

We awaited our favorite festivals with much anticipation. Long before the day of *Id Ul Fitr* (a sacred Muslim festival) dawned, we began preparing for it. We celebrate *Id Ul Fitr* to commemorate the successful completion of 30 days of fasting, and prayerful meditation. (Babuji, of course, observed the fast rigidly with the rest of the household observing it in varying degrees).

After this period of voluntary discipline, we celebrate the actual festival all the more joyously. My mother would awaken us early in the morning. Already she and Asho would have spent many hours in the kitchen, helping Babuji to prepare for the big day ahead. The house was always fragrant with the wafting drifts of *agar batti* (incense sticks). The incomparable aroma of saffron would be in the air as the huge pot of *sivain*, a very thin kind of vermicelli, was cooking. There are different ways to prepare it. On this day Babuji always cooked it with lots of milk and cream, garnished with nuts and edible silver leaf.

A Dessert of ————————————————— *Sivain* —————————————————
Thin Vermicelli Cooked in Milk

8 cups milk	4 tablespoons *ghee* (see page 40)
¼ teaspoon *zafraan*, saffron threads	¾ to 1 teaspoon *kewra* water
1 tablespoon hot milk	4 tablespoons shredded almonds
3 to 4 tablespoons grated jaggery	1 tablespoon pistachio nuts
2¼ cups thin vermicelli	

Place the 8 cups milk in a heavy-based, 4-quart pot and cook over moderate heat until the milk thickens (about 40 minutes). Stir occasionally.

Meanwhile, soak the saffron threads in the 1 tablespoon of hot milk.

Add the jaggery and saffron threads to the 8 cups milk and continue cooking. Stir frequently.

Fry the vermicelli in 3 tablespoons *ghee* in a *karhai* or large skillet over moderate heat 6 to 7 minutes. Stir very carefully to avoid breaking the vermicelli into small pieces.

Add the vermicelli and *kewra* water to the milk, reduce the heat to low, and simmer until the vermicelli puffs up and comes to the surface (about 10 minutes).

Heat the remaining *ghee* and fry the nuts lightly. Stir into the milk and serve.

Serves 8 to 12

Remarks

Sivain *is delicious served hot or chilled. Refrigerated, this dessert keeps for almost a week and thickens when chilled. You may serve it thick or add a little milk (hot or cold) to each individual serving. On* Id *days, when we had a house full of visitors, Babuji would serve it with lots of extra, thickened milk.*

A Visit to the Mosque for Prayers

The most important thing in the early morning was for the men to go to the Mosque for community prayers. My father and Baba would be dressed in immaculate white pajamas and a silk, embroidered *sherwani* which is a long double-breasted oriental coat. Then Babuji would emerge smiling and smelling strongly of his own brand of *attar,* the essence of jasmine. Little Lama was also included, wearing a glittering new *sherwani.* Baba and Lama were given a pile of coins to distribute to the poor at the Mosque after prayers. Babuji had his coins already well wrapped, in stacks, in thin white kite paper. He would let me hold these, while he had a last look around the kitchen, before leaving for prayers.

 While the men were away, Mama, Asho, and I would carefully lay out all the prepared savories on a lovely white damask table cloth. There were *samosas* and two kinds of *kababs. Sivain* was, of course, the main sweet dish, but we also served *barfi, laddus,* and *suji ka halva.* Asho had made gallons of her special *masalla* tea, because every time any of us went into the kitchen we'd drink a cup of it. It was very popular with all our friends, too.

Suji Ka Halva I — *Halva* of Cream of Wheat, Nuts, and Raisins

1 cup Cream of Wheat	4 cups water
6 to 7 tablespoons melted *ghee* (see page 40) or melted butter	5 to 6 tablespoons honey
2 tablespoons slivered almonds	½ teaspoon *kewra* water or rose water
2 tablespoons raisins	
5 small buff or pale green cardamom pods	

Heat a *karhai* or large skillet. Then add the Cream of Wheat and stir over moderate heat 10 minutes. Stir in the *ghee* and fry over moderately high heat, while continuously stirring, until the Cream of Wheat becomes a pale golden brown. Then add the almonds and raisins and stir 2 or 3 minutes.

 Meanwhile, lightly pound the cardamom pods just until the skins crack. Bring the water to a boil with the cardomom pods, honey, and *kewra* water in a 2-quart saucepan. Reduce heat and simmer, covered, 2 to 3 minutes.

 Pour the water with flavoring into the Cream of Wheat. Continue cooking over low heat while stirring constantly. In a few minutes, the Cream of Wheat will absorb all the water. Remove from heat and serve immediately.

Serves 6

Remarks

 Suji Ka Halva I *is loved by everyone in India. It is soft and delicious and can be enjoyed by babies or toothless, elderly people!*

 It is at its best when served immediately. If you wish to serve the suji *later, just add a little boiling water to it when reheating.*

 The halva *may also be served cold. Since it tends to get thicker and a bit lumpy when refrigerated, simply whip by hand until smooth before serving. Then garnish each portion with a dollop of cream.*

Whole Wheat ————————————— *Keema Samosa* ————————————
Deep-Fried Triangle, with Savory Minced Lamb Stuffing

2 cups whole wheat flour	½ teaspoon chili powder (optional)
1 rounded tablespoon *ghee* (see page 40) or butter	3 to 4 tablespoons finely chopped coriander leaves or parsley
1 cup plus 3 tablespoons water	½ cup water
3 tablespoons vegetable oil	2 to 3 tablespoons lemon juice
2 cups chopped onions	½ teaspoon *garam masalla,* a spice mixture (see page 42)
1 tablespoon minced garlic	
1½ tablespoons scraped and minced ginger	4 to 5 cups vegetable oil for deep-frying
1½ pounds lean round of lamb, minced	

Sift the flour into a large bowl. Rub in the *ghee* gradually until the mixture resembles bread crumbs. Gradually add 1 cup plus 3 tablespoons water. Mix until a mass forms. Knead well until the dough is soft and pliable (about 8 to 15 minutes). Cover and set aside for 30 minutes.

In a large, heavy skillet, heat the 3 tablespoons oil. Fry the onions 3 minutes over moderately high heat. Stir occasionally. Add the garlic and ginger and fry over moderate heat until golden brown (about 6 to 8 minutes). Add the meat and chili powder (if used) and fry 2 minutes. Stir in the coriander leaves and ½ cup water and bring to a boil. Cover, reduce heat to low, and simmer 25 minutes. Uncover and cook over moderate heat until the moisture evaporates (about 8 to 15 minutes).

Add the lemon juice and *garam masalla,* stir well, remove from heat, and cool.

Lightly knead the dough again. Divide into 12 portions. Form each section into a ball, flatten, and roll on a lightly floured board until you have a thin round about 5 to 6 inches in diameter.

With a small sharp knife, cut down the center so that you have 2 half circles of rolled dough. Form a cone shape with each half circle by holding the dough with the straight edge toward you and folding one third of the dough over, then the other third over the first one. Moisten the edges and press lightly to seal. Fill with a tablespoon or more of the filling. Seal the top edges by moistening and pressing securely. Continue this process until you have 6 *samosas* ready.

Begin to heat the oil in a large *karhai* or wok. Test the oil by dropping in a tiny piece of dough and if it rises to the surface immediately, the oil is ready. Gently place the *samosas,* one by one, in the hot oil. Reduce the heat to medium and cook until golden brown. You will need to turn them once or twice during the cooking time. Remove with a slotted spoon and drain on several layers of paper towels. Keep warm until all the *samosas* are cooked.

Yields 24 *samosas*

Remarks

Serve Pudina Chutney, *Mint Chutney, or* Dhania Chutney, *Fresh Coriander Chutney (see Index), as a dip to accompany the* samosas.

Traditional Dress for the Festival

My mother and I would then go in and dress in our traditional Moghul costume, the *gharara*. It is a strikingly beautiful dress, with yards and yards of rich silk made into two loosely joined skirts. A *kurta* (chemise) is worn on top and then the yards of chiffon or muslin that make the *dupetta*, a kind of large scarf or shawl, are draped around the head and shoulders, according to individual fancy. Wearing the *gharara*, one has to take small dainty steps, and the nature of the traditional billowing costume conspires to make one feel elegant and special.

It was the custom to have open house on the occasion of the *Ul Fitr*. Our friends (of all religions) would visit, to celebrate this auspicious day with us. We, in turn, visited our Muslim friends in the evening, or the next day.

As M. B. and company returned from the *masjid* (mosque), our first visitors would begin to arrive. We would be at the doorstep to greet them in typical fashion, with an embrace and then a touch of our favorite *attar gulab* (rose) behind the ear. My mother would do this, with smiling grace. She would dip her hand into the heavy silver *attar daan*, and dab a tiny bit of *attar*, soaked in cotton on each new welcome

For the festival, an Indian woman wears the traditional Moghul costume, the gharara.

The men would go to the Mosque for community prayers, dressed in a sherwani *(coat) and* tang pajama *(pants).*

guest. The mention of *Id* which we spent together in Shillong always conjures up the remembered fragrance that surrounded us that day. It is, to me, a symbol of shared happiness. Even now, whenever I use rose water to flavor any particular dish, I feel I am part of a tradition shared with Babuji, and never forgotten.

The Festival of Lights

Divali, known as the festival of lights, is one of the most beautiful Hindu religious events in India. Songs and verses are sung as they have been from time immemorial, to commemorate this day. A well-known, sad song from a famous film says, *"Ghar ghar meh Divali hah, mere ghar meh andhera"*—"Each house is lighted up to celebrate *Divali,* but there is darkness in my home." Of course, to have darkness is unthinkable on *Divali* night. The rich illuminate their homes with thousands of candles, *diyas,* or colorful electric lights. Even the poorest home will have at least one *diya* shining on the doorstep.

The *diya* or candle on the doorstep is an invitation to *Lakshmi,* the goddess of wealth, to enter our homes and bring us of her bounty. As the sun sets and evening begins, the flickering *diya* lights begin giving off a lovely glow from every home in India. The warmth of the little lights seem to envelope everyone's heart on that glad occasion.

Together with our Hindu friends, we have always celebrated this happy day. We had a little forest of bamboos growing along the hedges, at the bottom of the garden. Hansraj was busy for days beforehand, slitting the long bamboos into halves.

He would erect strong bamboo posts at intervals, from our front door, going straight down, hundreds of yards, to the lower garden gate, leading to the beautiful Shillong Ward lakes opposite our house. On these stakes he would tie the splintered bamboos, with the cut side facing upwards. As soon as he had done this, Lama Madhu, Baba, and I, with the elders, would place candles or *diyas* at regular intervals on the bamboo supports. At the first hint of darkness, we would begin the task of lighting up our "long string of jewels," one by one. It was much more fun to do this, slowly, savoring each moment, than to flood the place with electric lights.

Celebrating with Family and Friends

Divali is a time to spend with family and close friends. In the morning we would go to visit Jaya Parmasivan, a very dear south Indian friend. On her doorstep was an intricate, beautiful design, a religious symbol, made with rice flour and turmeric, involving many hours of eye-straining work. The result was breathtaking. We

──────────── *Shahi Badaam Ka Halva* ──────────── Royal Almond
Halva

4¾	cups water	8 drops *kewra* water
1	pound raw almonds, shelled	2 tablespoons lemon juice
2	egg whites	2 or 3 silver leaves
5	tablespoons honey	¼ cup pistachio nuts

Bring 4¼ cups of water to a boil in a 4-quart pot. Drop the almonds into the water and remove pot from heat. Allow the almonds to remain in the water for 10 to 15 minutes. Pick up one of the almonds and if you can easily remove the skin, then drain the water and peel the skins from all the almonds. Otherwise, let them remain in hot water until the skins peel off easily.

Place the nuts in another pot or bowl, add cold water to cover, and soak for at least 30 minutes. Drain and place the nuts in two thicknesses of kitchen cloth. Pound with several blows of a mallet. Then place the almonds in a blender in small batches and blend until they are crushed but not blended to a puree. Set aside in a large bowl.

Beat the egg whites until fluffy but not stiff. Fold into the almonds.

Bring ½ cup water to boiling point in a small pan. Stir in honey and continue stirring over moderate heat until the water becomes thick and sticky. Add *kewra* water and lemon juice and remove from heat. Then thoroughly stir the honey mixture into the nuts and transfer to a serving bowl.

Place 2 or 3 silver leaves carefully over the surface of the almond *halva*. Shell the pistachio nuts, chop into small pieces, and sprinkle lightly over the silver leaves. Press down gently with your fingers until the pistachio nuts are firmly anchored. Chill until ready to serve.

Serves 8 to 12

Remarks

This royal dessert is very rich. Only a small amount is needed for an individual serving.

would remove our shoes and go with her to her *puja* (prayer) room, which she had converted into a flower-bedecked haven. The pictures and statues of the gods which she particularly revered were adorned with garlands of flowers. A *diya* was lit at their feet. We would say a small prayer in private, yet together, and then *thalis,* full of *prasad,* or holy offerings, were extended to us, with coconuts and *laddus.*

In the evening, after lighting our *diyas,* we would celebrate *Divali* together, often with our neighbors, the Trivedi's. Mr. Trivedi is a wonderful man, good, kind, knowledgable, with the twinkle in his eye reflecting his capacity for fun. His infectious smile seemed even brighter that day, as he would urge Baba to set off a *patakha* (little bomb) or to light another *phuljari* (the word *phuljhari,* for sparkler, is very appropriate; it means "showering flowers"). Then, as is customary, we would be invited in to share a few homemade sweets. Mrs. Trivedi is an excellent cook, and her table would be laden with traditional sweets such as *barfi, rasgulla, laddus,* and *halva.*

Invited to the Extravaganza

To wind up the day, Asho would take Lama, Madhu, Baba, and me to "Police Bazaar" in the evening. Police Bazaar is the name of our local shopping center in Shillong. It is a large, sprawling affair, with main lanes crisscrossed by little side lanes, each with their own specialty shops. Our destination was the Goenkas' home. The Goenkas are rich, Marwari businessmen living in the heart of town in a huge extended family. My friend, Leela, was a member of this family and each *Divali* she invited all her school friends to an extravaganza held at her home. Her friends however, were not the only ones heading for her home! It seemed that half of Shillong was jam-packed into those narrow lanes in front of her house.

Everyone wanted to see the firework display that the Goenkas would put on, from late in the evening to almost midnight. We, the invited guests, would be led to their top terrace, many stories high, overlooking the town. Here, all kinds of firecrackers would be distributed. After an hour of lighting Catherine wheels, sparklers, bombs, snakes, and other fireworks and watching the neighbors trying to match the Goenkas' endless sparkling display, we would retreat downstairs, to the huge dining room, and eat again! Their numerous cooks had been busy for days, preparing for *Divali.* We especially enjoyed the soft *Dahi Baras,* deep-fried rissoles, served with *Sonth.* Food was sent to temples and distributed to the poor. Homemade sweets were sent in gaily wrapped packages to relatives and friends. Then, all the visitors had to be fed! Really, *Divali* in their home was more like a colorful fair than a family celebration.

American readers may wonder, "Are Indians always eating?" I wish to explain that the feeding of family and friends is one of our greatest joys, and yes, even a preoccupation.

The values of charity, generosity, and an extraordinary feeling for hospitality are surprising in a world where lack of time, a consequence of the frenzied modern lifestyle, has prompted us to regard such actions as "extravagance." I am happy to say my memories, at least, are extravagant ones!

———————————————— *Dahi Bara* ———————————————— Deep-Fried
Rissoles Made from Lentils, in Yogurt

1 cup *safed urad daal,* a lentil	vegetable oil for deep-frying
1¾ cups water	3 cups well-mixed Homemade Yogurt (see page 41)
½ tablespoon scraped and coarsely grated ginger	½ teaspoon freshly ground black pepper
¾ to 1 tablespoon lemon juice	
1 teaspoon crushed cumin seeds	2 or 3 small green chilies, minced
¼ to ⅓ teaspoon chili powder	

Wash the *daal* thoroughly. Place in an open jar or other narrow vessel and soak in the water for 24 hours.

Drain the *daal* and reserve the soaking water. Place the *daal* and ⅔ cup of the soaking water in a blender. Add the ginger and blend for a few seconds. Stir carefully and blend again until the mixture becomes a smooth, thick puree.

In a bowl, mix together the blended *daal,* lemon juice, cumin seeds, and chili powder.

In a *karhai* or wok bring the oil to almost the smoking point. Reduce heat to low. Drop in a small amount of batter, and if it rises immediately to the surface, the oil is ready. Slide either a tablespoonful or teaspoonful of batter into the oil. (If a tablespoon is used, the batter will yield 18 to 20 fried lentil balls; if a teaspoon is used, it will yield over 30.) Continue until there are 6 to 8 balls in the *karhai* at one time. Increase the heat to moderately high and cook until the lentil balls are golden brown (about 6 to 12 minutes). If the balls brown too quickly, lower the heat to moderate.

Remove from the *karhai* and drain on paper towels. When the *baras* cool, soak them thoroughly in water for at least 30 minutes. Squeeze the excess water from the *baras* and set aside.

Mix the yogurt and black pepper. Stir in the lentil balls until they are well mixed with the yogurt. Sprinkle with green chilies and chill for 30 minutes before serving.

Serves 6

Remarks

This nutritious and delicious preparation is popular all over India. The baras *are often topped with* Sonth, A Tamarind, Jaggery, Ginger Sauce *(see Index).*

A Tamarind, ———————————————— *Sonth* ————————————————
Jaggery, Ginger Sauce

½ cup tamarind pulp

1½ cups hot water

1 tablespoon scraped and finely
   slivered ginger

1½ tablespoons jaggery

pinch of *heeng,* asafetida

1 teaspoon freshly ground cumin
   seeds

1½ tablespoons raisins

Soak the tamarind pulp in the water for 30 minutes. Squeeze the pulp firmly between your fingers to extract as much juice as possible. Strain the liquid, collect the juice, and discard the pulp and any seeds.

Heat the tamarind juice over moderate heat in a skillet. Add the ginger, jaggery, *asafetida,* and cumin seeds. Cook until the juice thickens to a sauce and is reduced to just under ¾ cup (about 20 minutes). Stir occasionally. Add the raisins, reduce heat to low, and simmer 2 minutes. Remove from heat, allow to cool, and serve in a sauce boat or bowl.

Yields ¾ cup

Remarks

Traditionally, kala nimak *(black salt) and dried ginger are used for making this heavenly sweet-sour sauce. A family friend, Mr. Dharam Vir's sister, who is an excellent vegetarian cook, taught my mother this recipe. We love it! We serve it to accompany* Dahi Bara, *Deep-Fried Rissoles Made from Lentils, in* Yogurt *(see Index)—poured as a garnish over the* baras *or served separately.*

Sonth *is also very nice served with plain yogurt.*

Chakli I

Deep-Fried Snack of Rice Flour and Lentil Flour

2 cups rice flour

½ cup *urad daal* flour, a lentil flour

2 teaspoons white sesame seeds

1 teaspoon *ajwain,* oregano seeds

½ teaspoon cumin seeds

2½ tablespoons vegetable oil

pinch of *heeng,* asafetida

½ tablespoon scraped and grated ginger

½ tablespoon grated garlic

1¼ cups water

vegetable oil for deep-frying

A *soria* (see Index), a special tool that works like a cookie press or an icing tube. (Either of the latter two can be used in place of the *soria.*)

Mix the rice flour, *urad daal* flour, and sesame seeds together in a bowl.

Wrap the oregano seeds and cumin seeds in thick paper toweling and pound until they are coarsely ground.

Heat the 2½ tablespoons vegetable oil in a small skillet over moderately high heat and drop in the asafetida. Remove the skillet from the heat.

Add the pounded spices, the asafetida in oil, ginger, garlic, and 1 cup water to the flour. Mix together with your hands. Gradually add the remaining ¼ cup water, pressing and mixing the flour until a thick batter is formed.

Heat oil in a *karhai,* wok, or deep-frying pan over moderately high heat. Test the oil by dropping in a tiny bit of batter and if it rises to the surface quickly, the oil is ready for deep-frying. Adjust the heat between moderately high and moderate while frying.

If you use a *soria,* carefully push the plate that has a single hole—or one with 3 large holes—into place inside the bottom end of it. Be sure to have the slightly curved surface of the plate arranged so that the slight bulge is face-down inside the *soria.*

Dip a spoon into a cup of water and scoop some batter into the *soria.* I use my fingers, dipping them into the water before I pick up the batter. Continue until you have about ¾ cup of batter in the *soria.* Attach the lid securely but not too tightly. (If you use a cookie press or icing tube, use the large, round scalloped head.)

Position yourself just above the oil and carefully begin to turn the handle of the *soria,* making a circular shape with smaller circular spirals inside. As you finish one circular spiral, stop turning the handle. Move the *soria* to begin the next spiral quickly. Turn the *chaklis* after 3 to 4 minutes and cook until they are golden brown. Stack in a dish lined with 2 layers of thick paper toweling until ready to serve.

Serves 6

Remarks

This very popular Maharastrian snack derives its name from the word chakli, meaning "circle" or "round." It was taught to me by Ganga Bai.

Chaklis will keep for weeks in an airtight container.

Chakli II

Deep-Fried Snack of Rice Flour and Chick-Pea Flour

2 cups rice flour

¾ cup *besan,* chick-pea flour

2 teaspoons white sesame seeds

1 teaspoon *ajwain,* oregano seeds

½ teaspoon cumin seeds

2½ tablespoons vegetable oil

    pinch of *heeng,* asafetida

⅛ teaspoon tumeric powder

⅛ teaspoon chili powder (optional)

½ tablespoon scraped and grated ginger

½ tablespoon grated garlic

½ tablespoon lemon juice (optional)

1¼ cups water

    vegetable oil for deep-frying

A *soria* (see Index), a special tool that works like a cookie press or an icing tube. (Either of the latter two can be used in place of the *soria.*)

Mix the rice flour, chick-pea flour, and sesame seeds together in a bowl.

Wrap the oregano seeds and cumin seeds in thick paper toweling and pound until they are coarsely ground.

Heat the 2½ tablespoons vegetable oil in a small skillet over moderately high heat and drop in the asafetida, tumeric powder, and chili powder (if used). Remove the skillet from the heat.

Add the pounded spices with oil, ginger, garlic, lemon juice (if used), and 1 cup water to the flour. Mix together with your hands. Gradually add the remaining ¼ cup water, pressing and mixing the flour until a very thick batter is formed.

Heat the oil in a *karhai,* wok, or deep-frying pan over moderately high heat. Test the oil by dropping in a tiny bit of batter and if it rises to the surface quickly, the oil is ready for deep-frying.

If you use a *soria,* carefully push the plate that has a single hole—or one with 3 large holes—into place inside the bottom end of it. Be sure to have the slightly curved surface of the plate arranged so that the slight bulge is face-down inside the *soria.*

Dip a spoon into a cup of water and scoop some batter into the *soria.* I use my fingers, dipping them into the water before I pick up the batter. Continue until you have about ¾ cup of batter in the *soria.* Attach the lid securely but not too tightly. (If you use a cookie press or icing tube, use the large, round scalloped head.)

Position yourself just above the oil and carefully begin to turn the handle of the *soria,* making a circular shape with smaller circular spirals inside. As you finish one circular spiral, stop turning the handle. Move the *soria* to begin the next spiral quickly. Turn the *chaklis* after 3 to 4 minutes and cook until they are golden brown. Stack in a dish lined with 2 layers of thick paper toweling until ready to serve.

Serves 6

Remarks

Besan *has a different flavor than the* urad daal *used in* Chakli I. *It is a very nutritious flour and forms the base for dozens of snacks and savories in India.*

Chewra or *Poha*

Pounded Rice Flakes

2 or 3 small green chilies	1 cup *chewra*, pounded rice flakes
1 coconut	½ cup raw peanuts
ghee (see page 40) or vegetable oil for deep-frying	pinch of turmeric powder (optional)
5 to 6 tablespoons green coriander leaves	¼ teaspoon *garam masalla*, a spice mixture (see page 42)
3 tablespoons finely sliced onions	2 tablespoons lemon juice (optional)

Slit the chilies into halves and deseed under cold running water. Dry and slit each half into 2 or 3 thin slivers or chop.

Break the coconut. (For procedure, see page 40.) Cut 3 tablespoons coconut into ½ inch slices.

Begin to heat the *ghee* in a *karhai* or wok for deep-frying.

Wash the coriander leaves with stems. Coarsely chop and fry in the hot *ghee* for a few seconds. Remove immediately with a slotted spoon and set aside.

Fry the chilies for a few seconds. Remove immediately and drain on paper towels. Fry the onions until red and crisp and drain on paper towels. Fry the sliced coconut until lightly browned and drain on paper towels also.

Fry the *chewra* in several batches. Fry only for a few seconds until it puffs up and comes to the surface. Do not allow it to brown. Drain thoroughly on paper towels.

In a large bowl, mix together the chilies, coconut, coriander leaves, onions, hot *chewra*, peanuts, turmeric powder (if used) and *garam masalla*. Serve in a large bowl or in individual *katoris* (small bowls). Sprinkle with a few drops of lemon juice, if desired.

Serves 6

Remarks

Chewra, *made with different combinations of spices, is one of the most popular Indian snacks. When cool, it can be stored in an airtight container for several days.*

Daal Va

A Lentil Snack

1 cup *chana daal,* a lentil	1 to 2 tablespoons lemon juice
2 cups water	¼ cup minced spring onions
2 tablespoons milk	1 small green chili, minced (optional)
2½ to 3 cups vegetable oil	1 teaspoon cumin powder (optional)

Remove any stones or sticks from the *daal.* Wash thoroughly and soak in water and milk for at least 12 hours.

Drain the *daal,* then spread it out on a cloth or paper towels to dry.

Heat the oil in a *karhai,* wok, or deep-frying pan. When it is almost at smoking point, reduce the heat to low. Spoon about 2 or 3 tablespoons of the *daal* into the oil and increase the heat to moderate. Fry 1 to 2 minutes. It will rise to the surface and puff up slightly. Remove with a slotted spoon and place in a dish lined with several layers of paper towels. Repeat this process until all the *daal* is cooked.

In a bowl, mix the lemon juice, onions, and chili (if used) with the *daal.*

If cumin powder is used, roast it 10 seconds on a heated *tava* or griddle, while stirring. Add to the *daal,* stir thoroughly, and serve.

Serves 6

Remarks

This nutritious, quick snack is usually served in a bowl. We help ourselves by picking up small handfuls at a time.

Matar

Lightly Curried Peas

4 tablespoons vegetable oil	½ teaspoon turmeric powder
1 cup finely sliced onions	¼ teaspoon chili powder
2 cups peas, fresh or frozen	1 tablespoon lemon juice (optional)
⅓ cup water	

Heat the oil in a *karhai* or wok and fry the onions over high heat until brown (about 8 to 10 minutes).

Add the peas and water. If frozen peas are used, add only 1 tablespoon water. Stir in the turmeric powder and chili powder and cover tightly. Cook over moderate heat about 15 to 20 minutes. If peas are not tender, continue cooking. Add 1 tablespoon of water if needed.

Uncover and cook 1 to 2 minutes to allow excess liquid to evaporate. Stir in lemon juice, if used.

Serves 6

Remarks

This light, tasty teatime snack is enjoyed throughout north India, especially when fresh, tender peas are in season.

———— *Matthi* ————

Whole Wheat Biscuits with Peppercorns

1 cup whole wheat pastry flour	¼ cup cold water
⅛ teaspoon baking soda	vegetable oil for deep-frying
2 tablespoons melted *ghee* (see page 40) or butter	30 to 40 peppercorns
1 teaspoon *ajwain,* oregano seeds	

Sift the flour into a bowl. Add the baking soda, *ghee,* and oregano seeds and mix well. Gradually add the water and mix. Form into one mass and knead a few times. The dough will be very stiff and will tend to crumble. Continue pressing together and kneading.

Separate the dough into 8 portions. Form each portion into a tight ball and roll out until it is about 3½ inches in diameter. Fold the flat round in half, then into a quarter. Shape into a ball again, flatten, and roll until it is about 3 inches in diameter and about ¼ inch thick.

Since the dough will be rather difficult to work with, you may have some jagged edges. Trim them. Make criss-cross lines (wafflelike) on both sides.

Heat the oil in a *karhai,* wok, or deep-frying pan. Carefully stick 4 or 5 peppercorns into each biscuit.

Test the oil by dropping in a tiny piece of dough. If it rises immediately to the surface, the oil is ready. Fry the biscuits, two at a time, until golden brown. Remove with a slotted spoon and drain on paper towels. Serve when completely cooled.

Yields 8 *matthis*

Remarks

Matthis *will stay fresh for over a week in an airtight container.*

———— *Papard* ————

A Tortillalike Lentil Savory

vegetable oil for deep-frying	12 *papards,* any flavor you prefer (see Remarks below)

In a *karhai* or wok, heat the oil. It is ready when a tiny piece of *papard* dropped in rises immediately to the surface.

Deep-fry 1 *papard* at a time. Slide the papard in and press it down with a slotted metal spatula. It will puff up and come to the surface immediately. Remove and drain on double layers of paper towels. When cool, it will become crisp and ready to serve.

Serves 6

Remarks

Papards *are a very typical Indian savory made from ground lentils and seasoned with a mixture of spices. They are often served immediately after the meal. However, some people serve them with the main course, others serve them as an appetizer broken into halves or quarters.*

Papards *are available at most Indian stores. They come flavored with different spices, such as pepper, chilies, or garlic. When asking for* papard, *it might be helpful to pronounce it "pah-purr!"*

Saag Ka Pakora

Deep-Fried Spinach Leaves in Batter

½ pound spinach leaves

2 cups *besan,* chick-pea flour

3 tablespoons lemon juice

¾ to 1 teaspoon chili powder

1 teaspoon ginger powder

¼ teaspoon turmeric powder

½ teaspoon black pepper

1 cup water

vegetable oil for deep-frying

Trim all but 1 inch of the stems from the spinach leaves. Wash and let drain in a colander.

In a bowl, mix together the chick-pea flour, lemon juice, chili powder, ginger powder, turmeric powder, and pepper. Slowly add the water and stir well. Continue stirring and mixing until you have a smooth, slightly runny batter.

Heat the oil in a *karhai,* wok, or deep-frying pan over high heat. Test the oil by dropping in a tiny piece of batter. If it rises to the surface immediately, the oil is ready.

Dip a spinach leaf in the batter so that it is lightly coated and drop into the oil. Repeat this process quickly until you have 4 or 5 leaves in the *karhai.* If the first leaf browns too quickly, reduce the heat to moderately high. Cook until golden brown on all sides. Remove with a slotted spoon and place in an ovenproof dish lined with paper towels. Keep the *pakoras* in a warm oven until all the spinach leaves are cooked. Serve immediately.

Yields 28 to 30 pakoras

Sabudana Cha Usarh

A Sago, Peanut Savory Snack

1 cup *sabudana,* sago

8 tablespoons thick Homemade Yogurt (see page 41)

1 cup peanuts

4½ tablespoons *ghee* (see page 40)

1 teaspoon white sesame seeds

1 tablespoon chopped small green chilies

Place the sago in a bowl. Add the yogurt and mix thoroughly. Cover the bowl and set aside for about 30 minutes or until the sago will break when pressed between your fingers.

Wrap the peanuts in several layers of paper toweling and pound with a mallet until the peanuts are crushed.

Heat the *ghee* in a large skillet and fry the peanuts until lightly browned. Remove with a slotted spoon and add to the sago and yogurt.

In the same skillet, using the same *ghee,* fry the sesame seeds and chilies for a few seconds. Stir in the sago mixture, reduce heat to the lowest point, and leave covered 12 to 15 minutes. Uncover, stir thoroughly, and serve hot.

Serves 6

Remarks

We often serve this quick and nutritious Maharastrian snack for lunch. This is another recipe taught to me by that wonderful cook, Ganga Bai.

Shakar Para

Sweet Pastry Bits

1 cup whole wheat pastry flour	6½ tablespoons jaggery, grated
¾ teaspoon baking soda	1 cup plus 1 tablespoon water
1½ tablespoons melted *ghee* (see page 40) or butter	vegetable oil for deep-frying

Sift the flour into a bowl with the baking soda. Add the *ghee* and 1 tablespoon jaggery. Mix well and slowly pour in ¼ cup plus 1 tablespoon water. Mix and form into a dough.

Knead the dough thoroughly. Divide the dough into 2 sections. Shape each section into a long, thick "sausage" shape.

Roll out one of the sections until it is about 8 to 9 inches long. Fold it in half, then fold again so that you have 4 layers. Repeat this process once again, ending with rolled dough that is about ½ inch thick.

Cut the dough into squares, each less than ¾ inch. You should have 12 to 15 squares.

Repeat the same with the other half of the dough.

Heat the oil in a *karhai,* wok, or deep-frying pan.

In a saucepan bring ¾ cup water to a boil with the remaining jaggery. Cook over moderate heat until you have a syrupy consistency. Keep warm.

Test the oil by dropping in a tiny piece of dough. If it rises immediately to the surface, the oil is ready. Fry the squares, a few at a time, over moderate heat until golden brown. Remove with a slotted spoon and drain on paper towels for a few seconds.

Gently put the cooked *paras* into the syrup and simmer 15 minutes. Then spread the *Shakar Paras* on a lightly greased metal tray or dish. Serve when thoroughly cooled. Store in an airtight container.

Yields 24 to 30 *paras*

Remarks

While Shakar Paras *are usually served as a snack in India, you may serve them as a dessert. Properly stored, they will remain fresh for more than a week.*

Uppamma

A Light, Quick, Cream of Wheat Delight, with Yogurt and Cashew Nuts

3½ cups cold water	20 whole cashew nuts, unsalted
1 cup well-mixed Homemade Yogurt (see page 41)	¾ tablespoon scraped and minced ginger
1 to 1½ tablespoons lemon juice	1 to 3 small green chilies, minced
6 tablespoons *ghee* (see page 40) or vegetable oil	3 tablespoons chopped coriander leaves or any herb
1½ teaspoons black or red mustard seeds	4 tablespoons minced onions
12 *kardi patta,* curry leaves	2 cups Cream of Wheat
2 teaspoons *safed urad daal,* a lentil	

Mix the water, yogurt, and lemon juice thoroughly and set aside.

In a 4-quart pot, heat the *ghee* over moderate heat and drop in the mustard seeds. Cover the pot. When the mustard seeds sputter, quickly uncover and add the curry leaves and *urad daal.* Reduce the heat to low and stir occasionally until the *daal* becomes golden brown.

Add the cashew nuts and stir 1 minute. Stir in the ginger, chilies, and coriander leaves and fry ½ minute. Add the onions, increase the heat to moderately high and fry until the onions just begin to turn brown. Stir occasionally.

Stir in the yogurt mixture, cover, and bring to a boil. Lower heat and allow the liquid to simmer 4 to 5 minutes. Gradually add the Cream of Wheat and stir continuously. Cover and cook over low heat until the liquid is absorbed (about 5 minutes).

Serves 6

Remarks

This nutritious and tasty dish is a great favorite of the Indian housewife because it is easy to cook and is loved by everyone. It often takes the place of the lunch time sandwich that is common in America.

desserts

Aam Kulfi

A Mango Ice Cream

2 mangoes	5 egg yolks, slightly beaten
2 cups milk	2 cups heavy cream
1 tablespoon arrowroot	¼ teaspoon *kewra* water
½ to 1 cup honey	¼ teaspoon ground cardamom seeds

Wash mangoes, remove the skin and stones, and dice. Place the mangoes in a double boiler and steam until tender. Then place in a blender and puree. Set aside in refrigerator.

Bring milk to a boil. Take out 1 tablespoon of milk, blend with the arrowroot, then add back into the milk, and cook over low heat, while stirring, until mixture is of pouring sauce consistency.

Combine honey and egg yolks. Add milk gradually, while mixing well, and heat over high heat in double boiler until mixture coats spoon (about 5 minutes).

Cool mixture for 10 minutes in freezer, then add mangoes, heavy cream, *kewra* water, and cardamom seeds.

Freeze in *kulfi* dishes (see Remarks below) or a covered bowl until ice cream has desired texture (about 4 hours). Halfway through freezing time, stir ice cream once before it sets for best results.

Yields 2 quarts

Remarks

Other crushed fruit may be substituted for the mangoes. Pineapple adds a very nice touch.

Kulfi dishes are cone-shaped aluminum molds, 4 to 5 inches in length. The narrow end is slightly flattened and the other end has a tight-fitting cap. When ready to serve, unscrew the top of the kulfi dish and roll the mold between the palms of your hands to slightly loosen the ice cream. Then unmold on serving dish.

If the ice cream is placed in the freezer in a covered bowl for an extended period of time, move it to the refrigerator for a few hours before serving for best results. This allows the dessert to become softer, smoother, and easier to eat.

Beheshti Golay

Heavenly Chick-Pea Flour Balls with Almonds

2 cups water

4 ounces whole raw almonds, shelled

1 egg white

8½ to 10 tablespoons honey

¾ teaspoon *kewra* water

1½ teaspoons lemon juice

3 cups *besan*, chick-pea flour

6 ounces melted *ghee* (see page 40) or butter

4 to 6 small, pale green cardamom pods

2½ tablespoons desiccated coconut

2 tablespoons white sesame seeds

Bring 1⅛ cups of water to a boil in a 2-quart pot. Drop the almonds into the water and remove pot from heat. Allow the almonds to remain in the water for 10 to 15 minutes. Pick up one of the almonds; and if you can easily remove the skin, then drain the water and peel the skins from all the almonds. Otherwise, let them remain in hot water until the skins peel off easily.

Place the nuts in another pot or bowl, add ¾ cup cold water to cover the nuts, and soak for at least 30 minutes. Drain the water and place the nuts in two thicknesses of kitchen cloth. Cover the nuts securely by wrapping the cloth over and around. Pound with about 20 to 30 blows of a mallet. Then place almonds in a blender container and blend until they are broken into minute pieces but not blended to a puree. Set aside in a large bowl.

Beat the egg white until fluffy, but not stiff. Fold into the almonds.

Bring ⅛ cup water to boiling point in a small pan. Stir in 2½ tablespoons honey and continue stirring over moderate heat until the water becomes thick and sticky. Add ¼ teaspoon *kewra* water and the lemon juice and remove from heat. Then thoroughly stir the honey mixture into the nuts and transfer to a serving bowl.

Heat a large skillet, add the chick-pea flour and stir over moderate heat 1 minute. Add the *ghee* and fry, while stirring, over moderate heat 10 to 15 minutes. The chick-pea flour should become a golden brown and give out a lovely fragrance. Remove from heat. If your skillet is not large enough, use 2 skillets or cook the chick-pea flour in 2 separate batches.

Wrap the cardamom pods in cloth and pound vigorously. Carefully remove the pounded seeds, sprinkle them over the chick-pea flour and then quickly stir in 6 tablespoons honey, ½ teaspoon *kewra* water, and coconut. Add more honey if a sweeter taste is desired. Work quickly; do not allow the mixture to get cold. Start picking up lumps of the mixture and shape quickly into a flat circle about 2 inches in diameter. Place about ¾ teaspoon of the almond *halva* (filling) in the center and immediately wrap the chick-pea dough around it to form a ball. The dough will not form into solid balls unless it is very warm.

Heat a clean skillet over moderate heat, add the sesame seeds, and stir until they become pale brown. Scoop them onto a flat surface. Quickly roll the balls over the seeds, a few at a time, until some of the seeds are sticking to each of the balls and cool.

Yields 36 to 40 balls

Remarks

Beheshti Golay *may be served at room temperature immediately after they are made or a week or two later. To keep the golay fresh, store them, when completely cooled, in airtight glass containers.*

We serve Beheshti Golay *on festive occasions. They are rich and look very attractive. This recipe has been a special family secret, until now. My great aunt invented the exotic variation from a form of* Laddu, Cream of Wheat, Chick-Pea, Honeyed Balls *(see Index). They were so rapturously greeted that she laughed and said, "Achaa to tumey meray Beheshti Golay pasand aayay!"—which means, "Ah, so you liked my round sweets of heaven!" This is how they were named.*

The chick-pea balls can also be made without the filling.

Dalia Kheer

Cracked Wheat Dessert Cooked in Milk with Jaggery and Nuts

5½ cups milk	3½ tablespoons *ghee* (see page 40)
½ cup *dalia,* cracked wheat	1 tablespoon chopped pine nuts (optional)
3 to 3½ tablespoons grated jaggery	5 tablespoons slivered almonds
½ teaspoon *kewra* water or rose water	1 to 2 tablespoons raisins

Bring the milk to a boil in a 3-quart saucepan with a heavy bottom. Stir in the cracked wheat, jaggery, and *kewra* water, reduce heat to low, and simmer, uncovered, until the milk thickens (about 45 to 50 minutes). Stir frequently with a wire whisk, scraping the creamy milk from the sides of the pan and stirring it back into the cracked wheat.

In a skillet, heat the *ghee* and fry the pine nuts (if used), 4 tablespoons almonds, and raisins until the nuts are golden brown. Stir the fried nuts into the mixture and then transfer to a warm serving dish.

Heat a *tava* or griddle and roast the remaining almonds, while stirring, until lightly browned. Sprinkle the almonds over the *kheer* as a garnish. Serve immediately for best flavor.

Serves 6

Remarks

Dalia, *or cracked wheat, is very popular in north India. It is not served as a dessert, however, but as a sort of porridge. I have added* kewra, ghee, *and nuts to an otherwise very plain recipe.*

Being a simple nutritious food, dalia *is very popular with the people who have restricted diets. My father-in-law often has just* dalia *cooked in milk for his evening meal when he wants a change from our normal, richer fare.*

If you want to cook this ahead of time, refrigerate it when cool. You may want to thicken an extra cup of milk and stir it into the dalia *before serving since the* dalia *will thicken considerably when refrigerated.*

Dalia Kheer *is also delicious served chilled.*

Chukandar Halva

Beet *Halva*

¾ pound medium-size beets

1 cup powdered milk

2 cups water

3 tablespoons jaggery

6 tablespoons *ghee* (see page 40) or butter

⅛ teaspoon nutmeg powder

⅛ teaspoon cinnamon powder

1 tablespoon honey

2 to 3 tablespoons chopped pistachio nuts

sour cream (optional)

Boil the beets in just enough water to cover 20 minutes. Drain, peel, and dice.

Mix together the powdered milk and 2 cups water and pour into a *karhai* or wok. Add the beets and jaggery and bring to a boil. Reduce the heat to low, cover, and simmer 1½ hours.

Uncover and cook over moderate heat 30 minutes. Increase the heat to moderately high and cook, while stirring, until the liquid is absorbed. Add the *ghee* and fry 1 minute, while stirring. Stir in the nutmeg powder, cinnamon powder, honey, and nuts and remove from heat. Stir 1 minute. Serve hot, garnished with a dollop of sour cream (if used).

Serves 6

Remarks

This halva *is a nice, deep wine color and can be served with either whipped cream or sour cream.*

Gur Ki Taffee

Soft Jaggery and Peanut Toffee

6 tablespoons *ghee* (see page 40) or butter

1¼ cups grated jaggery

¾ cup peanuts, split in halves

In a large skillet, melt the *ghee* and jaggery over low heat. When the jaggery begins to bubble, add the nuts. Stir 2 minutes.

Grease a tray, 6 × 12 inches. Pour the melted jaggery with nuts onto the tray and allow the toffee to spread evenly over the surface. If necessary, spread with a greased knife.

When the toffee cools and begins to set, cut into 2-inch diamond shapes. Cut parallel straight lines in one direction, then cut parallel lines diagonally across the first set of lines.

Allow the toffee to cool and harden before lifting the pieces from the tray.

Yields 24 diamond-shaped toffees

Remarks

Babuji used to cook the jaggery for a longer period of time, until it turned a dark chocolate color. His toffee was hard and crunchy and he used to make it every week for Baba and me. I have never known a child who did not love this toffee.

The jaggery usually comes in walnut-size lumps. Break up the lumps completely to a coarse powder, or grate it, before measuring.

Payasam

Milk Pudding with Sago and Vermicelli

⅓ cup *sabudana,* sago

2 tablespoons *ghee* (see page 40) or butter

¾ cup vermicelli, measure by breaking into quarters and packing loosely

7 cups milk

1 tablespoon raisins

2 tablespoons blanched slivered almonds

7 small buff or pale green cardamom pods

6 to 7 tablespoons honey

Heat a 5-quart pot over moderate heat. Fry the sago with 1 tablespoon *ghee,* while stirring, 1 to 2 minutes. Remove the sago and set aside. Add the remaining tablespoon of *ghee* to the pot and fry the vermicelli 2 minutes. Stir once or twice.

Return the sago to the pot, pour in the milk, and stir over moderately high heat. Add the raisins and almonds to the milk.

Peel the cardamom pods. Wrap the seeds in thick paper towels and pound until the seeds are reduced to a coarse powder. Add the cardamom powder to the milk and bring slowly to a boil over moderate heat. Stir occasionally.

Stir in 6 tablespoons honey, reduce heat to low, and cook until the pudding thickens and becomes light brown in color (about 20 to 30 minutes). Stir frequently.

Pour into a serving dish or small individual bowls and serve hot.

Serves 6 to 9

Remarks

Payasam *is a rich dessert from Andhra Pradesh and is good either hot or cold. It is similar to the north Indian* kheer.

Refrigerated, the Payasam *will remain delicious for days. If it becomes too thick and you prefer it thinner, add some milk and simmer for a few minutes before serving.*

_____ *Phal Ka Salaad, Rabri Kay Saath* _____

Fruit Salad with Thickened Milk

4½ cups milk

⅓ to ½ cup finely grated jaggery

1 teaspoon *kewra* water or rose water

3 ripe mangoes

1 Golden Delicious apple

1 banana

1 orange

2 tablespoons finely shredded almonds (optional)

2 tablespoons finely shredded pistachio nuts (optional)

In a heavy-based, deep saucepan, bring the milk to a boil. Reduce heat to moderately high and stir continuously with wire whisk until the milk is reduced to a quarter of the original amount. Scrape the cream from the sides and stir it back into the milk.

Add the jaggery and stir until it completely dissolves. Remove from heat and cool. Scrape the cream from the sides again, add *kewra* water, and stir. Pour into a delicate serving bowl.

Peel the mangoes and cut into ¾-inch cubes. Core the apple and dice. Peel the banana and slice into ¼-inch rounds. Peel the orange and cut in half. Remove the seeds and cut each half into 6 pieces.

Gently stir all the fruit into the bowl with the *rabri.* Garnish with the shredded nuts, if desired. Refrigerate and serve chilled.

Serves 6

Remarks

If this dessert is prepared the day before you plan to serve it, do not add the banana until a half hour before serving time. I usually make the rabri *a day or two ahead of time and add the fruit the day I am serving the dessert.*

_____ *Srikand* _____

Light Dessert with Yogurt, Saffron, and Almonds

5 cups Homemade Yogurt or thick Homemade Yogurt (see page 41)

¼ teaspoon *zafraan,* saffron powder

½ teaspoon milk

8 or 9 small pale green cardamom pods

2 to 4 tablespoons honey

2 tablespoons slivered blanched almonds

Spoon the yogurt into a thick cloth and tie up the ends of the cloth. Hang the tied yogurt, with a container below to collect the draining whey, until the texture is thick like cream cheese (about 14 hours).

Soak the saffron powder in the milk for a few minutes.

Peel the skin from the cardamom pods. Wrap the seeds in thick paper toweling and pound with a mallet until the seeds are ground to a coarse powder.

Mix the thickened yogurt, dissolved saffron powder, cardamom powder, and honey in a medium-size bowl. Whip with an electric beater until the mixture becomes smooth, soft, and creamy.

Stir in the almonds and spoon into 6 individual serving bowls. Chill until ready to serve.

Serves 6

Suji Ka Halva II

Halva of Cream of Wheat, Milk, Cream, and Nuts

1 cup Cream of Wheat

6 tablespoons melted *ghee* (see page 40) or melted butter

5 tablespoons slivered almonds

1 tablespoon pistachio nuts

¼ teaspoon *zafraan,* saffron threads or powder

1 tablespoon lukewarm milk

4 cups milk

6 small pale green cardamom pods

⅛ teaspoon *kewra* water or rose water

6 to 7 tablespoons honey

¼ to ½ cup heavy cream

Heat a *karhai* or large skillet. Then add the Cream of Wheat and stir over moderate heat until lightly browned (about 10 to 15 minutes). Stir in the *ghee,* almonds, and pistachio nuts and fry 4 to 5 minutes.

Meanwhile, soak the saffron threads in the 1 tablespoon lukewarm milk. Then bring the dissolved saffron threads and the 4 cups milk slowly to a boil. Lightly pound the cardamom pods with just several blows of a mallet and add them to the milk along with the *kewra* water and honey. Once the milk reaches a boil, remove from heat and keep covered for 5 minutes to allow the milk to absorb all the flavors.

Pour the milk into the Cream of Wheat mixture, while stirring, and then add the cream. Cook over low heat just until the milk is absorbed by the Cream of Wheat mixture. Stir occasionally.

Serve immediately in *katoris* (small bowls).

Serves 6

Remarks

Suji *is a rich source of protein. So, while you are indulging in this rich dessert, it is also doing good things for you! You may also serve* Suji Ka Halva II *as a teatime snack. In fact, in India it is more often used as a snack than a dessert. I've found that my American friends love this* suji *as much as those of us in India who have enjoyed it all our lives!*

glossary

I. General

Attar: A fragrance, or an essence of a perfume.

Attar daan: A container to hold the *attar,* usually ornate and beautifully hand-carved silver.

Ayah: A woman who cares for the children.

Bhagavad Gita: The *Gita* is a section from the *Mahabharata,* an ancient religious epic. This beautiful piece of poetic prose (the *Gita*) often described as "the celestial song," deals with Lord Krishna's discourse to Arjun at the onset of a great battle, and embodies the essense of Hindu philosophy.

Bibi: An affectionate term for a young girl, used by Muslims. (*Bivi* is a Muslim word for wife.)

Dada: An older brother

Didi: An older sister.

Diya: A small tear-shaped oil lamp, lighted by a handmade cotton wick. *Diyas* are traditionally little earthen lamps, but are also made of brass or other metals.

Katori: A small bowl usually used for individual servings of food.

Khadoh: A *khadoh* is the youngest daughter in a *Khasi* family. Among the mainly matriarchial society of the *Khasis,* the *khadoh* inherits most of the family fortunes.

Khasi: A hill tribe living in the state of Meghalaya (formerly part of Assam) in northeast India.

Nepali: A person from Nepal.

Paisa: An Indian coin of small denomination, equivalent to approximately ⅛ of a cent.

Punjabi: A person from the province of Punjab, in India.

Rishi: A man learned in philosophy and religion who devotes his life to meditation.

Rupee: An Indian *rupee* is roughly ⅛ of a dollar.

Thali: A round metal, silver, brass, stainless steel, or stone plate, with a raised rim.

Walla: An expression similar in meaning to "fella."

II. Food

Baghar (or **Chonk** or **Tarka**)**:** A cooked Indian garnish of selected spices quickly fried in oil.

Barfi: Sweetmeats made from *Khoya* (thickened milk), flavored with coconut, rose water, cocoa, fruit, or nuts.

Bhaji or **Bhujia:** A cooked vegetable, curried, usually without any gravy.

Bhara or **Bhari:** Stuffed.

Bharta: A cooked vegetable that is mashed, or cooked to a consistency resembling a thick puree.

Biryani: A rich rice and meat (fowl or fish) preparation, with varied spices.

Chutney: A seasoned preparation made from raw, or sometimes cooked fruit or vegetables, traditionally served as a relish with meals or, in modern homes, as a dip with savory snacks.

Garam Masalla: *Garam* means hot and *masalla* means spices. Thus, the term *garam masalla* is a blend of (hot) spices (see page 42 for recipe).

Ghee: Clarified butter. A cooking medium made from cooking butter over low heat and straining it to obtain purified oil *(ghee). Ghee* solidifies when stored in cool temperatures (see page 40 for recipe).

Halva: A rich, thick dessert made with vegetables, fruit, or cereals, generally cooked in milk.

Idli: Steamed cakelike bread made from fermented rice and lentils. To be made successfully, *idlis* need a special utensil for steaming. I have, therefore, not included this typical south Indian recipe in this book.

Kababs:

> **Seekh Kabab:** Rolls made of uncooked minced meat and spices, put on skewers and charcoal broiled.
>
> **Shami Kabab:** Patty-shaped kabobs made from cooked minced meat, lentils, and spices and shallow fried.
>
> **Tikka Kabab:** Small pieces of seasoned meat, fish, or fowl, skewered and broiled over a charcoal fire.

Kacha: Raw.

Kardi: The English word "curry" is probably derived from this word, meaning a seasoned sauce.

Keema: Minced meat.

Kheer: A sweet dessert made by cooking rice, lentils, sago, tapioca, vermicelli, or a combination of these, in milk flavored with rose water, raisins, and nuts. (See Index for *Payasam* recipe, a similar preparation.)

Kofta: Small balls or sausagelike shapes made from minced meat and spices, curried.

Korma: Meat curry.

Laddu: Round sweetmeats made from lentils, chick-pea flour, Cream of Wheat, nuts, and spices.

Lassi: A cool, refreshing yogurt-based drink (see Index for recipe).

Masalla: Spice.

Pakora: A savory snack of chopped vegetables, wrapped in batter and deep-fried.

Panir: Homemade Cheese (see Index for recipe).

Pullau: Pilaf. A savory rice dish cooked with meat, poultry, seafood, vegetables, or eggs.

Rabri: Dessert of sweet, thickened milk.

Raita: Yogurt with various types of chopped or grated vegetables or fruit, lightly seasoned with spices and herbs.

Roti: Generic term for Indian "breads."

Sabudana: Sago. Processed from any of several varieties of Indian palm, sago is bought in the form of whitish granules and is similar to tapioca.

Sabzi: A vegetable (either raw or cooked).

Salaad: Salad.

Samosa: A deep-fried snack, triangularly shaped. The filling is minced meat or cooked vegetables. The shell is made from flour.

Sharbat: Essence of flower, bark, herbs, fruit, or nut, made into syrup. In the Orient, a cool, refreshing drink.

Singara: Another name for *samosa* (see above). A kind of water chestnut is also known as *singara*.

Sivain: Thin vermicelli prepared from wheat flour and made into slender threads thinner than spaghetti.

Suji: Cream of Wheat, also Semolina. Rich in protein, a popular base for both sweet and savory dishes.

Tarkari: A vegetable (either cooked or raw) (see *Sabzi*).

Tehri: A rice preparation. Often eggs, jackfruit seeds, or other vegetables are added.

Tel: Oil

Tinda: A soft vegetable, about the size of a lemon, tasting similar to a soft squash. In the States I use frizzle squash instead, which is probably the nearest equivalent.

Tok: A sweet-sour tomato-based chutney.

III. Daals

Description of some commonly used Indian lentils

Daal (or *dal*): The generic Indian term for lentil (which includes all members of the pulse family). In this country I have noticed just a few kinds of lentil, whereas there are over sixty varieties of lentil (peas and beans) in India.

> *Arhar daal* (or *tuar daal*): The English name is pigeon pea. A small, yellow-beige split lentil.
>
> *Chana, gram:* There are many varieties of chana in India, one of which is very similar to chick-pea (garbanzo).
>
> *Chana daal:* Golden, split, pea-like lentil.
>
> *Hara chana:* Green gram. This is a fresh green gram (similar to chick-pea) that is a lentil and a vegetable at the same time. I have not included a recipe, since it is probably not available (in the green, fresh form) in this country.
>
> *Kabuli chana:* A large, white gram similar to chick-pea.
>
> *Kala chana:* Small dark chick-pea, harder than the common chick-pea.
>
> *Lobia daal:* Black-eyed peas.
>
> *Mah daals:* The terms "mah" and "urad" are often used interchangeably.
>
> > *Dhuli maash* (or *safed urad daal*): White split lentil (split from *kali mah daal*). When hulled, it is white. *Dhuli* means washed; thus, white hulled lentil.

Kali mah: small black whole beans. Not the same as the American black bean, which should not be substituted for the Indian lentil. (*Kala* or *Kali* means black.)

Raj mah: Literally translated, king of lentils (red kidney beans).

Masur daal: Bright orange or salmon-colored split lentil, hulled from *sabut masur* (or lentil).

Moong:

Sabut moong: Whole green mung beans.

Moong daal: Tiny, oval-shaped, pale yellow lentil hulled from the whole mung bean.

Sabut masur daal: The common American variety, known simply as "lentil" (the whole brown flat lentil available at most supermarkets) resembles the Indian *sabut masur daal* and can be safely substituted for it. (*Sabut* means whole.)

Urad daals:

Chilka urad: Small whole black beans. Split, not hulled. *Chilka* means skin or covering; thus, a split unhulled lentil.

Sabut urad daal (or **kali mah**): Whole small black beans.

Safed urad (or **dhuli maash**): Small white hulled lentil. Hulled from the *sabut urad daal.*

maíl-ordeR souRces

The following list offers the names, addresses, and phone numbers of retail and wholesale outlets where many of the ingredients which are called for in our recipes may be acquired. This list is merely intended to be a representative sampling of stores which have some of the necessary foods. Natural food stores, Chinese, Korean, Japanese, Spanish, and other Eastern stores also have many of the ingredients we use.

Antone's
805–901 Rhode Pl.
Houston, TX 77019
Phone: (713) 526-1046
   Minimum Order—$50.00

Aphrodisia
28 Carmine St.
New York, NY 10014
Phone: (212) 989-6440
   Catalogue—$2.50

Benjian's Grocery Inc.
4725 Santa Monica Blvd.
Hollywood, CA 90029
Phone: (213) 663-1503
   Minimum Order—$15.00

House of Spices
76-17 Broadway
Jackson Heights, NY 11373
Phone: (212) 476-1577

India Gifts and Foods
1031 W. Belmont Ave.
Chicago, IL 60657
Phone: (312) 348-4393

India Gifts and Foods
643 Post St.
San Francisco, CA 94109
Phone: (415) 771-5041

Indian Spices and Gifts
4110 Wilson Blvd.
Arlington, VA
Phone: (703) 522-1049

Indian Super Bazaar
3735 Rhode Island Ave.
Mt. Rainier, MD 20722
Phone: (301) 927-2224

Oriental Foods and Handicrafts
3708 N. Broadway
Chicago, IL 60613
Phone: (312) 248-8024

Siddhartha
1412 New York Ave., NW
Washington, DC 20005
Phone: (202) 638-6828

The Smile Herb Shop
4908 Berwyn Rd.
College Park, MD 20740
Phone: (301) 474-8791

In England:

Osaka LTD
17–17a Goldhurst Terr.
Finchley Rd.
London, N.W.6
Phone: 01-624-4983

index